# JAPAN AND CHRISTIANITY

# Japan and Christianity

## Impacts and Responses

Edited by

**John Breen**
*Lecturer in Japanese Studies*
*School of Oriental and African Studies*
*University of London*

and

**Mark Williams**
*Lecturer in Japanese Studies*
*University of Leeds*

First published in Great Britain 1996 by
**MACMILLAN PRESS LTD**
Houndmills, Basingstoke, Hampshire RG21 6XS
and London
Companies and representatives
throughout the world

A catalogue record for this book is available
from the British Library.

ISBN 0-333-58938-6

First published in the United States of America 1996 by
**ST. MARTIN'S PRESS, INC.,**
Scholarly and Reference Division,
175 Fifth Avenue,
New York, N.Y. 10010

ISBN 0-312-12872-X

Library of Congress Cataloging-in-Publication Data
Japan and Christianity : impacts and responses / edited by John Breen,
Mark Williams.
 p. cm.
Includes bibliographical references and index.
ISBN 0-312-12872-X (cloth)
1. Japan—Church history. 2. Japan—Civilization—Christian
influences. I. Breen, John. II. Williams, Mark, 1957– .
BR1305.J37  1996
275.2—dc20                                                   95-17862
                                                                CIP

Selection and editorial matter © John Breen and Mark Williams 1996
Text © Macmillan Press Ltd 1996

All rights reserved. No reproduction, copy or transmission of
this publication may be made without written permission.

No paragraph of this publication may be reproduced, copied or
transmitted save with written permission or in accordance with
the provisions of the Copyright, Designs and Patents Act 1988,
or under the terms of any licence permitting limited copying
issued by the Copyright Licensing Agency, 90 Tottenham Court
Road, London W1P 9HE.

Any person who does any unauthorised act in relation to this
publication may be liable to criminal prosecution and civil
claims for damages.

10  9  8  7  6  5  4  3  2  1
05  04  03  02  01  00  99  98  97  96

Printed and bound in Great Britain by
Antony Rowe Ltd, Chippenham, Wiltshire

# Contents

| | |
|---|---|
| *List of Plates* | vii |
| *Acknowledgements* | viii |
| *Notes on the Contributors* | ix |
| *Chronology* | xii |
| Introduction | |
| *John Breen and Mark Williams* | 1 |

1. Translations of Christian Terminology into Japanese, 16–19th Centuries: Problems and Solutions
   *Stefan Kaiser* — 8

2. Early Western-Style Paintings in Japan
   *Michael Cooper* — 30

3. New Perspectives on the Early Tokugawa Persecution
   *Ōhashi Yukihiro* — 46

4. Acculturation among the *Kakure Kirishitan*: Some Conclusions from the *Tenchi Hajimari no Koto*
   *Stephen Turnbull* — 63

5. Beyond the Prohibition: Christianity in Restoration Japan
   *John Breen* — 75

6. Christianity Encounters Buddhism in Japan: A Historical Perspective
   *Notto R. Thelle* — 94

7. The Religion of the West versus the Science of the West: The Evolution Controversy in Late Nineteenth Century Japan
   *Helen Ballhatchet* — 107

8. Written and Unwritten Texts of the *Kakure Kirishitan*
   *Christal Whelan* — 122

| | | |
|---|---|---|
| 9 | The Social Forms of Japanese Christianity<br>*Mark R. Mullins* | 138 |
| 10 | From Out of the Depths: The Japanese Literary Response to Christianity<br>*Mark Williams* | 156 |
| | *Select Bibliography* | 175 |
| | *Index* | 186 |

# List of Plates

1 *Mater Dolorosa*, oil on canvas, 52.5 × 40 cm. Nanban Bunkakan, Osaka.
2 *Our Lady of the Rosary*, colour on paper, 75 × 63 cm. Kyoto University.
3 *St Francis Xavier*, colour on paper, 61 × 49 cm. Kobe City Museum.
4 Nobukata, *Woman Playing the Lute*, colour on paper, 55.5 × 37.3 cm. Yamato Bunkakan, Nara.
5 'Two Figures in a Pastoral Scene', colour on paper; detail from a pair of six-panel screens, 93 × 302 cm. Private collection.
6 'The King of Rome', colour on paper; detail from *The Battle of Lepanto*, one of a pair of six-panel screens, 153 × 362.5 cm. Kōsetsu Art Museum, Kobe.
7 *Four Mounted Western Warriors*, colour on paper, four-panel screen, 166.2 × 460.4 cm. Kobe City Museum.
8 'The City of Rome', colour on paper, detail from *Four Great Cities of the West* (Rome, Lisbon, Seville, and Constantinople), one of a pair of eight-panel screens, 158.7 × 477.7 cm. Kobe City Museum.
9 *Map of the World*, colour on paper, detail from one of a pair of six-panel screens, 153 × 362.6 cm. Kōsetsu Art Museum, Kobe.

# Acknowledgements

This volume emerges from an international conference on Christianity and Japanese culture held at St Mary's College, Strawberry Hill, Twickenham, in September 1991. The conference, designed to coincide with the Japan Festival of that year, was the idea of Richard Tames and the Dean of Humanities, Mr Brian Firth. Had it not been for Mr Firth's enthusiasm and hard work, the good offices of the Department of Religious Studies at St Mary's and the generosity of the Great Britain Sasakawa Foundation, neither the conference nor the present volume would have got off the ground. The college authorities gave us the use of the Waldegrave Drawing Room for the conference; it could hardly have been bettered as a location for two days of papers and discussion! Thanks are due to all participants at the conference, some of whose papers could not be included in the present volume, but especially to Professor William Beasley, who opened the proceedings with a stimulating survey of the place of religion in Japanese history.

We are very grateful to the following institutions for permission to use photographs: Kobe City Museum, Kōsetsu Art Museum (Kobe), Kyoto University, Nanban Bunkakan (Osaka), Yamato Bunkakan (Nara), and to *Rekishigaku Kenkyū* for permission to carry Ōhashi Yukihiro's essay.

Charlotte Breen, Luci Davin and Ruth Jarrett helped with the typing of the manuscript and Bill Garrard translated Ōhashi Yukihiro's paper. Our thanks are due to our editors at Macmillan, Belinda Holdsworth and Annabelle Buckley, for their support, encouragement, and above all their patience. Our wives, Chika Breen and Ikuko Williams, endured much for the several months of frenetic work it took to get the volume ready for publication. To our children, Ken, Naomi, Nicholas, Simon and Thomas, this volume is dedicated.

# Notes on the Contributors

**Helen Ballhatchet** obtained her doctorate from the London School of Economics and is Assistant Professor in the Economics Department, Keio University, Tokyo. Among her recent publications are 'Baba Tatsui and Victorian Britain' in Cortazzi and Daniels, eds, *Britain and Japan 1859–1991*, Routledge, 1991, and 'British Missionaries in Japan' in I. Nish, ed., *Britain and Japan: Biographical Portraits*, Japan Library, 1994. She is currently preparing manuscripts on the treaty ports and on the history of Christianity in East Asia.

**John Breen** obtained his doctorate at the University of Cambridge and is lecturer in Japanese at SOAS, University of London. Among his recent publications are 'Shintoists in Restoration Japan', *Modern Asian Studies* (1990), 'Accommodating the Alien: Ōkuni Takamasa and the Religion of the Lord of Heaven', in P. Kornicki et al., eds, *Arrows from Heaven: Essays in Honour of Carmen Blacker*, CUP, 1995, and 'Ōkuni Takamasa, Shinshin Kōhōron', in *Readings in Tokugawa Thought*, Select Papers, University of Chicago Press, 1994.

**Michael Cooper** has been editor since 1972 of the quarterly *Monumenta Nipponica*, a journal published by Sophia University, Tokyo. He obtained his doctorate at the University of Oxford with a dissertation on João Rodrigues, a Portuguese missionary in Japan in the sixteenth and seventeenth centuries. His publications include *Rodrigues, the Interpreter*, Weatherhill, 1974 and 1994; *They Came to Japan*, University of California Press, 1965 and 1981, and *This Island of Japan*, Kōdansha, 1973, in addition to numerous articles on European–Japanese cultural relations in the sixteenth and seventeenth centuries.

**Stefan Kaiser** is Professor at the Institute of Languages and Literatures, University of Tsukuba. His research concerns are the Japanese language and writing system and their research histories. His recent publications include *Circumnominal Relative Clauses in Classical Japanese: an Historical Study*, 1991, Harrassowitz, and 'Japan: History of Linguistic Thought' in R.E. Asher, ed., *The Encyclopaedia of Language and Linguistics*, 1994, Pergamon Press.

**Mark R. Mullins**, a specialist in the sociology of religion, is Associate Professor at Meiji Gakuin University, Tokyo and Yokohama, and associate editor for *Japanese Religions* and the *Japan Christian Review*. He has published widely on the indigenisation of religion, and most recently co-edited *Religion and Society in Modern Japan*, Berkeley: Asian Humanities Press, 1993.

**Ōhashi Yukihiro** teaches at Musashi Junior High School, and specialises in pre-modern Japanese history with a particular interest in Japanese encounters with Christianity. Among his recent publications are 'Shūmon aratame no seidoka to Kirishitan minshū', (The Systemisation of the *Shūmon Aratame* and the Christian Populace), *Rekishi Hyōron*, 1992; 'Bakuhan Kenryoku ni totte Kirishitan Kinsei wa nan datta ka', ('The Importance of the Christian Persecution for Bakufu Power') in *Shinshiten: Nihon no Rekishi 5: Kinseihen*, Shinjinbutsu Ōraisha, 1993, and 'Bakuhansei Kokka ni okeru Minshū no Kirishitankan' (Popular views of Christianity in the *Bakuhan* State), *Rekishigaku Kenkyū*, 1993.

**Notto R. Thelle** is Professor of Systematic Theology at the University of Oslo, with special interest in interfaith studies. He was in Japan from 1969 to 1985 as missionary, Associate Director of the National Christian Council Centre for the Study of Japanese religions and editor of *Japanese Religions*. Among his recent publications are *Buddhism and Christianity in Japan: from Conflict to Dialogue, 1854–1899*, University of Hawaii Press, 1987, and, in Norwegian, a textbook on world religions for high-school students, and two collections of essays on the contemporary search for religion.

**Stephen Turnbull** is the author of numerous books and articles on Japanese military history, religion and related topics. He is currently taking a part-time PhD on the subject of the *Kakure Kirishitan* at Leeds University, working under the joint auspices of the Departments of East Asian Studies and Theology and Religious Studies. His thesis examines the evolution of the faith of the hidden Christians during the time of their persecution as well as its manifestation in their communities of the present day.

**Christal Whelan** is lecturer in English at Sophia University. Her main research interests are the Portuguese presence in Japan and the hidden Christians. Her recent publications include 'Religion Concealed: the *Kakure Kirishitan* on Narushima', *Monumenta Nipponica*, 1992;

'Wenceslau de Moraes – the Man and the Myth', *Japan Quarterly*, 1993, and 'Loss of the Signified among the *Kakure Kirishitan*', *Japanese Religions*, 1994. She is currently preparing for publication an annotated translation of the *Tenchi Hajimari no Koto*.

**Mark B. Williams**, a specialist in modern Japanese literature, received his doctorate from the University of California, Berkeley, and is currently lecturer in Japanese Studies in the Department of East Asian Studies at the University of Leeds. He is the translator of two novels by the contemporary Japanese novelist, Endō Shūsaku, and has published widely in English and Japanese on the relationship between Christianity and literature in Japan. He is currently preparing a critical study of Endō's major novels for publication.

# Chronology

| | |
|---|---|
| 1549 | Arrival of St Francis Xavier in Kagoshima |
| 1569 | Frois received in audience by Nobunaga |
| 1579 | Alessandro Valignano arrives in Japan |
| 1580 | Founding of seminaries in Arima and Azuchi; Nagasaki ceded to the Society of Jesus |
| 1582 | Mission to Rome |
| 1587 | Hideyoshi's first anti-Christian edicts |
| 1591 | Valignano received in audience by Hideyoshi; Barreto manuscript; *Sanctos no Gosagyō* |
| 1592 | *Doctrina Cristan* |
| 1593 | Arrival of the Franciscan Pedro Baptista and the beginning of Franciscan Jesuit rivalry |
| 1597 | Crucifixion of the 'twenty-six martyrs' in Nagasaki; Hideyoshi renews his Exclusion order |
| 1602 | Arrival of Augustinian and Dominican friars |
| 1612 | First Tokugawa anti-Christian edicts |
| 1614 | Tokugawa Ieyasu issues missionary exclusion order; general persecution begins |
| 1622 | Great Martyrdom in Nagasaki |
| 1629 | First *efumi* ritual takes place in Nagasaki |
| 1633 | 'Exclusion Edict' 1 |
| 1634 | 'Exclusion Edict' 2 |
| 1635 | 'Exclusion Edict' 3 |
| 1636 | 'Exclusion Edict' 4 |
| 1637–8 | Shimabara Rebellion |
| 1639 | 'Exclusion Edict' 5 |
| 1657 | Establishment of the *Shūmon Aratameyaku* |
| 1859 | Protestant mission to Japan begins |
| 1865 | Hidden Christians make themselves known to Fr Petitjean in Nagasaki |
| 1867 | Renewal of Catholic persecution |
| 1868 | Meiji Restoration; Urakami Christians exiled |
| 1872 | Kyōbushō established; creation of the Yokohama Band and of Japan's first Protestant church |
| 1873 | Lifting of anti-Christian proscription; Urakami Christians released from exile |
| 1875 | Founding of Dōshisha University |

| | |
|---|---|
| 1876 | Creation of the Sapporo and Kumamoto Bands |
| 1877 | Formation of the *Nihon Kirisuto Itchi Kyōkai* (United Church of Christ in Japan); Edward Morse arrives in Japan |
| 1880 | Publication of New Testament in Japanese translation; *Rikugō Zasshi* |
| 1888 | Publication of Old Testament in Japanese |
| 1889 | Meiji Constitution published; freedom of conscience guaranteed |
| 1891 | Uchimura Kanzō's refusal to perform obeisance to the Rescript on Education |
| 1894–5 | Sino-Japanese War |
| 1896 | Buddhist–Christian Conference |
| 1901 | Creation of *Mukyōkai* (no-church) Christianity by Uchimura Kanzō |
| 1904–5 | Russo-Japanese War |
| 1912 | Founding of Jōchi (Sophia) University in Tokyo |
| 1940 | Formulation of the *Nihon Kirisuto Kyōdan* (United Church of Christ in Japan) |
| 1941 | *Iesu no Mitama* founded |
| 1941–5 | Pacific War |
| 1948 | *Makuya* founded |
| 1952 | Founding of International Christian University in Tokyo |

# Introduction
John Breen and Mark Williams

There are well-known dangers in framing the encounter between 'West' and 'East' in terms of a Western 'impact' and an Eastern 'response' or even of a Western 'contribution'. Equally, however, there are dangers in being over-sensitive to charges of ethnocentrism. The initial stage in the encounter between Christianity and Japanese culture – that is the period between 1549 and 1639 when Catholicism was disseminated by European missionaries – offers ample evidence that a Christian impact, a Christian 'contribution' was one vital aspect of a dynamic cultural encounter. That it is nigh on impossible to measure the impact and quantify the contribution does not invalidate the point.

The fears of Christianity harboured by a succession of central and local rulers from Toyotomi Hideyoshi to the first Tokugawa Shoguns were, at the very least, 'contributory' to the series of edicts that, in the first few decades of the seventeenth century, banned Japanese passage overseas and blocked Catholic Europeans' access to Japan. There was, too, an important legacy of suspicion and hatred of foreign religion that this initial encounter created: it surfaced full-blown in anti-foreign tracts of the early and mid-nineteenth century and provided a key dynamic to the anti-foreign movement.[1]

Christianity had this political impact in the late sixteenth and early seventeenth centuries, provoking an extreme response, not because it was a 'superior' creed, nor because it was the carrier of a culture more technologically advanced, more 'modern'. It did so for two reasons above all: because it was an 'exclusivist' religion in a society whose religious culture was distinctly non-exclusivist; and because, like all pre-modern exclusivist creeds, it was inseparable from the politics of the culture in which it had been nourished;[2] it was, in short, a 'politicised' religion in the highly unstable political environment of late sixteenth and early seventeenth century Japan. The potential for a major, disruptive impact was ever present, and it increased in proportion as large numbers of Japanese of all classes, for a complex variety of political, social and psychological motives, sought to identify with it.

The large numbers of conversions and of martyrdoms point, of course, to a contribution and an impact of a very different order. As many as 300 000 Japanese, out of a total population of some twenty million, had by the first decade of the seventeenth century converted to Christianity. It is a figure all the more impressive given Boxer's estimation of a mere 143 missionaries in Japan at the time.[3] Still more indicative is the estimated total of between forty and fifty thousand native martyrs born of the persecution.[4] To be sure, this hardly permits us to speak of a 'Christian century' if we mean to imply by the term that the majority of the population of Japan had come under the sway of European missionary culture. Vast areas of Japan – the south-eastern half of Kyūshū, most of the island of Shikoku, the Japan Sea side of the *Chūgoku* region of Honshū and extensive tracts of land to the north of Honshu and, of course, the vast area of land now known as Hokkaidō – saw no missionary activity at all. Nonetheless, it remains that we are justified in talking of Christianity contributing, of Christianity 'impacting' on the lives and the deaths of many thousands of Japanese. The enduring quality of this is nowhere more striking perhaps than in the remarkable historical phenomenon of the *Kakure Kirishitan*. These communities of 'hidden Christians' survived in secret from the early 1600s until their discovery in the 1860s, a period more than twice the length enjoyed by the mission which they perforce replaced. Their number in the 1860s was estimated at some 40 000.[5]

The question of a lasting contribution in a more general cultural sense is complex. The intellectual historian Ebisawa Arimichi talks of a *Nanban gakutō*, a 'Southern Barbarian intellectual legacy' which, he asserts, contributed much to the 'development of the Tokugawa Japanese world view', helped 'nurture a practical spirit' and 'laid the ground for the spread of Dutch learning'. The cultural legacy of the European mission can take some credit, he believes, for 'cultivating an anti-feudal, anti-"closed country" school of thought' later in the Edo period.[6] This is a provocative and still controversial view, which probably merits more serious attention than it has so far received. For the present, though, Elison represents the established view when he writes that: 'Seen in strict terms, the sum of (the Christian missionaries') cultural contribution was nil'.[7]

The reverse dynamic of this first encounter between Christianity and Japanese culture merits attention, too, of course. For, if we are able to talk of Christian contributions and Christian impacts, it becomes clear we must also acknowledge a Japanese 'contribution' to Christian culture, a Japanese impact and a Christian response. Again, attempts to qualify and quantify will prove frustrating, but there exist some striking examples to prove the point. One of several can be seen in the 'drift' of exclusivist European Catholicism in the direction of non-exclusivity in the beliefs of the hidden Christians; another, from a later period, can be seen in the development of the 'non-church' movement of the theologian Uchimura Kanzō in the early twentieth century. Some cursory comments on each are in order.

The *Tenchi Hajimari no Koto* (Concerning the Creation of Heaven and Earth) was the one text to survive the persecutions and remain with the Christians of Nagasaki until their 'discovery' in 1865.[8] In a section styled 'Kirinto no Koto' (On the Credo), the unknown author of the text reformulates the orthodox Trinity of Father, Son and Holy Spirit, for example, to comprise 'the parent, that is *deusu* or *paateru* (*pater*), the flesh, that is the son or *hiiriyo* (*filio*) and the mother, that is *suheruto santo* (*spirito sancto*)...God is three bodies. Of course, though we speak in terms of three bodies, they are, in origin, but a single body'.[9] The Virgin Mary, of immense importance in the religious devotions of the *Kakure* – as indeed she was in the teachings of the seventeenth century missionaries – is here elevated to a privileged position within the Trinity. The mother figure takes her place alongside the father, breaching the exclusive theological mould.

Other breaches in the exclusivism of European Catholicism were taking place elsewhere. The very survival of the clandestine Christians was, of course, a testimony to the Japanese rejection of the exhortations to martyrdom set out in such texts as the *Maruchirio no Michi* (The Way of the Martyr):[10] "There is no difference in terms of the gravity of sin, of the loss incurred, or of the punishment to be inflicted upon the man who apostasises in his heart and he who apostasises merely on the surface.'[11] The hidden Christians in and around Nagasaki, who had all 'apostatised merely on the surface', rejected these and similar exhortations to martyrdom. They did so annually in the ritual known as the *efumi*, which required them to tread images of Jesus or the Virgin Mary. The novelist Endō Shūsaku is possibly right to relate the psychological dilemma occasioned by the annual denial of faith to the strong 'maternal' dimension of their faith, of which the elevation of the Virgin Mary to the Trinity is but one manifestation: only a mother figure, limitless in her compassion could understand the anguish caused by denial and, moreover, forgive it.[12] Whatever the reasons, the fact is that Catholic structures were being steadily eroded. This happened in the most obvious sense that Buddhist, Shinto and 'ancestral' elements were gradually incorporated within *Kakure* practices. It may well be, again as Endō and others have suggested, that it was the accommodation of the last of these, ancestor worship, within the corpus of *Kakure* beliefs that explains, as much as any other single factor, the durability of their hidden communities.[13] But the temptation to attribute this 'drift' *uniquely* to the peculiar circumstances of prohibition Japan, and to dismiss it as mere 'corruption' or 'deterioration' should be resisted. We do well to bear in mind that for Japanese Catholics and other Christians of the late twentieth century, ancestors retain a central significance.[14] What was happening in the *Kakure* communities was, perhaps, less 'corruption' than cultural adjustment to a more appropriately 'Japanese' form.

A second famous example of Japanese Christianity speaking with originality and eloquence to Western Christianity is to be seen in the early twentieth century *Mukyōkai* or 'no-church' movement of Uchimura Kanzō. *Mukyōkai* was Uchimura's response to the materialism, denominationalism and institutionalism of the Christianity brought to Japan by nineteenth-century American and European missionaries, following the removal of the proscription in 1873. For Uchimura, it was 'Christianity minus the churches' that constituted 'the Way, the Truth and the Life'.[15] His movement advocated a return to the primitive simplicity of the gospel and the early church, and was an attempt to accommodate 'the Oriental mind [which] in general tends to conceive of religion as a matter of the spirit, to grasp it as such, and to worship Jehovah who has no voice and no forms'.[16] It is early yet to pass judgement on the accuracy of Uchimura's prophecy that 'churchless Christianity is the Christianity of the future',[17] but *Mukyōkai* is but one manifestation of a cultural phenomenon that merits closer attention by non-Japanese students of Christianity than it has so far received.

The present volume is one of very few book-length studies in recent years to address the question of Christianity in its dynamic encounter with Japanese culture. The lack of scholarly interest in Christianity in Japan contrasts not only with the situation in contemporary Korean and Chinese scholarship; it also contrasts with the keen interest shown by scholars – Western and Japanese – in the indigenous new and so-called 'new new' religions of Japan. It can, of course, hardly be said of Japan that Christianity there is the major political and social issue that it is in contemporary Korea and that it threatens to be in China; nor is it difficult to share the enthusiasm of religious studies' students for Japan's indigenous creeds. It remains, nonetheless, that Japan's engagement with Christianity from the mid sixteenth century to the present day is a rich source not only for students of religions but for all students of the interaction between cultures. The essays in this collection constitute a preliminary exploration of some of the key themes in Japan's encounter with Christianity across more than four centuries.

In his 'Translations of Christian Terminology into Japanese 16th–19th Centuries: Problems and Solutions', Stefan Kaiser analyses an issue that lies at the heart of all cultural interaction, namely language. He examines critically the early Jesuits' abortive attempts to evolve a lexicon adequate to the task of communicating the essentials of the Christian faith. It was, Kaiser concludes, only with the second wave of missionaries in the nineteenth century that a language was finally wrought, capable of contributing to a clear understanding of the imported religion and of doing justice to the nuances that the Japanese themselves brought to the imported faith.

Michael Cooper considers the place of Southern Barbarian art in the cultural dialogue of late sixteenth and seventeenth Japan. His 'Early Western-Style Paintings in Japan' sheds light on a stimulating – if short-lived – cultural experiment that saw Japanese artists, some from the famous Kanō school, adding to their repertoire the most sophisticated European artistic techniques of the age. Cooper analyses the conspicuously successful application of these techniques by Japanese artists to themes religious and secular and Western as well as native.

Ōhashi Yukihiro is concerned in his 'New Perspectives on the Christian Persecution' to reassess the political response to the foreign religion. His analysis of the texts of successive anti-Christian edicts suggests, contrary to received wisdom, that the Tokugawa *Bakufu* was primarily preoccupied not with the general populace's allegiance to Christianity, but with converts from the warrior class. It was only in the wake of the rebellion in Shimabara, the eruption of which was evidence that popular Christianity had been driven underground but not finally eliminated, that the focus of *Bakufu* attention shifted decisively to the general populace.

Stephen Turnbull in his 'Acculturation among the *Kakure Kirishitan*: Some Conclusions from the *Tenchi Hajimari no Koto*' warns against too ready an acceptance of received knowledge about the beliefs of the hidden Christians of the Tokugawa period. He demonstrates that many of the distinctive events described in the *Tenchi Hajimari no Koto* were not a corruption of European Catholicism at all, but a faithful preservation of the teachings of the early missionaries. The missionaries had clearly been more assiduous than has been thought in accommodating the special needs of the Japanese audience to their methods of propagation. Turnbull's paper highlights just how complex an objective analysis of intercultural relations can be.

John Breen's chapter is one of three to concentrate on the nineteenth century. His 'Beyond the Prohibition: Christianity in Restoration Japan' discusses the political response to Christianity in the early Meiji period. He argues that the so-called 'Urakami incident' – which followed the 'discovery' of the hidden Christians in the 1860s – was of much more than diplomatic significance. It was responsible, rather, for forcing the early Meiji government to consider the entire state-religion question. His analysis suggests that Christianity in general, and the Urakami incident in particular, provide an important key to the whole of early Meiji religious policy.

Notto Thelle's essay 'Christianity Encounters Buddhism in Japan: A Historical Perspective' analyses the vital cultural dialogue that took place in the late nineteenth century between Christian missionaries from America and Western Europe and Japanese Buddhist clergy. He examines the key moments in the development of the dialogue, and demonstrates how participants went beyond the fierce rivalry for spiritual hegemony over the new Japan, and arrived at a new dimension of cooperation and understanding. This happened, he shows, long before the post-war period, to which the 'breakthrough' is typically attributed.

Helen Ballhatchet's chapter switches the focus to the approach of Japanese Christian intellectuals toward evolution during the same historical period. She argues in her paper, 'The Religion of the West versus the Science of the West: The Evolution Controversy in Late Nineteenth Century Japan', that Japanese Christians offered a response to the new science altogether more sophisticated than that of Western Christians. Evolutionary theory enabled Japanese Christians, in short, to see Christianity as essential to Japan's modern development, but it also, Ballhatchet concludes, enabled them to conceive of religion itself in evolutionary terms: indigenous Japanese creeds were an evolutionary preparation for the advent of Christianity which, in its Japanese form, promised to be superior to that of the materialistic West.

The three remaining essays in the volume are concerned primarily with 'contemporary' issues. Christal Whelan in her chapter, 'Written and Unwritten Texts of the *Kakure Kirishitan*', turns her attention to the hidden Christians as they survive today in the islands off the coast of Kyūshū. These are descendants of the Christians who were unable to accept the baptism offered them by the Catholic missionaries after they returned to Japan in the mid nineteenth century. Whelan's examination of a series of *Kakure* texts from both the oral and written traditions demonstrates how the hidden Christians of the twentieth century have turned to alternative religious currents, and indeed to orthodox Catholicism, in their search for meaning.

Mark Mullins, in 'The Social Forms of Japanese Christianity' focuses on the *Iesu no Mitama* (Spirit of Jesus) church in contemporary Japan. *Iesu no Mitama* offers a particularly striking example of the dynamics of the encounter between Christianity and Japanese folk religion. Mullins highlights *Iesu no Mitama* rituals for the dead as one of several key points of contact with traditional Japanese religiosity. His conclusion, from a comparison of the different contributions made to Christianity by the *Iesu no Mitama* church and by Uchimura Kanzō's *Mukyōkai*, is that there are many different ways to be Christian and Japanese.

In his essay, 'From Out of the Depths: The Japanese Literary Response to Christianity', Mark Williams examines the gradual evolution of a series of literary texts born of the often conflicting dictates of literature and religion. Identifying four stages in the development of a Japanese response to the widespread perception of incompatibility between the 'ways' of religion and literature, Williams concludes that the considerable acclaim accorded the works of several post-war authors with self-acknowledged affiliation to the Christian church, both Catholic and Protestant, provides further testimony of the extent to which the search for a form of 'Japanese Christianity' has resulted in an acknowledgement of the need for mutual compromise.

## NOTES

1. Elison, *Deus Destroyed*, p. 253.
2. Levy, *Modernization and the Structure of Societies*, vol. 2, p. 610. An exclusivist religion is here defined 'externally' as one whose adherents 'ideally and self-consciously speaking may believe in one and only one religion at any given point in time' (ibid., p. 610) and 'internally' as one whose teachings are 'fixed' and not open to interpretation.
3. Boxer, C.R., *The Christian Century in Japan*, p. 321.
4. Ciezlik, 'Kirishitansho to sono Shisō', p. 582. Cieslik's figures do not include the 30 000 killed in the Shimabara Rebellion of 1637–8.
5. Boxer, *The Christian Century in Japan*, p. 361. The number of 40 000 was that estimated by French missionaries in the 1860s and reported to the British diplomat, Sir Harry Parkes in 1868.
6. Ebisawa, *Nanban Gakutō no Kenkyū*, p. 4.
7. Elison, *Deus Destroyed*, p. 248.
8. Other texts earlier in their possession had been confiscated by the Nagasaki magistrate in a series of raids in the 1790s. See Breen, 'Heretics in Nagasaki'. See also Turnbull's essay in this volume.
9. *Tenchi Hajimari no Koto*, pp. 404-5.
10. *Maruchirio no Michi* is known to have been with the Christians of Urakami at least until the 1790s. See Breen, 'Heretics in Nagasaki', p. 15.
11. *Maruchirio no michi*, p. 333.
12. Endō, 'Nihon no Numa no Naka de – Kakure Kirishitan kō', pp. 37–42.
13. Ibid, pp. 37, 41–2.
14. On ancestor worship and contemporary Japanese Christianity, see, for example, Doerner, 'Comparative Analysis of Life after Death in Folk Shinto and Christianity', and Reid's more scientific study, 'Japanese Christians and the Ancestors'.
15. The best and most recent study of the *Mukyōkai* movement is Caldarola, *Christianity: the Japanese Way*. For the citation here, see p. 79.
16. Ibid., p. 78.
17. Ibid., p. 79.

# 1 Translations of Christian Terminology into Japanese 16–19th Centuries:
## Problems and Solutions
### Stefan Kaiser

EARLY STUDY OF JAPANESE BY WESTERNERS –
AN OVERVIEW

It is a well-known fact that the discovery[1] and subsequent study of the Japanese language by Westerners began with Francis Xavier's setting foot on Japanese soil in 1549 in order to preach the gospel, a few years after Portuguese traders were shipwrecked there. Xavier's two-year stay in the country led to a concentrated attempt by the Jesuits, and later Spanish Franciscans, to convert the Japanese to Christianity. Hugely successful (converts are said to have amounted to some 300 000 around the end of the sixteenth century), this was cut short after about 65 years when the Tokugawa government proscribed Christianity in 1614, closed the country in 1639, and eventually eradicated the religion by about 1643, just short of a hundred years after its introduction.

After initially using interpreters (a few Japanese individuals who had lived abroad), the Jesuits took to learning the language themselves, producing (with the help of Japanese converts) a substantial number of (often printed) materials for the study of Japanese, including dictionaries of the Portuguese, Latin and Japanese languages, of Chinese characters, texts and translations (some written in colloquial romanised Japanese), and grammars of the language. Their efforts in learning the language were of course motivated by the need to spread the gospel in an alien language and culture, and in the process they encountered endless problems in how to express and explain their faith and its concepts in Japanese.

After the Catholic Christians were expelled, the only Western presence tolerated for some two centuries was a small Dutch trading post, segregated to the artificial island of Dejima off Nagasaki. Being concerned with trade, and officially required to communicate through Japanese interpreters (Japanese language study was forbidden by the Shogunate), the

Dutch produced comparatively little material directly concerned with the Japanese language, although the numerous works taken back to Holland later served as materials for a Dutch grammar of the language. During the latter half of this period, however, the Japanese government actively encouraged the study of Western medicine, science and technology through the medium of Dutch (the so-called Dutch learning, or *rangaku*), resulting in some work on the Japanese language by Japanese using Western terminology.

Missionary activity, this time led by Protestants representing various denominations from the US and Europe, was resumed in 1859. However, this had to be done under the disguise of teaching English, as Christianity was still outlawed in Japan, and progress was slow for quite some time, even after the ban was lifted in 1873. However, translations of the Bible, which had already been attempted in part by various missionaries from about the 1830s, were now attempted with renewed vigour, and in very different conditions from those faced by the earlier Catholics since work done in Chinese by Jesuits (and more recently Protestant missionaries) eased their task considerably. Their efforts culminated in the New Testament translation of 1880, and the Old Testament in 1888.

The study of foreign languages other than Dutch had by then become well established in Japan, and Western studies of the Japanese language became plentiful.

Apart from the above mainstream developments there were some minor and more haphazard channels by which Japanese was introduced to Russia through castaways such as Denbei from about the beginning of the eighteenth century, and schools teaching Japanese were established, in St Petersburg and Irkutsk among other places. There was also the case of the American Ranald McDonald, who entered Hokkaido in 1848 and was sent to Nagasaki for repatriation, but taught English for several months to the interpreters there before being sent back to the US in 1849. Although not published until 1923, he produced *Japan: Story of Adventure*, which contains a glossary of Nagasaki dialect vocabulary.

In what follows, I will concentrate on the Christian connection, while referring at times to other developments in so far as they are connected or influenced by it.

## CHRISTIAN TERMINOLOGY AND JAPANESE

Francis Xavier, who appears to have had only an imperfect command of Japanese,[2] was aided in his missionary activities, which centred around

Kagoshima, by Yajirō (or Anjirō), a baptised native of that area whom he had brought back from Goa. Although the work is no longer extant, according to a letter Yajirō sent to Ignatius de Loyola, he translated the Gospel according to Matthew into Japanese in some form[3] and was therefore the first to encounter the problem of how to translate Christian technical terms into Japanese. Being originally a Buddhist, possibly of the Shingon sect, but not conversant with classical Chinese,[4] he used popular Buddhist terms to translate Christian vocabulary. This sometimes led those to whom they preached to believe that Christianity was a new Buddhist sect that had arrived from India. Initially condoned by Xavier and his fellow missionaries, Torres and Fernandez, it was soon recognised that this approach, while making the new religion appear more familiar to those exposed to it, had the danger of causing grave misunderstandings of its basic concepts. Baltasar Gago, who had arrived in Japan in 1552, recognised the need to institute a change of policy, as set out in his letter of 23 September 1555:

> These [Buddhist] Japanese have a number of words which they use in their sects. For a long time we preached them the truth through the medium of these words. Once I had become aware of them, however, I changed them immediately because, if one wishes to treat the truth with words of error and lies, they impart the wrong meaning. For all words, therefore, which I realised to be damaging, I teach them our own words. Even just the things that are new require new words. Besides, theirs have in essence very different meanings from what we mean.[5]

In accordance with the above sentiments, Gago was instrumental in substituting 'our own words' (Portuguese or Latin) for some of the earlier Japanese/Sino-Japanese 'tainted'[6] expressions, as in the examples below:

| *Hotoke* | → | *Dios* |
| *tamashii* | → | *anima* |
| *jōdo* | → | *paraiso* |
| *jigoku* | → | *infierno* |
| *tennin* | → | *anjo* |

However, there are indications that it was not always possible or advisable to follow this new policy to the letter; certainly Japanese documents such as Ōuchi Yoshinaga's *Licence to the Daidōji* of 1552 uses *buppō* (Buddha's Law) for the Christian faith and *sō* (Buddhist priest) rather than *patere* (padres).[7]

The above document was written as an official Japanese document, so the use of traditional Japanese terminology is perhaps not surprising; however, the Jesuits, too, requiring as they did a style of language that was easy to understand by the uneducated, needed to strike a balance between foreign and Japanese/Sino-Japanese terms when writing in Japanese, as we shall see below.

## Christian terminology in the Evola Screen fragments

One of the earliest extant Japanese translations of Christian literature are the fragments discovered in 1960 written on the inside layer of an old screen in the Evola Library. They are thought to be notes of Valignano's preaching taken down by Japanese novices in 1580 or 1581.[8]

This document contains short Latin sections from the Old Testament followed by their Japanese translations. The Japanese uses Buddhist terminology to translate Christian ideas:

*gongyō*[9]*-iwai*   (*quo mihi multitudo victimarum vestrarum*, etc.) (Isaiah I:11)
*mōnen*[10] *wo kiyome* (*auferte malum cogitationum vestrarum*)
*zenji wo shūseyo* (*discete benefacerlu*) (both Isaiah I:16)

In the first example, the Latin text is abbreviated, but *gongyō-iwai* may be thought to be a translation of a Latin word equivalent in meaning to offerings.

Direct loans are also found: before *gongyō-iwai* there is *sakirihishiyosu* (*sacrificios*), and in another section from the Gospel of John, *prophetavit* is rendered in Japanese as *poroheshia wo iheri*.[11]

## Christian terminology in the Manoel Barreto manuscript

The Barreto manuscript is an extensive handwritten romanised text that was discovered among the *Codices Reginenses Latini* of the Vatican Library; it is a copy in Manoel Barreto's own hand of various Christian works, dated 1591 (about one year after his arrival in Japan).

The 391-leaf manuscript is in four major parts, beginning with an account of the miraculous cross discovered in a tree in Obama (Kyūshū), going on to a book of gospels, setting out in the third part the benefits bestowed by the Guardian Angel and the Blessed Virgin, and ending in a collection of lives of saints. The source for the first three parts is unknown, but the last part bears a striking similarity to the *Sanctos no Gosagyō* (see below), with which it may share a common source.[12]

The manuscript uses a large number of Portuguese/Latin direct loans, but also a substantial number of Sino-Japanese (and some Yamato-Japanese) Buddhist terms. There is, however, a fair degree of variation between sections; especially the first one does contain Buddhist terms for some very basic Christian terminology:

*tera*[13] (Buddhist temple)
*gongyō*
*kimyō raisan*[14]

On the other hand, the same brief story also has many direct loans such as the following:

*anjo* (angel)
*arutaru* (altar)
*circuncisão* (circumcision)
*confissão* (confession)
*cruz* (the cross)
*Deus* (God)
*Ecclesia* (church)
*Escriptūra* (Holy Bible)
*gentio* (heathen)
*Irumão* (Brother)
*Missa* (Mass)
*Natal* (Christmas)
*Pādre* (Father)
*Providencia* (Providence)
*Santa Cruz* (Holy Cross)

Some direct loans that do not represent Christian items or concepts (even though they appear in the Bible) further illustrate the inability of Japanese at the time to accommodate unknown concepts, or perhaps lack of inventiveness on the part of the authors:

*deserto* (desert)
*mouro* (moor)

As far as the brief introductory story is concerned, Gago's policy seems to be largely adhered to, even though there are some glaring mismatches with Buddhist terms, as exemplified above. If we look further at other sections of the work, there are, however, many more Buddhist terms, making the matter of a 'policy' less clear.

The main terms are given below in noun form (i.e. *gedatsu-su* as *gedatsu*). Brief explanations of their meanings are given in parentheses (from Inagaki, *A Dictionary of Japanese Buddhist Terms*, unless otherwise indicated). Explanations taken from Japanese-language dictionaries are translated by the present author.

*akunen* (evil thoughts[15])
*dangi* (discussion of the principles and meanings; exposition, lecturing)
*gedatsu* (liberation, emancipation)
*hōji* (Buddhist service[16])
*jihi* (mercy, compassion)
*honzon* (object of worship; main image established in a temple[17])
*kago* (protection by a buddha, bodhisattva or other deity)
*kahō* (effect, reward or distribution of some acts done)
*kannen* (meditative thought)
*kuriki* (power of merit[18])
*kyō* (sūtra; a Buddhist scripture),
*kyōke* (to teach the proper and true faith; to convert to Buddhism[19])
*kyōmon* (passages of a Buddhist scripture),
*naishō* (inner realisation; enlightenment)
*raigō* (welcoming; the welcoming of an aspirant into the Pure Land by Amida and/or his attendant bodhisattvas),
*seppō* (exposition of the Dharma; sermon)
*shikishin* (a material body; physical form of a Buddha)
*shikitai* (substance of matter[20])
*shugyōsha* (a wandering ascetic)

## Christian terminology in the *Sanctos no gosagyō*

The *Sanctos no gosagyō no uchi nukigaki* is a Japanese translation of extracts from Acts of the Apostles by the Japanese *irmão* (Brothers) Paulo and Vicente. As its title suggests, it deals with the lives and deeds of the apostles, popular saints and certain martyrs.[21] It was printed at Kazusa in 1591 and written in a popular style.[22] It contains many Buddhist terms. Some examples are given in Table 1.1 below, which lists Buddhist terms on the left[23], and their Portuguese translation according to the 1603 *Vocabulario da lingoa de Iapam*:

Here, *mōnen* is used as in the Evola Screen fragments; by contrast, the Barreto MS does not use *mōnen* at all, using *akunen* instead. The lack of definite translation terms is discussed below.

## Christian terminology in the *Doctrina Cristan*

The *Doctrina Cristan* is a romanised Japanese catechism which was printed in 1592 in Amakusa by Jesuit missionaries. Another version (see below) bears the date 1600, but gives only *In Collegio Iaponico Societatis*

Table 1.1: Some Buddhist term from the *Sanctos no gosagyō*

| *Sanctos* term | Portuguese translation (*Vocabulario*) | English equivalent |
| --- | --- | --- |
| tenma | demonio | demon, devil[24] |
| mōnen | maos pensamentos | evil thoughts |
| bikuni | molher rapada, ou religiosa gentia | nun or religious heathen woman[25] |
| hōdan | predação da lei | prophesising the Law[26] |

*Iesu*, no place of publication. Both versions were also printed in Japanese mixed script in 1591 and 1600 respectively, providing us with four translations of the same work (all known in only one copy).

The stated aim of the work was to write in a style that was accessible to the masses:

> In order to enlighten everyone, irrespective of rank or standing, about this [Christian Doctrine], the words are [written] close to the commoners' ears, but the meaning investigates the mysteries of God.[27]

The use of a number of technical terms was, however, unavoidable for explaining Christian doctrine; to some degree, this was achieved by using foreign (Portuguese or Latin) words, such as *Ecclesia, Doctrina, Fides, Baptismo, Cruz, Penitencia*, etc. (written in capitals in the original text). For others, existing Sino-Japanese terms that often were not part of the general vocabulary of the spoken language were employed, as the following example shows (romanisation here and elsewhere is given in the Revised Hepburn system, unless otherwise indicated):

> ... wareraga nangi, daiji no jisetsu go saido riyaku arubeki tameni, IESUS no tattoki mi-na o tonae-tatematsuru nari[28]
> (because at hard and difficult times he can be expected to save us, we call his holy name.)

*Saido riyaku* is a Sino-Japanese Buddhist term; *saido* being saving and ferrying across (the sea of transmigration) and *riyaku*, benefit.[29] Here, the combination is used in the Christian sense of to give salvation, as is clear from the *Yawarage*[30], an appendix to the work consisting of a glossary explaining difficult terms in plain language, which deals with it as follows:

> Saido, riyaku. Tasukuru. Saluar, liurar.[31]
> (*Saido, riyaku*: To save; to save, liberate.)

There are many more examples of Buddhist terminology (in Chinese translation) in this work on Christian doctrine, e.g. *genze* 'the present world', *gose* 'the after-life', *gedatsu* 'freedom from the bonds of illusion and suffering in the three worlds'.[32] Obviously these were used because they were roughly similar to the intended meaning, thus compensating for the lack of appropriate terminology. Furthermore, some of them had the advantage of people being familiar with them – but not all, as can be seen from the fact that some are included in the glossary at the end of the volume.[33]

Apart from Buddhist terminology, archaic terms from the Japanese classics were also employed, e.g. *mi-yo* (His realm/kingdom) or *mi-oya* (Christ's father), and object-honorific auxiliary verbs like *tatematsuru*.

If we compare the 1592 and 1600 versions, there are various differences, which may just represent a revision, but can also be interpreted as evidence pointing to different traditions of translations (or different translators involved). Near the end of the work there is a section entitled *Benaventuranca wa yatsu ari* (Beatitudes), which is the same text (from Matthew V: 1–11) that the 1591 Barreto manuscript also contains (under a different heading), with yet again a partly different translation. Below is a comparison between the three texts for nos. 1 and 8:[34]

*Beatitude 1 (Matthew V: 1)*

1591: Spirito no hinja wa ten no kuni o motsu ni yotte Beato nari.
1592: Hitotsu ni wa, Spirito no hinja wa ten no kuni sono hito no naru ni yotte kahō nari.
1600: Hitotsu ni wa, Spirito no hinja wa, ten no kuni o motsu ni yotte, Beato nari.

*Beatitude 8 (Matthew V: 3)*

1591: Iusticia o sodaten tame shinrō o shinobu mono ten no kuni o shindai suru ni yotte Beato nari
1592: Yatsu ni wa, Iustitia tote goshō to, zen ni taishite sebameraruru koto o shinogu hito wa ten no kuni sono hito no naru ni yotte kahō nari
1600: Yatsu ni wa, Iusticia ni taishite shinrō o shinogu hito wa, ten no mi cuni o shindai subeki ni yotte, Beato nari.

There are some notable differences between the 1592 *Doctrina* and the other two works in that the former uses the Buddhist term *kahō*, as against *Beato* (one who has been beatified).[35] Otherwise, No. 1 is phrased quite similarly in the Barreto MS and the 1600 *Doctrina*, whereas the 1592 *Doctrina* is again quite different.

No. 8 shows differences between all three versions, but Barreto and the 1600 *Doctrina* are closer. The 1592 *Doctrina* again uses a Buddhist term, *goshō* (after-life; the future life).[36] The 1600 *Doctrina* is in all likelihood, as suggested by Ebisawa,[37] a revised version of the 1592 *Doctrina*, and it will therefore be useful to examine some of the differences between the two translations.

The Japanese version of the 1592 *Doctrina* was printed in 1591 as *Dochirīna Kirishitan*, and has an almost identical text to the 1592 romanised text.[38] As Kamei points out,[39] the *Dochirīna Kirishitan* seems to have been an edited translation of *Doctrina Cristā* (in Portuguese) by Marcos Jorge.

*Some differences between the 1591 (A) and 1600 (B) versions of the Doctrina*

The newer (B) version is not necessarily a more accurate rendition of the Portuguese original. For instance, (A) has a faithful translation of the original as follows:

> ... senam pola bondade & misericordia de Deus, & polos mercimentos de Christo.[40]
> ... tada Deus no go-Bondade to, on-jihi to, mata on-aruji Jesu Christo no kuriki o motte ... (A: A4)

(B) has a version that has been edited and abbreviated as follows:

> ... tada Deus no on-jihi no ue yori on-aruji Jesu Christo no go-kuriki o motte (B: A4)

Both the sentence structure and the one-to-one translation of terms are more faithful in the older translation.

There are, however, instances, where (B) is closer to the original, as in the following extract:

> ... mas todas hejam ordenadas pera honra, & gloria de Deus nosso Senhor.[41]
> ... sono shosa o ... Deus no go-hōkō to, on-homare to naritatematsure tame nari. (B: A10)
> ... mata sono shosa wa Deus no Gloria to naritatematsuru tame nari. (A: A8)

*Towards simplicity of expression: gains and losses*

It is said that (B) overall represents an improvement over (A) in that it aims for a clearer, simpler mode of expression, which is partly achieved by translating unusual foreign words into Japanese.[42] In some instances it was possible to do so by using everyday Japanese, as for instance in the following:[43]

*Oleo* (A: 5) *abura* (B: A5)
*Speransa* (A: 27) *tanomi* (B: C1)

However, in other cases it was not so easy to find a translation term that was untainted by Buddhism:

*Catechismo* (A: A3) *go-seppō* (B: A3)
*Benedicta* (A: 23) *go-kahō* (B: B4)
*go-Ontade* (A: 59) *go-naisho* (B: E1)

Although (B) here chooses translation terms that are familiar, the advantages are not clear, in that they are Buddhist, and in that sense belong to Gago's category of dangerous words.

Notwithstanding such comparative failure, (B) also often succeeds in replacing Buddhist terms with more general Sino-Japanese or Yamato-Japanese expressions:

*go-nyūmetsu*[44] (A: 82) *go-shikyo* (B: F8)
*gedatsu jiyū* (A: 7) *jiyū* (B: A6)
*zengon*[45] (A: 70) *zenji* (B: F3)
*go-saido riyaku* (A: 14) *sukuware-tatematsuru* (B: B1)

Another attempt to achieve greater clarity in (B) is achieved through a technique which we may call pseudo-*Monzenyomi*. *Monzenyomi* refers to a way of glossing Japanese *kanbun* for the Chinese classics as typically found in certain Japanese textual traditions of the *Wen-xuan*. Examples are found in *kunten* works (works written in Classical Chinese glossed by interlinear marks etc.) from the early Heian period.[46] Below is an example from a late eleventh century text of the *Shōmonki*

heikiku to nonoshiri kenka to kamabisushi.[47]

*Heikiku* and *kenka* are both two-kanji Sino-Japanese compounds. The former means 'to make a racket',[48] but the meaning of the latter is somewhat obscure, not being listed in the *Daikanwa jiten* as a compound. Its first kanji, however, means the sound of a carriage moving along;[49] the second, on the other hand, meaning 'to investigate a crime'.[50] The classical Yamato-Japanese verb *nonoshiru*, too, means 'to be loud', and the adjective *kamabisushi*, 'noisy'. Both *heikiku* and *kenka* use complex kanji and were clearly not part of everyday vocabulary. By reading the terms twice, once in the Sino-Japanese, followed by Japanese translation-equivalents, the meanings of the technique were applied only to difficult terms.[51]

Structurally speaking, the Sino-Japanese term (usually a two-kanji compound) always comes first, followed by the Yamato-Japanese reading. The two are linked by the particle *to* if the Yamato-Japanese term is a verb or adjective, whereas *no* is used where it is a noun, as in the following example[52]:

*sairō no ōkami* (wolf)

The relationship between the two sections of identical meaning in a *Monzenyomi* is a modificational one, effected by *to* (adverbial particle) or *no* (adnominal particle) depending on the nature of modification.

Initially, this technique was used for explicating difficult terminology, but later was clearly used for ease of memorisation as well as for basic educational texts such as the Thousand-Character Classic (*Senjimon*).[53] These two functions, serving as a crib for the understanding and memorising of difficult terms in the Chinese classics, can also be thought to have motivated the application of the pseudo-*Monzenyomi* to Christian terminology in the Latin or Portuguese original.

The (B) version applies this technique to explain unfamiliar foreign terms in a similar way, using (mostly) the particle *tote* (which functions in the same way as *to*). Below are some examples from the section entitled *Dos sete peccados* (Of the seven deadly sins) in the originals:

*Humildade.* (A: 72)
*Humildade tote herikudaru koto.* (B: F4)
*Temperança.* (A: 72)
*Temperança tote chūyō no koto.* (B: F4)
*Diligencia* (A: 72)
*Diligentia tote zen no michi ni yurugase naku susumu koto.* (B: F4)[54]

The Japanese explanatory equivalents range from a (nominalised) verb (*herikudaru*, 'be humble') or a noun (*chūyō*, 'moderation') to a whole phrase, as in the last of the above examples (*zen no michi ni yurugase naku susumu*, 'advance on the path of virtue without neglect').

The section titled 'On the Cardinal Virtues' shows similar differences: below are shown the text of the original, followed by the (A) and (B) translations:

As virtudes Cardeaes.
*As Virtudes Cardeaes*

*San quatro,*
*A primeira, he prudencia,*
*A segunda, justiça,*
*A terceyra, fortaleza,*
*A quarta, temperança.*[55]

Cardeales no virtudes wa yotsu ari.
Hitotsu ni wa, Prudencia.
Futatsu ni wa, Justicia.
mittsu ni wa, Fortaleza.
Yotsu ni wa, Temperança: kore nari. (A: G3)

*Cardinales Virtu(-)*
*des to iu yotsu no zen ari.*
Hitotsu ni wa, Prudentia tote kenryo no zen.
Futatsu ni wa, Justitia tote kenbō no zen.
Mitsu ni wa, Fortaleza tote tsuyoki kokoro no zen.
Yotsu ni wa, Temperança tote shikishin no ue ni chūyō o
mamoru zen, kore nari. (B: H1)

The pseudo-*Monzenyomi* technique is applied from the outset, here using *to iu* to modify *yotsu no zen* ('four virtues'), but elsewhere *tote*, which may be considered a suspensive form of *to iu*. The first two virtues are translated by non-Buddhist Sino-Japanese terms, *kenryo* and *kenbō*,[56] but no direct translation equivalents could be found for the remainder, where explanatory translations are instead used (*tsuyoki kokoro*, 'strong heart', and *shikishin no ue ni chūyō o mamoru*, 'follow the middle ground for one's body').

The section *Os dões do Spiritu Sancto* (The gifts of the Holy Spirit) in the original takes this technique to such extremes that one can no longer argue that there is the one-to-one correspondence in meaning that characterises the technique of *Monzenyomi*.[57] Whether this represents efforts at rewriting and editing shorter versions is not clear, but it clearly goes beyond anything we could call translation, and in a sense can be seen as an acknowledgement on the part of the translators of the impossibility of translating some areas of Christian doctrine by the means that were available at the time. Let us look at the gulf between versions (A) and (B) for the first two gifts:

Hitotsu ni wa, Sapiencia.
Futatsu ni wa, Entendimento. (A: 98)

Hitotsu ni wa, Sapientia tote genze no koto o omoisage, goshō no gi o fukaku omonji, ajiwai ni motozukase-tamō on-atae nari.

(Firstly, the gift called Sapientia, which makes one think less of this world, attach great importance to the after-life, and base things on its attractions.)

Futatsu ni wa, Entendimento tote, Fides no ue yori shinzuru kotowari o yoku wakimayuru tame ni funbetsu o akirame-tamō on-atae nari. (B: H1)
(Secondly, the gift called Entendimento [understanding], which provides one through Faith with the judgment in order to discern the truth.)

As may be seen from the above examples, this technique was generally made use of in the (B) version in sections where concepts are listed in the foreign language(s), so as to explain their meaning and implication in Japanese. However, even though the style is increasingly aimed at the uneducated,[58] Sino-Japanese terms are not accorded the same treatment, even though they may be thought to have been well beyond the understanding of the masses (see below).

*Retention of Buddhist terminology*
Despite the attempts to create a simpler, more transparent terminology, a great many Buddhist terms were left unchanged. For instance, *kuriki, kyōke, genze, goshō, shikisō, shikishin, shikitai, jihi, mōnen.*[59]

Another glaring example of this is the case of the Seven Deadly Sins, which are listed in the original and the two translations as follows:

...
O primeyro he Soberba,
  O segundo Auareza,
  O terceiro Luxuria,
  O quarto Ira,
  O quinto Gula,
  O sexto Enveja,
  O septimo Preguiça.[60]

...
Hitotsu ni wa kyōman.
Futatsu ni wa ton'yoku.
Mitsu ni wa jain.
Yotsu ni wa shin'i.
Itsutsu ni wa tonjiki.
Mutsu ni wa shitto.

Nanatsu ni wa kedai. Kore nari.
Kore o subete Mortal toga to iu nari. (A: 69)

...

Hitotsu ni wa kōman. Futatsu ni wa ton'yoku. Mitsu ni wa jain.
Yotsu ni wa shin'i. Itsutsu ni wa tonjiki. Mutsu ni wa shitto.
Nanatsu ni wa kedai kore nari. Kore o subete Mortal toga to iu nari.
(B: F2)

Here, there is no attempt to explain the meanings of the terms; the majority of them are listed in the (A) *Yawarage*, indicating that there was a perceived need to explain them in simpler words for the uneducated:[61]

Tonyocu. Yocuxin. Auareza.
　(Desire. Greed.)
Xiny. Icari. Ira.
　(Anger. Fury.)
Tonjiqi. Xocu uo musaboru. Gula.
　(Crave food. Gluttony.)
Xitto. Sonemi, sonemu. Enueja.
　(Envy, to envy. Envy.)
Qedai. Itazzura ni iru coto. Priguiça.
　(Being idle. Indolence.)
　　(A: *yawarage*, given in original spelling)

The (B) version, while being in many respects superior to the earlier (A), was presumably still not regarded as a definitive version. The problem first faced by Xavier of how to translate Portuguese/Latin and Buddhist terminology into workable Japanese, had made some progress but had not really been solved, as is evident from the obvious state of flux in the *Doctrina* and other works.

Another piece of evidence demonstrating this lack of definitive translation terms is that the *yawarage* lists *bu'nyō*,[62] but this term, which was used in the earlier mixed-script version, had in fact been changed to *vōqinaru tocu* (original spelling) in the text, making the *bu'nyō* entry redundant, as the word is not used anywhere else in the (A) text either.[63]

The state-of-flux theory is also supported by the fact that the (B) version uses quite a variety of different translations for a single term in the original. For instance, for *gloria* we find *keraku, on-homare, on-ikuhō, keraku mandoku* and *Gloria*.[64] Similar tendencies are also observed in other works, such as the 1596 *Contemptus Mundi*, which has four different wordings for Matthew XI: 28.[65]

To what degree such differences were overcome in the Kyoto translation of the New Testament, which existed in some form (possibly as a summary) according to a variety of sources[66], is unfortunately impossible for us to tell, but the odds are that one-to-one translation equivalents for Christian terminology were never achieved before the authorities finally suppressed the activities of the Jesuit missionaries and their press.

## PORTUGUESE/LATIN TERMS: ERADICATED BY THE AUTHORITIES

The expulsion of missionaries and persecution of Christianity had the effect of eliminating all the work that had been done in Japanese within Japan. The disappearance of the Portuguese tradition is perhaps best illustrated by the fact that early translations of parts of the New Testament by Protestant missionaries in the nineteenth century were clearly unaware of the Jesuit achievements.[67] The persecution in Japan also eradicated the terminology (given the fact that it never seems to have been definitive, one had perhaps better use the plural, terminologies) that had been so painfully created.

Some Portuguese words denoting everyday foreign objects, such as *pan* (*paõ* = bread) and *bīdoro* (*vidro* = glass), did of course survive in popular parlance, but most technical terms, even those not in any way connected with Christianity, became the victims of the persecution of this foreign culture. Curiously, some Portuguese medical terms survived under the guise of Dutch for some time because the Portuguese medical tradition (*Nanban-ryū*), was merged with the Dutch medical tradition in the mid-seventeenth century.[68] For instance, in the 1681 *Tōryū Denki Yōsatsu Nukigaki* or in the list of medical terms (*Orandakō wage*) in the 1696 *Oranda Gekasho,* the majority of terms are still from the Portuguese, despite the word *Oranda* (Holland) in the title, alongside some Latin and Dutch.[69] In the former work, Latin and Dutch terms are in fact identified as such, whereas Portuguese terms are not, suggesting that they were still regarded as the established layer of technical terms in this area.

There were also some isolated instances through which Christian terms were reintroduced into Japanese, the best known of which is Arai Hakuseki's *Seiyō Kibun*, which contains an account of Christianity based on his interrogation of the Italian Jesuit missionary Sidotti, who had secretly entered the country in 1708.

The manuscript of this work seems to have been revised several times, and was not published until 1807, but is thought to have circulated to a degree in secret.[70]

Hakuseki (who incidentally is the first Japanese to have consistently used *katakana* for transcribing foreign words)[71] uses many notes (*warichū*) in the text to explain unfamiliar terms and proper names. To a degree, they give us an indication of the fate of the earlier Christian terminology in Japan:[72]

deusu, Kan ni tenshu to yakusu.
(*Deus*, in China translated *tienzhu*.)

haraiso to wa, Kan ni yakushite, tendō to iu, Busshi no iwayuru gokuraku sekai no gotoshi.
(*paraiso* is translated in China as *tientang*. It is similar to *gokuraku sekai* in Buddhism.)[73]

anzerusu wa Busshi no iwayuru kōon tenjin[74] no tagui, Porutogaru no go ni, anjo to iu nari.
(angels are the type of thing the Buddhists call *kōon tenjin*; in Portuguese they are called *anjo*.)

anima wa, tamashii nari.
(*anima* is soul.)

konchirisan to wa, koko ni zange to iu.
(*contrição* is what we call *zange*)[75]

yeizusu kirisutos, Kan ni sēsu to yakusu, ware zoku ni zesu to iishi wa, kanyaku no oto tenjinamareru nari.)
(Jesus Cristos is translated as *sēsu* in China; what we used to call *zesu* in popular parlance is a corruption of the Chinese translation.)

kirisutyan, kore yeizusu no hō nari, ware zoku ni, kirishitan to iu wa, Porutogaru no go
(Christian, this is the Law of Jesus; what we call *kirishitan* in popular parlance is the Portuguese word).

Three facts can be inferred from the above examples: firstly, that educated Japanese at the time were aware of Christian terminology through Chinese translation (Matteo Ricci's name in Chinese transliteration is mentioned elsewhere in the work); secondly, that Buddhist terminology is generally used to explain what Christian terms mean; and, thirdly, that there were a few Christian terms that had survived the eradication of Christianity and were used colloquially.

It is not clear what the implications of the different tenses in the last two examples are. It may indicate that *zesu* was already obsolete at the time. *Kirishitan*, however, appears to have been still in use, although possibly only as a derogatory term, as indicated for instance from a 1779 work quoted in the *Edogo Daijiten*, where *Kirishitan goteretsu* is used as a term of abuse.

## THE IMPORTANCE OF A TRADITION

The difficulties faced by the Jesuit mission in translating Christian terminology into Japanese are symptomatic of a situation where there was virtually no tradition or previous work available, even though there are some indications that there may have been earlier translations of Christian literature, perhaps for internal uses,[76] and glossaries or vocabulary lists that were used in the Japanese language learning process by the Jesuits were available.

Unlike the Protestant missionaries in Japan in the nineteenth century, the Jesuits had no access to earlier Chinese works (translations of Western works and Christianity were not produced by Matteo Ricci and others until a decade later, as woodblock prints).

Given the fact that works such as the *Doctrina* were no doubt used in day-to-day missionary activities by a number of different people and/or at times their Japanese assistants, it is also likely that constant adjustments were being made. Nevertheless, the fact that no definitive translation equivalents had been established even after some fifty years indicates that the task at hand was simply too daunting without a tradition of terminology, or some other means.

### The role of Chinese translations for Japanese terminology

The above situation contrasts sharply with the situation faced by the Protestant missionaries who entered Japan from 1859 in that they could avail themselves of the intermediary of Chinese. The crucial importance of this difference is briefly outlined below.

Jesuit missionaries in China produced hundreds of Chinese translations and adaptations dealing not only with Christianity but also astronomy, geography, history, mathematics, and so on. Despite the ban on such books (pronounced in 1603, tightened further in 1685, but relaxed somewhat between 1720 and 1839), many of these works appear to have increasingly circulated in Japan, often in handcopied versions and created a bedrock of technical and religious terms.[77] The 1787 *Kōmō Zatsuwa*, for instance, quotes a Chinese translation of the (equivalent of) the Dutch *gasutohoisu* as follows:

> Minjin byōin to yakusu. (*Kōmō Zatsuwa* 1787/1980: 57)
> (The Ming Chinese translate it as *byōin*)[78]

As demonstrated by Itō, even a scholar of National Learning like Hirata Atsutane was able to plagiarise arguments from works on Christianity by Aleni (*Sanshan Lunxueji*), Ricci (*Jiren Shipian*) and Pantoja (*Qike*) in his *Honkyō Gaihen* (written 1806). Influences from Christianity, therefore, now took place through the medium of Chinese rather than directly through the Japanese language as the earlier Jesuits had attempted. This was possible as learned Japanese were of course highly proficient in classical Chinese.

Chinese translations of Western works date back to seventeenth century Jesuit works dealing with scientific and religious matters; many of these early Chinese translations circulated among the intelligentsia in Japan during the period of prohibition of Christian books.[78] There is also evidence that like Japanese men of learning, translators of Western works in Japan also consulted Chinese translations of Western learning.[79]

Protestant missionaries had entered China over fifty years before they could gain access to Japan in 1859. Introducing Western learning in Chinese formed an important part of their work, and they and their Chinese assistants produced some 800 works between 1807 and 1867,[80] dealing with a great variety of topics ranging from Christianity via history and geography to mathematics.

Many of these missionaries came to Japan after having actively published in Chinese, and often brought with them (and sold) multiple copies of these works. Japanese also travelled to Hongkong or Shanghai and purchased such works there. For instance, Namura Gendo's *Akō Nikki* states that he purchased *Xiaer Guanzhen*[81] and *Luhe Congtan*[82] in 1860.[83]

Such Chinese translations were already circulating in Japan before the first Protestant missionaries arrived in 1859, and Japanese editions (with *kaeriten*, etc) were being published. For instance, parts of Muirhead's 1847 *Haiguo Duzhi* (*Kaikoku Zushi* in Japanese) came out in Japanese editions from 1854.[84]

Chinese–English dictionaries such as Lobscheid (1866–9) also served as a valuable translation aid.[85] Lobscheid's dictionary was widely consulted because it represented the culmination of a tradition of Chinese–English dictionaries[86] and sought to incorporate technical terms,[87] whereas Dutch–Japanese dictionaries such as *Yakken* and *Oranda Jii* were more concerned with *explaining* the meaning of words in simple, easy-to-understand Japanese.[88] In Japan, it was in fact not until the 1872 *Yōgo On'yakusen*, using Chinese translation sources in Japanese editions, that translation terms were actively included in Japanese dictionaries.[89] Until then, translators had to rely on Dutch–Japanese and English–Chinese dictionaries.

26  *Japan and Christianity*

It is significant that both J.C. Hepburn and S.R. Brown, who were the central figures in (probably) the first full translation of the New Testament into Japanese in the 1870s, had been living in China and could read classical Chinese, and their Japanese assistants had all been trained in Chinese and/or Buddhist studies.[90] As Morioka shows, influence from the 1861 *Xinyi Quanshu* (translators E.C. Bridgman and E.C. Culbertson, published by the Meihua Shuguan in Shanghai), was enormous, and enabled the translators to come up with a translation of the New Testament, famous for its flow and beauty, barely 20 years after the first Protestant missionary entered Japan.[91] As Ebisawa puts it:

> When one mentions the Bible in Japan, one must not overlook the Chinese translation of the Bible. That is because even though a policy of being faithful to the [Hebrew/Greek] originals was adopted, the Chinese translation was not only consulted: there are extremely numerous (*kiwamete ōi*) instances where it was followed with respect to the titles of its chapters and to Christian terminology.[92]

Haugen has made the axiomatic assumption that in order to cope with unknown linguistic situations, people will use known linguistic patterns wherever possible.[93] In light of what we saw above about the differences between the magnitude of problems the early Jesuits had to deal with in Japan and the speedy achievements of the later Protestants, we may take Haugen's statement a little further and suggest that unknown linguistic situations without the possibility of using known linguistic patterns present almost insurmountable problems, particularly in a language and culture that is as distant for Europeans as was that of Japan at the time.

NOTES

1. The existence of Japan had, of course, been known in the West for some centuries through Marco Polo's brief account of *Zipangu*, which was based on hearsay information obtained in China.
2. Schurhammer, *Das Kirchliche Sprachproblem*, p. 11.
3. Cieslik, 'Shūkyō Shisōshi kara mita Bareto shahon', p. 49.
4. Schurhammer, *Das Kirchliche Sprachproblem*, p. 20.
5. Ibid., p. 61. The English given here has been translated by the author from Schurhammer's German rendition.
6. Gago called these terms 'the dangerous words' (ibid.)
7. The interlinear Latin translation of the Japanese original uses (*ad declarandum*) *legem faciendi sanctos* (to make known the law which makes saints) and *patres*.
8. Ebisawa, *Nihon no Seisho*, p. 37.

9. Diligent practice; effort; practice of the Buddhist way (Inagaki, *A Dictionary of Japanese Buddhist Terms*).
10. An illusory thought; a wanton thought; an illusion (ibid.).
11. Ebisawa, *Nihon no Seisho*, p. 39.
12. Laures, *Kirishitan Bunko*, p. 105.
13. *Tera* is an old cultural loan from Korean that entered Japanese with Buddhism.
14. *Kimyō* = embrace Buddhism and devote one's body to the Buddha; *Raisan* = worship the Three Treasures and praise their merits (Iwamoto, *Nihon Bukkyōgo Daijiten*.)
15. Ibid.
16. Ibid.
17. *Japanese-English Buddhist Dictionary* (Revised).
18. Iwamoto, *Nihon Bukkyōgo Daijiten*.
19. *Japanese-English Buddhist Dictionary* (Revised).
20. Nakamura, *Bukkyōgo Daijiten*.
21. Laures, ed., *Kirishitan Bunko*, p. 40.
22. Fukushima, *Santos no Gosagyō*, p. 370.
23. Ibid., pp. 114–15.
24. 'A heavenly devil; the king of the Paranirmitasavartin Heaven is so called because he causes hindrances to those who follow the Buddhist Way' (Inagaki, *A Dictionary of Japanese Buddhist Terms*).
25. A Buddhist nun (ibid.).
26. Preaching the Dharma; expounding the Buddhist teaching (ibid.).
27. Hashimoto, *Kirishitan Kyōgi no Kenkyū*, p. 6. The Japanese text reads as follows:
    Jōge banmin ni tayasuku kono mune (mane) o shirashimen (shirasen) ga tame ni, kotoba wa zoku no mimi ni chikaku, gi wa tenmei (Deus) no soko (takaki kotowari) o kiwamuru (arawasu) mono nari.
    (Sections in parentheses indicate revisions in the later 1600 version.)
28. Hashimoto, *Kirishitan Kyōgi no Kenkyū*, p. 14.
29. Inagaki, *A Dictionary of Japanese Buddhist Terms*.
30. *Doctrina no uchi kotoba no yawarage* (Explanations in easy-to-understand words for terms used in the *Doctrina*) is the full heading.
31. The 1603 *Vocabulario da lingua de Iapam* explains the term as follows:
    Saido riyaku. Saluacao, Vt. Saido riyakuno go goon. Beneficio da redepcao, ou saluacao.
    (*Saido riyaku* (salvation), e.g. *saido riyaku no goon* (benefit of redemption, or salvation)
32. *Japanese–English Buddhist Dictionary*.
33. Hashimoto, *Kirishitan Kyōgi no Kenkyū*, p. 296 argues that this use of Buddhist terminology may have been due to the numerous converts to Christianity from Buddhism.
34. See also Ebisawa, *Nihon no Seisho*, p. 53 for a comparison between the three texts of nos 3 and 4.
35. Taylor, *A Portuguese–English Dictionary*.
36. Inagaki, *A Dictionary of Japanese Buddhist Terms*.
37. Ebisawa, *Kirishitansho, Haiyasho*, p.477;
38. See, however, Kamei, *Nihon Iezusukaihan Kirishitan Yōri*, p. 72 for a discussion of some (minor) differences between the mixed-script and romanised versions.

39. Ibid.
40. Reproduced in Kamei, *Nihon Iezusukaihan Kirishitan Yōri*, p. 20.
41. Reproduced in ibid., p. 29.
42. Ebisawa, *Kirishitansho, Haiyasho*, p. 477; Kamei, *Nihon Iezusukaihan Kirishitan Yōri*, p. 173.
43. The following comparison between versions (A) and (B) is based on the textual differences listed in Ebisawa, *Kirishitansho, Haiyasho*, pp. 477–89, but several of the differences are also discussed in Kamei, *Nihon Iezusukaihan Kirishitan Yōri*. The numbers in parentheses indicate the pages in versions (A) and (B); for (B), where the pages are not indicated, numbers are supplied by the present author by counting forward from the last one given. Also, the usual order of B, B1, B2... is standardised here as B1, B2, B3... Note further that these numbers refer to leaves, i.e. two sides.
44. Passing into Nirvana; the passing away of a Buddha or revered priest (Inagaki, *A Dictionary of Japanese Buddhist Terms*).
45. A root of goodness; a meritorious, good act (ibid.)
46. Tsukishima, ' "Monzenyomi" Kō', pp. 38–45.
47. Ibid., p. 39.
48. 'Kamabisushiku sawagu' (Morohashi, *Daikanwa Jiten*).
49. Morohashi, *Daikanwa Jiten*.
50. Ibid.
51. Tsukishima, ' "Monzenyomi"-kō', p. 40.
52. Ibid., p. 41.
53. Ibid., p. 43.
54. Reproduced in Kamei, *Nihon Iezusukaihan Kirishitan Yōri*, p. 92.
55. Reproduced in ibid., p. 110.
56. The *Vocabulario* has entries for these terms as follows: *Qenrio. Caxicoqu vomonbacaru* (consider wisely). *Prudecia. Qenbo. Iustica.*
57. Kamei, *Nihon Iezusukaihan Kirishitan Yōri*, p. 111.
58. There are various indications of this, which include the much-simplified way of writing in the Japanese (mixed script) version (B), but also the use of plain Yamato-Japanese expressions instead of more literary Sino-Japanese in the (A) version, that is, *shōji no hito* (A: 30); *ikitaru hito, shishitaru hito* (B: C2)
59. Kamei, *Nihon Iezusukaihan Kirishitan Yōri*, p. 136.
60. Reproduced in ibid., p. 94.
61. Hashimoto, *Kirishitan Kyōgi no Kenkyū*, p. 295.
62. The entry reads *Bunho. Yutaca. Prosperidade.* in the original.
63. Kamei, *Nihon Iezusukaihan Kirishitan Yōri*, p. 73.
64. Ibid, p. 61.
65. Ebisawa, *Nihon no Seisho*, p. 54
66. Ibid., p. 56
67. Guntzlaff's 1837 translation (made with the help of Japanese shipwrecked individuals) of the Gospel According to John, which influenced later translators such as J.C.Hepburn is one example. It uses *kawaigaru* for love, and *gokuraku* for God (Ebisawa, *Nihon no Seisho*, p. 108.)
68. This development was partly due to the eradication of Catholicism, which made use of the word *nanban* difficult.
69. Sugimoto, *Kaitai Shinsho*, p. 21.

70. Ebisawa, *Nihon no Seisho*, p. 71.
71. Matsumura, 'Arai Hakuseki to Gaikokugo'.
72. All citations are from Arai, *Seiyō Kibun*, p. 783–7.
73. Amida's 'World of Utmost Bliss' (Inagaki, *A Dictionary of Japanese Buddhist Terms*).
74. *Kōon-ten*. The third of the three heavens comprising the second group of *dhyana* heavens (*nizenten*) in the *rupa-dhatu* (*shikikai*, world of form) (*Japanese-English Buddhist Dictionary* (Revised).)
75. 'To repent of one's sins' (Inagaki, *A Dictionary of Japanese Buddhist Terms.*)
76. Laures, *Kirishitan Bunko*, p. 2.
77. See, for example, Itō, 'Kinsho no Kenkyū' (*ge*), and Ebisawa, *Nanbangakutō no Kenkyū*.
78. See Ebisawa, *Nanban Gakutō no Kenkyū*, pp. 301–17 for a list of works that can be documented.
79. According to Matsui, 'Bakumatsu Kango no Imi', p. 104, n. 7, the 1843 *Kaijo Hojutsu Zensho* (published 1853) gives a Chinese translation as the source for the word *jugaku* as follows:
*Anzuru ni jugaku no go, Minjin yakusho ni izu.*
(Note that the word *jugaku* is found in Ming-Chinese translations.)
80. Ozawa, *Bakumatsu Meiji Yasokyōshi Kenkyū*, p. 141.
81. *News from Near and Far*: a monthly magazine, published 1855–56, initially by W.H.Medhurst.
82. A gazette in Chinese with various contributors, edited by Alexander Wylie, published in China 1857–8.
83. Furuta, p. 551.
84. Matsui, 'Kindai Nihon Kango', p. 36.
85. See Morioka, *Kindaigo no Seiritsu*, p. 116ff. for an account of Lobscheid's influence on various Japanese translations.
86. Morioka, *Kindaigo no Seiritsu* lists 14 earlier 'major' English–Chinese dictionaries.
87. 'The author has deemed it imperative to translate and explain in this work, all the scientific words which have been added to the English language during the present century …' (Lobscheid, *English and Chinese Dictionary*. (Preface)).
88. Sato, *Kokugo Goi*. p. 376.
89. Matsui, 'Kindai Nihon Kango', p. 35.
90. Ebisawa, *Nihon no Seisho*, p. 212.
91. Morioka, *Kindaigo no Seiritsu*, p. 183ff.
92. Ebisawa, *Nihon no Seisho*, p. 98.
93. Haugen, 'The Analysis of Linguistic Borrowing'.

# 2 Early Western-Style Paintings in Japan
## Michael Cooper

Impact, influence, and cultural contribution are terms notoriously difficult to assess, as regards both quantity and quality, when studying transcultural relations between two civilisations. To make one's point, there is always a tendency to exaggerate the effect that a culture has had upon another society, to see ideal results that perhaps were not nearly so significant as might be fondly supposed. Such a danger is certainly present in the study of *nanbanjin*, or the Southern Barbarians, as the Japanese unflatteringly dubbed the early Spaniards and Portuguese who came to their country.

The early Christian missionaries in Japan sent back an immense quantity of letters, reports and writings. Many of these are of considerable historical value for they offer a comparative insight into things Japanese, but their sheer number may give the mistaken impression that the sun rose and set on European activity in Japan, that the European presence made itself felt throughout the country and in every aspect of Japanese life. To counteract this view, it is well to bear in mind that the early Europeans, both missionaries and merchants, in Japan were few in number, that many Japanese never once caught a glimpse of them, let alone were in any way influenced by them. Additionally, it is surely significant that references to the Europeans living in or visiting the country are few and scanty in Japanese official records and private writings of the time.

It would be a mistake, however, to go to the other extreme and believe that the Westerners left no mark at all during their nearly a hundred years of residence in Japan. They certainly did so in the religious sphere, for despite extended and relentless persecution Christianity continued to exist, at least in attenuated form, in outlying regions for centuries after all the missionaries had been expelled or martyred. And in a peculiar but limited way Western painting made a small contribution to the cultural scene in that for a limited period some local artists painted in the Western style. Although this artistic phenomenon was short-lived, it has at least left behind some examples as proof positive that the Western cultural tradition did manage to obtain a tenuous foothold on Japanese soil for a brief time. This daring experiment was cut short by political factors and not allowed to mature, put down roots and flourish. But thanks to the examples that have fortunately survived to the present day, it is impossible to hold that the West made no cultural impact at all on Japan in the sixteenth and seventeenth centuries.

A word of clarification is perhaps needed here. *Nanban bijutsu*, or Southern Barbarian art, can be divided into two general categories. The first includes screens (or *byōbu*), usually sixfold and in pairs, that depict European missionaries, merchants and ships, and sometimes even the foreign port, that is, Goa, from which they embarked for their voyage to Japan. Some sixty of these fascinating screens are extant, both in Japan and elsewhere, and they are painted in purely Japanese style, usually by artists belonging to the Kanō school. These works are classified as *nanban bijutsu* simply because of their exotic content, not because of their artistic style. The second general category embraces works painted in the Western style by Japanese artists, who for the most part produced copies based on European exemplars. The present chapter deals with this second category.

## MISSIONARIES

At the end of the thirteenth century Marco Polo included a brief hearsay description of the legendary island of Zipangu (as he called Japan) in his celebrated book of travels through Asia.[1] His account of the mysterious country would have probably gone unnoticed except that the author mistakenly dwelt on the abundance of gold in Zipangu, a fact that aroused the interest, not to say cupidity, of European merchants. But it was not until 1543 that three Portuguese traders were shipwrecked off the small island of Tanegashima, to the south of Kyushu, and thus unwittingly inaugurated the century of Western relations with Japan.

Only six years later Francis Xavier and two Jesuit companions sailed into Kagoshima determined to bring the country into the Christian fold. Although this dream was never realised, Xavier's successors achieved some remarkable results in view of their exiguous numbers, and within a matter of 30 years some 100 000 Japanese had been baptised. As the Jesuit mission in the country became better organised and administered, more and more churches were inaugurated throughout Kyushu and parts of Honshu (especially Kyoto). Many of these foundations, however, were probably little more than houses converted for the purpose. Those that were especially built were constructed in typical Japanese style, as can be seen in Kanō Motohide's fan-painting of the church in Kyoto.[2]

As Buddhist temples were often generously decorated with statues and paintings, so the missionaries too wished to embellish their own places of worship to encourage the fervour of the local Christians. The fact that the Portuguese, Spanish and Italian priests came from a cultural milieu in which the interiors of churches were lavishly decorated obviously increased this desire. In addition, religious pictures would obviously have been useful as gifts to recent converts and as visual aids when missionaries, some of them less than fluent in Japanese, gave sermons or catechism instruction. Scattered through the Jesuit correspondence are references to religious paintings and statues that served either to decorate churches or as objects of personal devotion. Such items were liable to be abused by anti-Christians. Reports in 1565 and 1566 tell of an official in Kyushu who seized an imported *The Assumption*, painted out the eyes of the figure, wrote an obscene expression across the painting, and derisively put it on display in his mansion.[3]

To help the missionaries in their apostolic work, a call went out to Europe for religious pictures and paintings. In 1584 Luis Frois reported that even 50 000 pictures would not satisfy the requirements of the missionaries and begged his brethren in Europe to send as many as possible. At different times requests were made for prints and pictures of Rome, European knights, sea and land battles.[4] The Jesuits in Japan were at a disadvantage, for Nagasaki was the last port of call of the annual Portuguese carrack, or *não*, on its two-year voyage from Lisbon to Japan, and there is evidence that some pious pilfering of religious items took place when the ship wintered at Goa. Although the carrack was the largest vessel afloat at the time, luggage space was limited, and it is likely that pictures and paintings destined for Asia were small in size. Further, lack of financial resources probably meant that the items sent East were not of the highest artistic quality, nor, in view of the purpose of their dispatch, was there any real need that they should have been.

A number of these imported European paintings still exist today in Japanese museums. They are, naturally, religious in inspiration, and usually depict either Christ or the Virgin Mary. *Mater Dolorosa* (oil on canvas, 52.5 × 40 cm, Nanban Bunkakan, Osaka) is perhaps one of the best examples from the artistic point of view. *Virgin and Child* (oil on metal, 21.8 × 16.6 cm, Tokyo National Museum), on the other hand, is of decidedly inferior quality and was somewhat crudely retouched by an unknown artist. All of these examples are from the Italian and Spanish schools of painting.[5]

Whether or not the imported paintings were of high quality, there can be no doubt that the Western style of painting produced a deep impression among the Japanese. For the first time they encountered artistic techniques such as chiaroscuro, perspective, shading and foreshortening, and the resulting realism could not help but cause wonder among the viewers. At the very beginning of the mission, Xavier showed a fine illuminated bible to Ōuchi Yoshitaka, *daimyō* of Yamaguchi. He reports that Shimazu Takahisa, *daimyō* of Kagoshima, fell to his knees (although admittedly he was probably sitting on the tatami flooring at the time) when shown a painting of Our Lady; his mother, expressing her admiration, later requested a copy.[6]

Even some sixty years later, the same effect was caused when the Spanish envoy Sebastian Vizcaino visited the court of the *shōgun* Tokugawa Hidetada in Edo in 1611 and showed portraits of the family of his king, Philip III. According to Vizcaino, the shogun's ladies marvelled at the realistic depiction and inquired whether the facial colouring of the figures was natural or not. The Spaniard subsequently donated the paintings to Tokugawa Ieyasu when he visited his court at Suruga.[7] The astonishment of the Japanese is hardly surprising when we consider the stereotypical, standard depictions in portraits of their nobles at the time; the seated posture varies hardly at all, and often only the face differentiates one portrait from another. Small wonder, then, that the more realistic Western painting produced a deep impression.

Although some of these Western paintings still exist there are documentary references to other Western works introduced at the time. In 1582 four teenage Japanese youths set out for Europe under Jesuit patronage to deliver the respectful greetings of three Christian *daimyō* of Kyushu to the pope. During the course of their journey in Europe they were twice received in audience by Philip II. In Rome, the boys were greeted with much kindness and pomp by the ailing Gregory XIII in March 1585 and with no less warmth by his successor Sixtus V. The party then made what can only be described as a triumphal progress through Italy. While in Padua the Japanese were given copies of Abraham (Wortels) Ortelius' celebrated atlas, *Theatrum Orbis Terrarum*, first published in Antwerp in 1570, and the first three volumes of Georg Braun and Frans Hogenberg, *Civitates Orbis Terrarum*, a collection of bird's-eye views of cities such as Rome, Lisbon and London.[8] The significance of the latter work will be seen later. They also took home to Japan various paintings presented to them on their travels: a self-portrait by Vicenzo Gonzaga; a portrait of Bianca Capello, Duchess of Tuscany, by Alessandro Allori; and *The Funeral of Emperor Charles V*. As far as is known, none of these works has survived.

The donation of paintings was not, however, entirely one-sided. On 3 April 1585, during a private papal audience, the boys presented to Gregory XIII a magnificent pair of screens, showing Azuchi Castle and city; the screens were possibly the work of the master painter Kanō Eitoku. Unfortunately no trace of this work, of such historical and artistic value, can now be found.[9] In addition, while at the court of Philip II later in the same year, the legation donated two religious paintings, *Ecce Homo* and *The Saviour*, executed 'by one of the best Christian painters in Miaco [Kyoto]'.[10] The identity of this artist is not known, but as the boys left Japan in 1582 and the Italian art teacher Giovanni Niccolo, introduced below, arrived there in the following year, it is clear that the Japanese painter had not been one of his pupils.

So far we have briefly dealt with some of the known examples of Western art that found their way into Japan during the period under review. Their significance lies not so much in themselves as works of art (some of them were of indifferent quality) but in the fact that they were used as exemplars by Japanese artists painting in the Western style.

## PAINTING IN THE WESTERN STYLE

Although the missionaries in Japan were begging their confrères in Europe to send religious pictures and paintings to decorate churches and to use as teaching aids, Japan could hardly be more geographically remote from Europe, and the vast distance between Lisbon and Nagasaki, not to mention the danger of shipwrecks, pirates, typhoons and fire, contrived to make the supply of such works irregular at the best of times. If, then, Europe could not provide this desired material in sufficient quantity, then another solution was possible – the missionaries should train local artists to paint in the Western style and produce religious pictures in Japan itself. In 1581 Francisco Cabral wrote to Rome pointing out that 'for the love of God' an instructor in painting was urgently needed.[11] With such a teacher, the local church would become largely independent, at least as regards the supply of art work, of the annual ship from Portugal.

The operation was masterminded by an Italian missionary. Alessandro Valignano (1539–1606) was appointed Visitor, or Inspector, of the Jesuit missions in Asia (with exception of the Philippines) in 1573, and in that capacity he visited Japan three times. During his first visit, 1579–82, he devised the plan to found Jesuit high schools, called *seminarios*, for the education of the sons of Christian gentry. In so doing, he hoped that the solid Christian education offered by the institutions would foment vocations to the religious life, as well as protect the boys from the influence of Buddhist monks. The original plan called for the setting up of three such schools, although in the event only two were founded. The school in Azuchi, the city of Oda Nobunaga, lasted only a brief time and was dispersed soon after the violent death of that warlord in 1582.

The school in Kyushu also suffered various vicissitudes and was transferred from place to place owing to the changing political situation, but despite these upheavals it managed to survive. A good deal is known about this establishment, including the daily timetable and lists of pupils. For the present purposes, however, what is important is that, in addition to the standard curriculum of Japanese language and literature, science and mathematics talented pupils were given the opportunity to study Western music, printing, engraving and painting. As regards music, the standard must have been reasonably high, for two of the boys who went to Europe played the organ at Evora Cathedral in September 1584 as they passed through Portugal, and then all four performed as a quartet in an impromptu concert in the presence of the ruler Toyotomi Hideyoshi, 1537-98, at his Juraku palace in Kyoto on their return from Europe.[12]

While it is possible that various Jesuit teachers were capable of teaching Western music to some degree, instructing students in the techniques of Western painting obviously required the services of a specialist. The Jesuits' entreaties for such a teacher were finally met when the Neapolitan Giovanni Niccolo (1560-1626) arrived in 1583. For someone who was the first to teach Western art in Japan, Niccolo remains a disappointingly shadowy figure, and sources of information about him consist, for the most part, of laconic entries in the catalogues listing the members of the Japanese mission.[13] According to the scant records, Niccolo had indifferent health, was talented at painting, mathematics, clock-making and other manual skills, and taught art at the Kyushu school throughout most of his 31 years in Japan. None of his own work is known to exist, although some non-extant items have been attributed to him on somewhat tenuous grounds.[14]

Niccolo certainly painted *The Assumption of the Virgin* three years after his arrival in Japan. According to Frois, in December 1586 disturbances in Bungo obliged the Jesuits to abandon their residence and church in Usuki and take refuge in the local castle. The missionaries carried away with them as many possessions as they could, but among the items left behind was a large clock and 'a very lovely, large, and accomplished painting of Our Lady of the Assumption, which Brother Giovanni Niccolo, the Neopolitan, had finished only a few days earlier for the Usuki church. As it was painted in oils on a large and heavy board, it was impossible to carry it to the castle; and even if they had wanted to do so, there was no entrance there through which they could take it inside.'[15]

After the missionaries were expelled from Japan in 1614, Niccolo continued his teaching activities at the Jesuit college in Macao and it was there that he died. He was a versatile man and his talents were not limited to painting. In 1606, the Jesuits presented Tokugawa Ieyasu at Suruga with a bamboo striking clock that told not only the time but also the days of the month and the movements of the sun and moon – most probably the work of Giovanni Niccolo. In the following year the missionaries visited Edo Castle and gave another Western clock, 'made in Nagasaki', to the shogun Tokugawa Hidetada. Niccolo is also credited with making bamboo organs and other musical instruments.[16]

Only limited information is available regarding the teaching of Western art in the Kyushu *seminario*. In his report about mission activity in 1594 Luis Frois mentioned the school, then located at Hachirao in Arima, and after praising the pupils' musical talent he observed:

> With no less fruit do some of them progress in painting and engravings. Some of the boys are engaged in oil painting. We cannot help greatly admiring them because some copy so dextrously the finest paintings brought back from Rome by the four Japanese nobles. They do this with such skill as regards colour, exactness, shading, and precision, that many of the Fathers and Brothers cannot distinguish which are their paintings and which are the paintings done in Rome, and some insist that those done by the Japanese are those brought from Rome. Without knowing that they had been made in Japan, some Portuguese saw these paintings and were greatly astonished, declaring afterward that they looked like the paintings brought from Rome. So in this way, with God's help, Japan will have from now on people who can fill many churches with fine pictures and also satisfy many Christian lords.[17]

Two years later, on his arrival at Nagasaki in August 1596, Bishop Pedro Martins made a tour of inspection of the school, then located at nearby Arie in Arima. He was first entertained by an allegorical play performed by the students in Latin, Japanese and Portuguese in which Christian virtue triumphed over evil spirits attempting to impede the evangelisation of Japan. Duly edified by this uplifting spectacle, the bishop and his party then went to visit the school's printing shop and art studio. In the latter he inspected the pupils' work and members of his retinue exclaimed that the boys' reproductions were in no way inferior to the original European imported works; it was difficult, they declared, to distinguish between the two.[18]

The repeated observation that the boys were engaged in copying European originals underscores an essential feature of the works painted in Western style: as the pupils had never left the shores of Japan, their paintings were inevitably imitations of European imports. While it is true that the students were later obliged to create enlarged versions of these imports so as to fill the ample area of *byōbu*, their artistic contribution for the most part consisted of reproductions, with varying degrees of faithfulness, of European works, although there were a few exceptions.[19]

The names of some of the Japanese Jesuit lay-brothers who were occupied in painting are listed in catalogues and it is probable that they cooperated with Niccolo in his teaching duties – Brothers Mancio Joan of Usuki in Bungo; Thadeu (b. 1568) also from Usuki; Pedro João (b. 1566) of Kuchinotsu in Arima; Mancio Taichiku (b. 1574) of Uto in Higo; Leonardo Kimura (1574–1619) born and martyred in Nagasaki; Luis Shizuoka (b. 1577) of Nagasaki; and the Chinese-Japanese Jacobo Niwa (1579–1638) who later worked as an artist in Macao and China.[20] The names of various other painters working in the Western fashion are also known from written sources. Yamada Emonsaku was still alive in 1638 at the time of the Shimabara Uprising. An artist of considerable talent was the mysterious Nobukata, about whom nothing is known except for his seal that appears on various paintings. Finally, there is a reference to a painter named Pedro Kanō who was seeking reconciliation with the Church, and it is possible that, although belonging to the traditional Kanō family of painters, he worked in the Western style.[21]

## WESTERN-STYLE PAINTINGS

The extant work of these native artists can be divided into two general categories: religious and secular paintings. In all probability the former were executed while they were still students at the *seminario*; obviously their Jesuit mentors would encourage them to devote themselves to pious illustrations as an integral part of their education as well as to supply the needs of local churches. The secular paintings on screens were often on a large scale and therefore required more skill than a teenage pupil would probably possess. Once the boys had left the college, they were presumably free to paint whatever they pleased, and the short-lived craze for things Western in the 1590s meant that commissions for screens depicting life in the exotic West would be in profitable demand.

Of the extant religious paintings, two may be mentioned here. The first is by an unknown artist and is titled *Our Lady of the Rosary* (colour on paper, 75 × 63 cm, Kyoto University). Although the composition of the work is obviously overcrowded, the individual parts show considerable skill in execution. In the centre Our Lady is depicted holding a flower in her left hand and the Infant Jesus in her right; the child in turns holds an orb in his left hand and raises his right in blessing. The pose is, of course, quite common, and in this case is probably based on *Nuestra Señora de Antigua*, a mural painting in Seville Cathedral.[22] Across the middle of the composition runs the legend in Portuguese, 'Praise be to the Blessed Sacrament', an invocation that has no particular relevance to the subject matter of the painting. Below are featured four saints: the two men prominently shown in the centre are St Francis Xavier and St Ignatius Loyola, founder of the Society of Jesus (thus indicating that the painting was probably executed under Jesuit auspices). For good measure, although again with little apparent relevance, Saints Matthias and Lucy are somewhat awkwardly shown on either side. The names of all four saints are written in roman letters at the bottom of the composition.

It is not difficult to determine the model for Xavier, as a similar portrait with an identical pose appears as the frontispiece in Horacio Turselino, *Vida del P. Francisco Xavier*, Valladolid, 1600, a work first published in Latin at Rome in 1594 and copies of which were presumably introduced into Japan. Finally, around three sides of *Our Lady of the Rosary* are illustrated the fifteen Mysteries of the Rosary, the Joyful and Glorious mysteries running down the left and right sides, and the Sorrowful across the top. These miniature scenes, executed with no little skill, were presumably based on European originals, and such quaint illustrations may be found in ancient churches and cathedrals in Europe even today.

Yet another religious painting, a portrait of Francis Xavier, appears to have some connection with the frontispiece in Turselino's biography, for both pictures have the saint uttering the Latin words, 'Satis est, Domine, satis est.' Although the portrait is painted in Western style, it is interesting to note that the hands are depicted weakly, a feature often encountered in portraits executed in traditional Japanese fashion. Beneath the portrait is written with considerable skill the saint's name in ancient *man'yōgana* script, followed by the Japanese name, 'The Fisherman'. In view of the golden background, it has been suggested that the artist may have been a member of the Kanō school of decorative art, and, further, may have been Pedro (the fisherman) Kanō, mentioned above. The title beneath the portrait refers to *St* Francis Xavier, and as Xavier was not canonised until 1623, the picture was probably painted sometime after that date, perhaps in Macao. Alternatively the title may have been added some years after the portrait was completed, thus making it possible for the work to have been produced long before 1623.

While it is only too easy to criticise various aspects of both paintings, it must be borne in mind that the artists were utilising a foreign style that had been introduced only shortly before, that in all probability they belonged to the first generation of Japanese painters working in the Western fashion. Seen in this light, both works are creditable and have comparative merit. In addition, the artists were presumably using Japanese brushes, or *fude*, and were painting on paper; neither of these features would lend itself to high-quality Western art.

There are a few other extant examples of religious painting, but a couple, bearing Nobutaka's seal, are of particular interest. As stated above, nothing is known about Nobukata (indeed, we cannot be absolutely sure of the reading of his artistic name), but his output shows considerable talent; his *Woman Playing the Lute* (colour on paper, 55.5 × 37.3 cm, Yamato Bunkakan, Nara) is skilfully executed, and the figure shows a pleasing suppleness missing in the work of other artists.

But Nobukata has another claim to fame inasmuch as he did not base all his compositions on European paintings. Two of his portraits are unique in that, although executed in Western style, they depict Buddhist figures and therefore are not copies of imported European exemplars. One shows Nikkyō, 1552–1608, a Nichiren monk (colour on paper, 112 × 60 cm, Seirenji, Hyōgo Prefecture), complete with the Nichiren invocation *Namu Myōhō Rengekyō*, while the other depicts a stylised Daruma (colour on paper, Yōchiku-in), or Bodhidharma, the Indian monk who introduced Zen into China – two paintings that were obviously not produced under Jesuit auspices. The realism and delicate treatment of the beard in the latter work are particularly striking. It is worth noting that, although painted in the Western style, both portraits show elongated ears, the conventional Buddhist symbol of sanctity in East Asia. Nobukata showed an admirable spirit of artistic independence, for he also painted the Christian *Cleric and Two Children* (colour on paper, 115 × 54 cm, Kobe City Museum).

## SECULAR THEMES

If extant religious pictures painted in Western style are relatively few in number, possibly because of the subsequent anti-Christian persecution, we are fortunate to be still able to examine a variety of paintings depicting secular subjects, many in the form of six-panel screens. Some of them are devoted to Western pastoral scenes; the exemplars of these *byōbu* have not been identified, but the screens are obviously based on imported European pictures in which splendidly robed courtiers and nobles frolic in the countryside, with not a puddle or mosquito to spoil their languid enjoyment. The Japanese screens generally depict young Europeans, dressed in brightly coloured costumes, standing or sitting in a garden, talking and gesticulating to one another. Often one or more of the figures is playing a Western musical instrument, such as a harp or lute. The subjects adopt wooden, somewhat theatrical poses, but then the courtiers peopling

European paintings of pastoral scenes are often enough shown with a similar lack of realism.

If the people depicted in the Japanese screens appear unnatural, it must be recalled that the artists were copying from relatively small exemplars and were therefore obliged to increase their size considerably to fill up the extensive surface of the *byōbu*; such enlargement, unless undertaken with experience and skill, can easily deprive figures of their original vitality. And as will be seen below, various details of these highly coloured screens were taken from monochrome copperplate prints, thus adding to the artists' problems. Ships sail in a bay or lake in the middleground, and generally the depiction of the mountains and sky in the background appears oriental in inspiration, suggesting that the artists copied the central figures from European pictures but supplied their own background based on the Asian tradition.

The popularity of these colourful but unrealistic screens depicting daily life (as the Japanese probably believed) in the exotic West was probably considerable, and there doubtless existed a demand for such works. The screens were painted over a period of only, at most, 30 years, and the number still extant after nearly three centuries indicates that they must have been produced in quantity. In fact, few themes in the history of Japanese painting were reproduced so often in so short a time.[23]

Two screens show mounted warriors on a terrace, which is so unnaturally tilted that in reality the horses would not be able to remain standing. The human figures and the size of their mounts leave something to be desired, as also does the general perspective. But the overall effect of these colourfully robed, exotic warriors would doubtless have provided pleasing decoration in a noble's mansion.[24]

The most spectacular example of all, and unique of its kind, is the six-panel screen titled *The Battle of Lepanto* (colour on paper, 153 × 362.5 cm, Kōsetsu Bijutsukan, Kobe). That memorable conflict pitting Don John of Austria against the Turkish forces took place on 5 October 1571 and was, of course, a naval engagement. But to depict a battle at sea was possibly beyond the capabilities of the Japanese painter and he took the artistic liberty of setting the conflict on dry land, with the sea and ships, however, in the background. Occupying three panels on the right are the massed forces of the Turkish warriors, some shooting arrows from the howdahs of three suitably fierce-looking elephants. The ranks of the Christian forces are locked in violent combat and some of the soldiers are mounted on rearing horses with bulging, foreshortened haunches. A wounded soldier, fallen from his mount, lies pitifully in the foreground, while officers urge on their troops to greater efforts in the frenzied conflict.

To the left, sitting calmly in a horse-drawn chariot with a forest of upraised spears as background, a regal figure stares imperturbably out of the picture and is identified as the King of Rome. To emphasise the Roman element, flags on the ships and on land bear the motto SPQR (*Senatus Populusque Romanus*). Great art this is not, but battles scenes on traditional *byōbu* are not uncommon, although never quite so overwhelming as this depiction, and doubtless this screen attracted a great deal of attention in its time as, in fact, it still does today. And for all the Japanese then knew, this was an outstanding example of Western art.

As in the case of *Our Lady of the Rosary*, the artist seems to have borrowed from a variety of sources. The chariot, horseman, and horses of the 'King of Rome' are obviously based on those of the Four Graces in a European print depicting *The Wedding of Louis XIII*. As for the elephants, an animal seldom seen in Japan, one of them in the Lepanto screen, together with its driver and the soldiers in its howdah, has exactly the same posture as an elephant seen in a European print showing *The Battle of Zama*, an engagement between the Romans and Carthaginians that took place in the Second Punic War in 202 BC.[25] Thus if the artist copied these relatively small portions of the screen from such diverse sources, we can only wonder how many European works he used as models to complete all six panels.

Other screens or panels depicting a single monarch, courtier, or warrior are also extant, but unlike the religious pictures mentioned above, it has so far proved impossible to track down all the original European works on which they were undoubtedly based. A good deal of research has been devoted to this end and this detective work has met with some limited success. Screens sometimes show miniature pictures of people dressed in the costumes of different countries and some of these are based on the figures within cartouches of European maps of the time.[26] It is easy to see where the Japanese artists obtained their inspiration in this regard. Although admittedly too late to have been used as an exemplar, Willem Blaeu's *Asia Noviter Delineata*, 1662, contains around its edges miniature illustrations of ten couples garbed in the robes of different countries, as well as bird's-eye views of nine cities.

The origins of small portions of other screens have been traced to European pictures. A small mounted figure in one screen is identical with a European copperplate print of the Emperor Vespasian, while another is perhaps based on a print of Emperor Otto. In the pastoral *byōbu* in Osaka and Itami, a fortress-like building, leaning with an alarming tilt in the Itami example, is copied from a castle seen in the European print *Pyramus and Thisbe*. The Itami screen also features a gazebo, complete with a statue inside and, outside, two trumpeters and a woman carrying a dish on her head, and all this has its original in a detail from a Flemish work depicting the eremitical life. In these and other cases the artists, while undoubtedly copying the European exemplars, have considerably simplified the original pictures and rendered them with a good deal less skill.[27] Hopefully more exemplars of Japanese paintings will come to light in time, probably not so much through systematic search as by chance discovery.

If we have yet to trace completely the origins of the pastoral pictures, some of the exemplars of the screens depicting Western cities and maps of the world have been identified. As regards the cities, it was noted above that the four boys brought back to Japan Braun and Hogenberg's illustrated *Civitates Orbis Terrarum*, and it is on record that they displayed their European gifts to interested parties. For example, on their way to Kyoto for the audience with Toyotomi Hideyoshi in 1591, they stopped at Morotsu and there showed the *daimyō* Mōri Terumoto and other visitors astrolabes, maps, charts, a map of Italy, and a plan of the city of Rome. These works, especially *Civitates Orbis Terrarum*, subsequently provided models for Japanese artists to copy.[28]

Thus an eight-panel screen in Kobe displays bird's-eye views of Rome, Lisbon, Seville and Constantinople, one each to two panels. The depiction of Rome is impressively accurate, and it is easy to identify landmarks such as the Colosseum (more intact than it is today), the Church of the Gesù, the Roman College, the bridges over the Tiber, Castel Sant'Angelo, and the obelisk in St Peter's Square. This enlarged picture is admittedly only a copy, but it was produced with remarkable fidelity by a Japanese artist who had never left his country.

Even more ambitious is a screen in the possession of the Imperial Household that shows miniature paintings of no less than 28 cities, including Rome, Frankfurt, London, Lisbon, Moscow and Paris. Although the small depictions are executed with care, the numerous places represented in the limited space make the screen less interesting than the Kobe *byōbu* showing, on a far larger scale, only four cities.[29]

Somewhat related to these screens illustrating cities are those decorated with a map of the known world. Unlike Matteo Ricci's celebrated *Mappa Mundi*, third edition, 1602, which diplomatically places China in the centre of the world, Japan is usually located at the far right.[30] In some maps the country's remote location is compensated by its exaggerated size, for Japan is made to appear about half the size of neighbouring China. The maps are of interest as they illustrate the extent of European knowledge of world geography at that time. Europe, West Africa, India and South America are depicted with fair accuracy, while North America and Australia remain largely undefined. Given that these paintings were produced in Japan, it is disappointing that both that country and China are not depicted with greater accuracy, although the screens improve on Western versions by correctly depicting Korea as a peninsula. In addition, Hokkaido is usually shown; in some cases it does not appear, but as Japan is located on the extreme right-hand edge of the screen, it may be that there was no room to include the island or else the painting was trimmed to fit on the screen.[31]

## CONCLUSION

It is a tempting but ultimately fruitless exercise to speculate how the new school of Western painting would have developed in Japan had it been allowed to continue, develop and mature. Would it have been a passing phase, a mere fad, that once initial enthusiasm had cooled would have died out on its own accord? Would the native tradition have eventually prevailed and swallowed up the imported artistic innovations, leaving no trace? Would some sort of composite Western-Japanese style have evolved, borrowing the best features from both traditions? Would artists have continued to paint in the European fashion and eventually established an independent art form that would have lasted to our own day? There is no way of telling. It is enough to report that the anti-Christian persecution beginning in the second decade of the seventeenth century, followed by self-imposed national seclusion up to the mid-nineteenth century, effectively brought to an end this East–West cultural experiment.

We are finally left with the problem raised at the beginning of this chapter – how significant was the impact of the Western art introduced in the latter half of the sixteenth century? However much sentiment may prompt us to exaggerate its importance, we must inevitably admit that it was a passing phenomenon, a barely discernible ripple on the surface of Japanese art history. At the same time we can allow that it was a stimulating cultural experiment. While we may regret its abrupt and artificial termination, we can rejoice that at least for two or three decades there was a tentative meeting between European and Asian cultures.

## NOTES

1. Masefield, ed., *The Travels of Marco Polo*, 3:2, pp. 323–5.
2. Colour on paper; width, 50.3 cm; Kobe City Museum. The three-storey Church of Our Lady of the Assumption was inaugurated in 1576.
3. Frois, *Historia de Japam*, 2, pp. 80, 155–6.
4. Okamoto, *The Nanban Art of Japan*, pp. 97–8.

5. Illustrations of these and other paintings are found in Sakamoto et al., *Nanban Bijutsu to Yōfūga*, Gutierrez, 'A Survey of Nanban Art' and Okamoto, *The Nanban Art of Japan*.
6. Frois, *Historia de Japam*, 1, p. 40; Francisco de Xavier, in Ruiz-de Medina, ed., *Documentos del Japon*, pp. 156–7.
7. Vizcaino, *Relacion del Viaje*, pp. 129–30, 141.
8. According to a contemporary Latin account, the boys received Ortelius' atlas plus three volumes of 'the world's cities depicted with much skill'. Almost certainly these were the first three volumes of Braun and Hogenberg's famous work, published in 1572, 1575 and 1581. The three succeeding volumes (1588, 1598 and 1617) would not have been available at the time of the Japanese visit. De Sande, *De Missione*, p. 323, Frois, *La Première Ambassade*, p. 233, n. 815.
9. Frois, *La Première Ambassade*, p. 184.
10. Frois, *La Première Ambassade*, pp. 94, 107.
11. Francisco Cabral, 3 September 1581, in Jesuit Archives, Jap.Sin. 9 (1a), f.19v.
12. Frois, *La Première Ambassade*, pp. 43–4; Cooper, *Rodrigues the Interpreter*, p. 80.
13. For these catalogues, see Schütte, ed., *Textus Catalogorum Japoniae*. Further details about Niccolo's career in Japan are given in Schurhammer, 'Die Jesuitenmissionare', pp. 771–2.
14. Okamoto, *The Nanban Art of Japan*, p. 100.
15. Frois, *Historia de Japam*, 4, p. 302. I thank Professor John R. Kelly for this reference.
16. Cooper, *Rodrigues the Interpreter*, pp. 210–11, 216.
17. Frois, *Historia de Japam*, 5, pp. 479–80; Okamoto, *The Nanban Art of Japan*, pp. 103, 113. According to a 1593 report, eight pupils were painting in oils, five were engraving copper plates and eight were painting with Japanese colours.
18. Manoel Frias, letter dated 1597, in British Library, Add. MSS.9860,f.52; Gutièrrez, 'A Survey of Nanban Art', p. 140; Cooper, 'Teatro Jesuitico no Japao', pp. 141–3.
19. Introducing a note of realism into the general chorus of praise, one of the missionaries wrote in 1599 that, despite their imitative skill, the students lacked creative originality when it came to producing their own work. Gutièrrez, 'A Survey of Nanban Art', p. 148.
20. Schütte, *Textus Catalogorum Japoniae*; Schurhammer, 'Die Jesuitenmissionare', pp. 773–4.
21. Jesuit Archives, Rome, Jap.Sin. 20(1),ff.162v–163. The document is in the form of an official retraction, signed by Kano and dated Kyoto, 6 March 1603. The ecclesiastical notary who witnessed the deed was Martin Hara, who had been one of the four boys who visited Europe.
22. A similar depiction of the *Virgin and Child*, although more crudely executed, appears as an engraved print on paper (22 × 14.5 cm, Ōura cathedral, Nagasaki); according to the inscription, it was produced at the Kyushu *seminario* in 1597.
23. If the *nanban* screens featuring Europeans and the Portuguese carrack, but painted in the traditional Kano-school style, are included in the total, this

*Cooper: Western-Style Paintings* 45

number grows considerably, for there are no fewer than 60 of these works still extant.

24. The exemplars of most of these mounted warriors can be found in an illustrated world map, 'Nova Orbis Terrarum Geographica', published by William Blaeu, 1571–1638, in Amstersdam in 1607. The map is shown in the exhibition catalogue *Seiyōjin no Kaita Nihon Chizu*, p. 181.
25. Sakamoto, *Nanban Bijutsu to Yōfūga*, p. 187.
26. Vlam, 'Kings and Heroes' and Vlam, 'Western-style Secular Painting'.
27. Sakamoto, *Nanban Bijutsu to Yōfūga*, pp. 184–91, and Sakamoto, *Shoki Yōfūga* contain valuable illustrated accounts of this subject.
28. Frois, *Historia de Japam*, 5, pp. 280–1; Okamoto, *The Nanban Art of Japan*, p. 80.
29. Braun and Hogenberg's first three volumes were not, as is sometimes supposed, the sole source of these copied pictures. While the views of some cities in Volume 1 (for example, Rome, Paris, Frankfurt and Venice) are almost certainly the exemplars of the Japanese copies, others (such as Amsterdam and London), also in Volume 1, are entirely different. The picture of Lisbon was included in Volume 5, 1598, long after the boys' return to Japan. The depiction of Rome in the screens is similar to Braun and Hogenberg, but Jesuit institutions, such as the Church of the Gesù, and the Roman College, have been added prominently to the Japanese version. Although the German volume does not show the obelisk in St Peter's Square, the monument is clearly seen in the Kobe screen.
30. There are exceptions. Two screens in the Nanban Bunkakan, Osaka, have the country squarely in the middle of the world map, and the same is true of *Bankoku Sōzu*, 'World Map', woodblock print, Kobe City Museum.
31. As late as 1646, Jan Jansson's 'Iaponiae Nova Descriptio' shows no sign of Hokkaido and depicts Korea as an island.

# 3 New Perspectives on the Early Tokugawa Persecution
Ōhashi Yukihiro

## INTRODUCTION

The banning and suppression of native Christians that took place in the early seventeenth century as the Tokugawa political structure was being erected is familiar enough to all students of Japanese history. A number of questions about the proscription remain, however, unanswered. There appears, especially, to be very little corroborative evidence for the view held by Kataoka and others, that the suppression of Christians was, despite some regional variations, applied thoroughly throughout Japan after the issue of the first Tokugawa anti-Christian edict in 1612.[1] This chapter endeavours to shed light on the process of qualitative change in the proscription following the first of the Keichō edicts, taking as its material the Christians of the Shimabara and Amakusa areas.

The Christian prohibition was enforced because quite simply, in the eyes of the *Bakufu*, the Christians posed a threat. The established view holds that the Christian threat was twofold: firstly there was the fear of the 'colonisation' of Japan through the military might of Portugal and Spain on whom the Christian missionaries were seen to rely,[2] and secondly there was fear of the outbreak of popular uprisings inspired by Christians.[3] This position is not, however, easily reconciled with the well-known facts that (a) the Christian missionaries were anxious, for the most part, to be seen to conform to the ruling structures of the time,[4] and (b) Christian thought, as disseminated by the Iberian missionaries, sought no disruption of the temporal order of things.[5]

The failure of earlier studies to explain this 'tension' between the apparent acceptance by Christians of the temporal order, on the one hand, and the *Bakufu*'s perception of Christianity as a threat, on the other, is a consequence perhaps of misunderstandings about the meaning of the term *Kirishitan* in the steady application of the Christian proscription from the end of the sixteenth through to the early seventeenth century. In short, existing studies of Christianity in the period reviewed here have all too often overlooked the class structure within the Christian community. We tend to talk loosely of *Kirishitan*, but on closer inspection it becomes clear that the so-called '*Kirishitan* community' comprised a multi-layered class structure. It is unwise, therefore, to lump all Christians together as *Kirishitan*. The present essay focuses on the internal class system within Christian communities as a means of approaching the broader issue of the dynamics of the proscription process. Part I reveals the existence of a qualitative change in the Christian prohibition of the early seventeenth century, while Part II, drawing on the conclusions of Part I, attempts a reassessment of the Shimabara Rebellion from the perspective of the changing nature of the proscription.

## I   PROCESSES OF CHANGE IN THE CHRISTIAN PROHIBITION

It has already been suggested that the contradiction between Christian acceptance of the temporal order and the Tokugawa *Bakufu*'s perception of a Christian threat may be solved by an analysis of the internal Christian class structure. Let us focus first, then, on the anti-Christian edicts promulgated by Toyotomi Hideyoshi and subsequently by the *Bakufu* in an attempt to uncover the changing nature of the Christian proscription. The following analysis of the terminology in the anti-Christian edicts suggests that the Shimabara Rebellion marks a major break, and this points in turn to a substantial shift along class lines in the primary target of the persecuting authorities. I then delineate, on the basis of primary source material, those targets *prior* to the Shimabara Rebellion, before analysing *Bakufu* understanding of Christianity in the same period. The final section points up the critical nature of the Shimabara Rebellion for an understanding of the development of the prohibition.

### The target of the Christian proscription

Table 3.1 is a chronology of anti-Christian edicts promulgated up until the Kan'ei period (1624–44). Kan'ei 15 (1638) is notable for the decisive change that it marks in the terminology employed by the *Bakufu* in its edicts to denote Christians. For example, the Tokugawa *Bakufu*'s first anti-Christian law, promulgated in Keichō 17 (1612), refers to Christians as '*bateren* sectarians', where *bateren* is a corruption of the Portuguese '*padre*'. Thus: 'Item – *Bateren* sectarians are now proscribed. Any breaches of this law of proscription shall be dealt with with the utmost severity.'[6] Table 3.1 makes it quite clear that this terminology prevailed up until Kan'ei 15 (1638) and that, thereafter, the term *Kirishitan* is to be found in its place. What significance, though, can we read into this change?

*Table 3.1* Chronology of anti-Christian edicts

| Date | Source | Terminology for Christians | Terminology for Christian leaders | Notes |
|---|---|---|---|---|
| 18/6/1587 (Tenshō 15) | Oboe | Bateren monto | | Issued by Toyotomi Hideysohi |
| 19/6/1587 | Sadame: Bateren tsuihorei | | Bateren | ibid. |
| 6/8/1612 (Keichō 17) | Jōjō | Bateren monto | | |
| 12/1614 (Keichō 19) | Bateren tsuihōbumi | | Kirishitan no totō; Bateren totō | |
| 8/8/1616 (Genna 2) | Bateren shūmon goseikin hōsho | Bateren no monto | | |
| 5/1628 (Kan'ei 5) | Oboe | Kirishitan | Bateren | |
| 28/2/1633 (Kan'ei 10) | Nagasaki Bugyō e no hōsho-oboe | Bateren shūshi | Bateren | First Exclusion edict |
| 28/5/1634 (Kan'ei 11) | Nagasaki Jōjō | Bateren no shūshi | Bateren | Second Exclusion edict |
| | Nagasaki seirei kinsei | | Bateren | |
| 9/1635 (Kan'ei 12) | Furegaki | Bateren narabi ni Kirishitan shūshi | | |
| | Nagasaki Jōjō | Bateren no shūshi | Bateren | Third Exclusion edict |
| 19/5/1636 (Kan'ei 13) | Sadame | Kirishitan shūshi Baterenhō | Bateren | Fourth Exclusion edict |
| 13/9/1638 (Kan'ei 15) | Oboe | Kirishitan | Bateren; Iruman | |

*continued*

*Table 3.1* Continued

| Date | Source | Terminology for Christians | Terminology for Christian leaders | Notes |
|---|---|---|---|---|
| 20/9/1638 | Furegaki | *Bateren monto* | | |
| 1/12/1638 | Kirishitan Gohatto no gi ni tsuki jōi no omomuki | *Kirishitan shūmon* | | |
| 21/2/1639 (Kan'ei 16) | Gojōmoku-oboe | *Kirishitan shūmon* | *Bateren* | |
| 5/7/1639 | Jōjō | *Kirishitan shūmon* | *Bateren* | Fifth Exclusion edict |
| | Kirishitan no gi ni tsuki uraura ashioki jōi no omomuki | *Kirishitan shūmon* | *Bateren* | |
| 5/1641 (Kan'ei 18) | Furegaki | *Kirishitan shūmon* | | |
| 5/1642 (Kan'ei 19) | Kono tabi itoma kudasaru daishōmyō ni ōseide nō omomuki | *Kirishitan shūmon* | | |
| | Goson shohatto | *Kirishitan* | | |

*Source*: Shimizu, 'Kirishitan Kankei Hōsei Shiryōshū'; Ishii, *Tokugawa Kinreikō*.

By way of an answer, let us consult the system of rewards for Christian informants. The reward system began in Genna 14 (1618) in Nagasaki; it was implemented in territories under direct *Bakufu* control from 1633, and was finally applied nationally after 1638.[7] We shall find in the regulations for this system changes that parallel precisely adjustments made to the terminology for Christians. The following clauses on rewards for informants have been extracted from four of the well-known exclusion edicts, and are revealing in this regard. The revelant clauses from the edicts for 1633, 1634 and 1635 are near enough identical. Their gist is as follows:

Item – Rewards for information leading to the discovery of *bateren*
Note: Informants are eligible for rewards of one hundred pieces of silver; rewards for those informing on other Christians will be determined in proportion to their loyalty.[8]

The 1636 edict differs only in that it offers three, two or one hundred pieces of silver to informants 'depending on the informant's social status'.[9] As these materials suggest, prior to the Shimabara Rebellion of 1637, the informant system specified the rewards for those denouncing '*bateren*', but for those denouncing members of the lower orders, rewards are disbursed 'according to the loyalty [of the informant]'. The priority here is clearly to expose *bateren* and not to expose Christians of lower social rank. After the Shimabara Rebellion, however, that is, after Kan'ei 15 (1638), important adjustments are made to the informant system. The following memorandum from 1638 makes this clear:

*Memorandum*
Item – informants discovering *bateren*: silver 200 pieces
Item – informants discovering other religious: silver 100 pieces
Item – informants discovering Christians: silver 50 pieces (or 30 pieces – depending on the informant)
Note well: It is hereby declared that even if the informants are themselves of the same *Kirishitan* religion, their crimes – as long as they have recanted – shall be forgiven, and they shall be rewarded as outlined above. Kan'ei 15 (1638), 9th month, 13th day'[10]

It is clear that only after the Shimabara Rebellion of 1638 are rewards for information leading to the arrest of Christians of the lower class spelt out in public notices.

What, though, are we to make of the following source, a petition from a senior *Bakufu* elder dated Genna 2 (1616)?

The strict prohibition on *bateren* sectarians was declared last year by Tokugawa Ieyasu. He has taken the utmost care to ensure that the religion does not penetrate the class of peasants and those below.'[11]

Christians are being referred to here as '*bateren* sectarians'. The section 'he has taken the utmost care to ensure that the religion does not penetrate the class of peasants and those below' would appear to confirm for us that the Keichō 17 (1612) edict marked the onset of the comprehensive proscription, targeted at all social classes. There are indications, however, that at this early juncture in the prohibition process, a certain class was being specifically targeted, whatever the stipulation as it stands in writing.

Evidence for this is to be found in an anti-Christian edict issued two days later on the 8th day of the 8th month, Genna 2 (1616). On this day, the Zen priest Konchiin (Ishin) Sūden, who exerted a great influence on the *Bakufu*'s policy decision-making, wrote in a letter to the *daimyō* Hosokawa Tadaoki, that he had heard from the *Shogun*'s scribe that 'an ordinance had been distributed (to all *daimyō*) demanding measures be taken to ensure *bateren* were eliminated from all *daimyō* territory'.[12]

The ordinance he cites can only be a reference to the anti-Christian edict of two days before, which Sūden interestingly summarises as referring exclusively to the elimination of *bateren* from *daimyō* territory. It serves, in other words, as confirmation that the emphasis of this pre-Shimabara anti-Christian edict lay *not* with the general populace – whatever the wording of the *Bakufu* elder's petition – rather with the elimination of the *bateren*. The Shimabara rebellion, we shall find, stands as a turning-point, marking qualitative change in the Christian prohibition from the *bateren* to the wider Christian population.

## The *bateren*

How, though, are we to interpret the term *bateren*, these specific targets of the pre-Shimabara Christian prohibition? Who were they? It transpires that usage of the term *bateren*, although derived, as we have seen, from the Portuguese *padre*, was by no means confined to the clergy. Contemporary edicts and other data reveal that *bateren* meant not only priests but Christians of the samurai class, too.[13]

In the early seventeenth century, the policy of dividing warriors from peasants was as yet imperfectly implemented, and the land-bound local gentry remained a military force to be reckoned with. It is this class of gentry that I refer to specifically when I talk of Christian warriors. Article 4 of the anti-Christian edict issued by Toyotomi Hideyoshi on the 18th day of the 6th month of Tenshō 15 (1587) is a case in point.[14] It reads: 'Item – persons owning land in excess of 100–200 *chō*, 2000–3000 *kan* who wish to become *bateren* may do so provided that they have the approval of the authorities.'[15] Converting to Christianity is here referred to as 'becoming a *bateren*' in the case of men above a certain degree on the landowning scale. A Tokugawa communication to the Uesugi family in Keichō 17 (1612) offers further confirmation that Christian warriors were referred to as *bateren*. It states that eight men mentioned in the communication had 'become *bateren*' and were, as a result, to be removed from their territory.[16] This communication, the first to a *daimyō* announcing the removal of *Bakufu* vassals on account of their Christian beliefs, was sent in the 3rd month of Keichō 17 (1612), some three months before the Tokugawa *Bakufu* published its first anti-Christian edict.[17] Anyway, it is quite clear that the term *bateren* refers here not to foreign missionaries at all, but to Christian converts of warrior status.

If further confirmation is required that, prior to Shimabara, the Christians specifically targeted by the proscription were 'gentry', we can consult the records of missionaries such as Pedro Morejon.[18] A couple of observations are in order here. The first is that the social status of almost all the martyrs in Morejon's list is 'high'; a second, to which we shall return below, is that there were considerably more martyrs in Shimabara than there were in Amakusa.[19]

Notwithstanding the possibility of a certain arbitrariness on Morejon's part, the list may stand as evidence that the majority were, indeed, either local gentry or their families. Martyrs of lower social status were extremely few and far between. The point to note in conclusion here is that the anti-Christian prohibition laws *prior* to the Shimabara Rebellion applied both to missionaries and also to local gentry-type warriors, but that they were not targeted specifically at the *general* Christian populace.

**The meaning of the term '*bateren* sectarians'**

What can we discern of the *Bakufu*'s stance from its application of the term *bateren* sectarians?

The term *bateren* sectarian used to signify Christians was not used for the first time in the *Bakufu*'s first regulations in Keichō 17 (1612). The term had appeared already some 25 years before in Tenshō 15 (1587) in a notice promulgated by Toyotomi Hideyoshi. The 'Notice', dated the 18th day, 6th month of that year, includes the following seven articles:

1. Item – The matter of becoming a sectarian of the *bateren* shall be the free choice of the individual concerned;
2. Item – That enfieffed recipients of provinces, districts and estates should force peasants registered in [Buddhist] temples, and others of their tenantry, against their will into the ranks of the *bateren* sectarian is unreasonable beyond words and is outrageous;
3. Item – Provinces and stipends are granted in fief with tenure limited to the incumbent. The recipient may change; but the peasants do not change. In case of unreasonable demands exerted upon any point, the recipient will be held in contumely. Act accordingly!
4. Item – Persons holding above 200 *chō*, 2000–3000 *kan* may become *bateren* sectarians upon obtaining official permission, acceding to the pleasure [of the lord of the realm].

5. Item – Persons drawing stipends below the aforementioned: in the matter of choice among the Eight Sects or Nine Sects, the head of the house shall decide as he pleases, for himself only.
8. Item – That *daimyō* in possession of provinces and districts or of estates should force their retainers into the ranks of the *bateren* sectarians is even more undesirable by far than the *Honganji* sectarians' establishment of temple precincts, and is bound to be of great harm to the realm. These individuals of no discretion shall be subject to chastisement.
9. Item – *bateren* sectarians by their free choice, [in so far as they] are of the lower classes, shall be unmolested, this being a matter of Eight sects or Nine Sects.[20]

As previous studies have pointed out, the purpose of this notice was to limit Christian activity while not amounting to a blanket ban. The law's basic attitude appears in Article 1, where the premise that belief in Christianity is a matter of free choice is set out. Articles 4, 5 and 9 then make a clear distinction, on the basis of class, between those who do and those who do not require official permission to convert to Christianity. It is noteworthy that the term *bateren* is used in Article 4 to refer to the men of the warrior class who had converted without court permission. Articles 2, 3 and 8 then forbid warrior-class Christians from enforcing Christian conversion on those under their control. In short, the notice attempts to put the brakes on efforts by these warrior-class converts to control sections of the population through the ideological medium of Christianity. So, although Christian belief is here declared to be fundamentally free, it means free from the irresistible pressures of warrior class *bateren*.

From this we can suggest that the expression '*bateren* sectarian' means specifically Christian followers of Christian missionaries *and* warrior-class Christians. These usages that we find in Hideyoshi's edicts were inherited by the Tokugawa *Bakufu*, and were applied consistently until the Shimabara Rebellion of 1637.

**Christian Prohibitions and the Shimabara Rebellion**

Prior to the outbreak of the Shimabara Rebellion, the Toyotomi regime's regulations and the subsequent *Bakufu* edicts were targeted at the missionaries and Christians of the warrior class. It is frequently pointed out that these local gentry were still firmly entrenched in the early seventeenth century; the *Bakufu*'s vision of a society in which warrior and peasant were clearly separated from one another had yet to materialise in areas beyond the five home provinces. When such gentry were Christian converts, there would typically be large numbers of Christians in the local populace, too.

Quite simply, the typical Christian attitude of respect for those in a position of power led to the phenomenon of group conversions.[21] To the *Bakufu*, the source of all political authority in the land, the ability of these local Christian warriors to use Christianity as an ideological bolster in the control of their own territories posed a major threat. It was precisely for this reason that the anti-Christian laws of this time were targeted at the gentry.[22] And it was from Keichō 17 (1612) onwards that the thorough suppression of not only Christian missionaries but this warrior class of Christian was implemented. Martyrdoms of men of this class followed in large numbers, and this in turn forced upon the Christian populace at large a grim choice: follow the *bateren* in death or recant. These, then, were the historical conditions under which, in Kan'ei 14 (1637), some years after the apparent elimination of Christianity, the Shimabara Rebellion broke out.

The point here, as Fukaya Katsumi has pointed out, is that all the Christians of the Shimabara and Amakusa area had, by 1633, four years before the rebellion, gone through the motions of recanting and converting to Buddhism, and Christian suppression had come to an end.[23] This is a point of some significance for our understanding of the character of the rebellion.

The Shimabara Rebellion provided the opportunity for the *Bakufu* to direct its Christian suppression towards the lower Christian orders. This shift is manifest, *inter alia*, in the changing terminology in the edicts – from *bateren* sectarians to *Kirishitan* – and in corresponding adjustments to the reward system for informants.[24] The Shimabara Rebellion was a watershed, then, after which the weight of suppression shifted gradually to the populace.

As Senmoto and others point out, the anti-Christian edicts from Keichō 17 (1612) did, on paper, take away the religious rights of the populace.[25] Of this there can be no doubt. But the present investigation shows that until the rebellion, the target of the *Bakufu* was quite clearly the *bateren* – in the sense of missionaries and *samurai*-class warriors – and, further, that it was only *after* the rebellion that the populace became the target of a major *Bakufu* assault.[26]

## II  LOCAL CONDITIONS IN SHIMABARA AND AMAKUSA AND THE SHIMABARA REBELLION

It was observed above that martyrdoms in Shimabara were overwhelmingly greater in number than those in Amakusa. There were important local differences at work here, and these differences prove, in turn, to be relevant to an understanding of *Bakufu* attitudes towards both territories and also to the dynamic process leading up to the Shimabara Rebellion.

## Changes in *daimyō* control prior to the Shimabara Rebellion

Table 3.2 makes possible a comparative look at *daimyō* control in Shimabara and Amakusa, and the significance that this might have had for developments in the Christian persecution.

The Shimabara region since the middle ages had been under the control of the Arima family. The *daimyō* Arima Harunobu swore allegiance to Toyotomi Hideyoshi, and subsequently to Tokugawa Ieyasu. The Arima family was, however, implicated in the Okamoto Daihachi incident in Keichō 17 (1612), as a result of which their territory was confiscated.[27] Harunobu's son, Naozumi, however, married Ieyasu's adopted daughter Kunihime, and Naozumi was dispatched from Suruga to assume charge of the domain. Just prior to Naozumi's entry into the domain, in either Keichō 12 (1607) or 16 (1611), the Arima family had completed a cadastral survey. Shortly after, in Keichō 19, the new lord Naozumi was transferred from the fief to a new territory in Nobeoka, Hyūga, having ultimately failed in his attempts to bring to heel members of the local gentry class. Naozumi left behind his band of personal retainers. Thereafter, the domain became, for a time, directly administered territory under the immediate supervision of the Nagasaki magistrate, Hasegawa Sahyōe. Throughout this period, Christians in the domain were subjected to the fiercest suppression, and there were many martyrdoms. In Genna 2 (1616), the domain was placed under the charge of a new *daimyō*, Matsukura Shigemasa. In the normal course of events, the ensconcement of a new lord with his vassals would produce keen tensions with the local gentry (in this case the old retainers of Arima Naozumi), but this time not only was there no attrition, but Matsukura's Kan'ei 7 (1630) cadastral survey – always a potential flashpoint – also went smoothly.

Two years before the cadastral survey, in Kan'ei 5 (1628), Matsukura's anti-Christian persecution had proved, apparently, 100 per cent successful in achieving the apostasies of the local Christians. The *Arima kiroku* reported: 'the Christian proscription was strictly reinforced throughout Japan, and all of the peasants in the domain of Matsukura, too, abjured their faith in the 5th year of Kan'ei.'[28] That there was subsequently a major revoking of apostasy is implied by the outbreak nine years later of the Shimabara Rebellion.

The situation in Amakusa was rather different. In Tenshō 17 (1589), there had been a rebellion against the *daimyō* Konishi Yukinaga, known as the Battle of Amakusa. Unable to put this down with his own resources, Yukinaga had had to rely on reinforcements from Katō Kiyomasa. Only through their joint efforts was the rebellion finally quelled. One result of

*Table 3.2* The process leading to the Shimabara Rebellion

|   | Year | Shimabara | Amakusa |
|---|---|---|---|
| 1. | Tenshō 17 (1589) | Under control of Arima Harunobu | Battle of Amakusa; under control of Konishi Yukinaga |
|   | Keichō 5 (1600) |  | Under control of Katō Kiyomasa |
| 2. | Keichō 6 (1601) |  | Under control of Terazawa Hirotaka |
|   | Keichō 12 (1607) | The Arima cadastral survey (Keichō 16 according to some records) |  |
|   | Keichō 17 (1612) | Under control of Arima Naozumi |  |
|   | Keichō 19 (1614) | Arima Naozumi transferred to Nobeoka, Hyūga. | Adam Arakawa martyred |
|   |  | Control rotating between Nabeshima, Ōmura and Matsuura families. Actual power in hands of Nagasaki magistrate, Hasegawa Sahyōe. |  |
| 3. | Genna 2 (1616) | Under control of Matsukura Shigemasa |  |
|   | Kan'ei 5 (1628) | Apostasy of all local Christians accomplished |  |
|   | Kan'ei 7 (1630) | Matsukura cadastral survey |  |
|   | Kan'ei 10 (1633) |  | Apostasy of all local Christians accomplished. |
|   | Kan'ei 14 (1637) | Shimabara-Amakusa Rebellion | Shimabara-Amakusa Rebellion |

*Source*: Fukaya Katsumi, 'Shimabara no Ran'.

this, however, was the annihilation of men of the local gentry class in Amakusa. Thereafter, Yukinaga allied himself to the western army in the Battle of Sekigahara in Keichō 5 (1600) and, for a while, came under Kiyomasa's command; later in Keichō 6 (1601), Yukinaga came under the command of Terazawa Hirotaka, the lord of Karatsu in Hizen. In

Keichō 8 (1603), Hirotaka implemented a cadastral survey, but met with no resistance since, as we have noted, the earlier Battle of Amakusa had eliminated the class of local gentry it was most likely to antagonise. On the subject of martyrdoms in the domain, Adam Arakawa, a Christian leader, died a martyr's death in Keichō 19 (1614), but thereafter there was no large scale anti-Christian drive in the area until Terazawa's thorough-going persecution in Kan'ei 10 (1633), which appears to have brought about mass apostasies.[29] It was just two years later, of course, that the Christians of Amakusa, spurred on by the actions of the once apostate Christians of Shimabara, revoked their own apostasies and themselves raised the flag of rebellion.

**Local society in Shimabara and Amakusa and the Christians**

The period leading up to the Shimabara Rebellion can be usefully broken down into the three stages set out in Table 3.2.

Prior to Matsukura's ensconcement, there had been no rebellion of the gentry class in Shimabara. There must have been many men of that class in the domain and the potential for violent reaction against his cadastral survey must have been great. It seems, however, to have proceeded with a minimum of resistance. Then, however, Arima Naozumi assumed charge of the territory. The following is recorded in the chronicle *Arima Harunobu Ki*:

> Arima Saeimon Naozumi's transfer from Kazuraki[30] in Hizen to Hyūga was connected with the fact that Kazuraki was full of Christian sectarians. The priest Honzui Shōnin was asked for his advice (by the *Shogun*) on how to deal with the religion. After consultation, Ieyasu recommended that the prohibition be enforced. As a result, Honzui was dispatched to Kazuraki. There, everybody from the *daimyō's* household down to the lowliest peasant was thoroughly questioned. Those who recanted were let be, but seven who refused to recant were subject to all manner of interrogation. They were then put to death by fire. Then, Ieyasu ordered that, as Kazuraki was close to Nagasaki and so Christianity was unlikely to die out [of its own accord], the young *daimyō* Saemon should be transferred to Hyūga, to spare him the hardship of having to carry out all manner of punishments. Naozumi was specially favoured by the *shōgun*, and had his territory increased by 13,000 *koku*.[31]

The *Arima Korō Monogatari* of Tenna 2 (1682), an account by a peasant of north Arima village, has the following account:

There were seven members of Arima Saemon's family who, it emerged after investigations, were Christians, and who refused to change their beliefs. Of those samurai in possession of land, there was a certain Takeji Jinzaemon who was burned at the stake. As a result of all this, Saemon requested the presence, from the Kantō, of a virtuous priest by the name of Honzui. For seventeen days, Honzui preached to congregations of people in Shimabara, but not a single one was there who listened with his heart. Soon, Honzui returned to the Kantō area. Saemon next consulted the *Ōmetsuke* of Nagasaki, a man called Hasegawa Sahyōe. Saemon was subsequently ordered to remove immediately to a new territory in Hyūga.[32]

The first problem for the new lord Naozumi – unresolved since the time of his father Harunobu – had been to wrench warriors, men of the local gentry class, that is, from the land, and recast them as 'modern' vassals. These men were, in significant proportion, Christian converts. Anyway, as we have seen, Naozumi's efforts to tackle them failed and, as a result, he was transferred to Hyūga. The *Tōdaiki* has this account:

(Keichō 19, 7th month) The castle of Takahashi Ukon in Hyūga was given to Arima son of Shūri Saemon. When Saemon removed to Hyūga not a single member of his vassal band followed him. This was because they were all *bateren* sectarians.[33]

The reason, then, that Naozumi's retainers did not accompany him to Hyūga in Keichō 19 (1614) was that they belonged to the *bateren* sect. The Arima retainers, staunchly *local* gentry, appear to have stayed put out of a belief that Christianity was an essential device for maintaining their own control over the land and its populace. The *Bakufu* – in the person of the Nagasaki magistrate – responded by carrying out a thorough suppression of Christianity after Naozumi's departure, which was aimed specifically at these old Arima retainers. (See Table 3.2). The subsequent success of Matsukura's cadastral survey can be seen, then, to have owed much to the fact that Hasegawa's persecution had obliterated most of the gentry class.

In Amakusa, on the other hand, there had already been a gentry uprising in 1589. This had taken place in the period corresponding to Stage 1 of Table 3.2. Because most of the principal players in that rebellion were Christian, Christian gentry had effectively been eliminated before Terazawa took possession of the fief in 1605. There was quite simply no scope, then, for large-scale martyrdoms in Amakusa of the sort that had taken place in Shimabara. In Shimabara, the division between the agricultural and the military was not as advanced as in Amakusa, so Christian suppression was perforce aimed at Christian gentry. We have already seen that, until the Shimabara rebellion, the specific target of Christian controls was *bateren*, namely missionaries and samurai-class Christians. We can suggest further, perhaps, that Christian suppression at this period, precisely because it was targeted at *bateren*, made a major historical contribution to the separation of the samurai and peasant classes.

Thus it was that the larger Christian populace of Shimabara and Amakusa, deprived of men of the gentry class, suffered repression from, respectively, Matsukura and Terazawa, and were forced to choose between apostasy or secrecy (Table 3.2, Stage 3.) Unlike the clandestine Christians of other regions, however, the depredations of the lords of Amakusa and Shimabara forced upon the hidden Christians of those areas a unique response.

Tsuruda Yasunari and others have argued that it was the excesses of Matsukura and Terazawa at this time in Shimabara and Amakusa – owing in part at least to the harsh military duties with which they had been saddled by the *Bakufu* – which were the major cause of the Shimabara Rebellion.[34]

The rebellion was, then, a turning-point beyond which the Tokugawa regime's perception of Christians changed. The target was no longer *bateren* but *Kirishitan*: this terminological shift representing a new perception that the threat lay no longer with Christian missionaries and the warrior-class Christians, but with the general populace. What the *Bakufu* feared was the cohesive quality of those who shared in common the Christian faith. The following clause from the exclusion edict promulgated in the year following the Shimabara Rebellion makes this clear:

> Item – Gatherings and assemblies of sectarians for the purpose of plotting evil shall be severely punished.[35]

CONCLUSION

That Christianity was accommodated by the populace owed much to its readiness to acknowledge the authority of government in secular matters. Caught in a dilemma between a desire to practice Christianity on the one hand, and a reluctance to rebel – for such was the nature of their faith – on the other, Christians had no choice but to recant or to go underground. It was the massive depredations of the domainal lords in Amakusa and Shimabara that brought these Christians to the surface and drove them to rebellion. The Christianity that they had only nominally relinquished they then took up again with a vengeance. Since the Christians did not rise up in response to *Christian* persecution, it is, of course, difficult to define the

Shimabara Rebellion as a *Christian* rebellion. It is better thought of as a peasant rebellion, in which Christianity played an all-important cohesive role.

What is important to note, in conclusion, is that the Shimabara Rebellion marks a turning point in the nature of the Christian suppression: the focus of government attention shifts demonstrably now from the *bateren* – which we have seen meant missionaries *and* Christians of the warrior class – to the general populace. At the same time, we have suggested that the enforcement of the persecution – at least in the Shimabara and Amakusa areas – was an important contributory factory in achieving the complete separation of the military and peasant classes. From the Shimabara Rebellion onwards, it was the Christian populace and the threat of rebellion that they posed which, to the *Bakufu* authorities, became the greatest Christian threat.

Against this background, then, the *Bakufu* in Meireki 3 (1657) after the Shimabara Rebellion, set up a *Shūmon Aratameyaku* – effectively a religious inquisition – as the centre-piece of new efforts to tighten controls on the Christian populace.[36] In Kanbun 4 (1664), it applied the inquisition to all fiefs;[37] in Kanbun 11 (1671), it ordered the application of population registers in *Bakufu* territories,[38] and in Jōkyō 4 (1687) set up the *Ruizoku Aratame* system, according to which children born of Christian parents before the parents apostatised are legally defined as Christian.[39] It is usually understood that these Christian control regulations were prepared at a stage when the actual threat of Christianity had already been eliminated. Yoshimura sees the point of these controls as lying specifically in the reorganisation and strengthening of feudal status;[40] Murai, for her part, sees *daimyō* control to be the major consideration.[41] We have demonstrated here, however, that the organisation of these controls took place not at a time when the Christian threat had disappeared but rather at a time when, with the elimination of the military threat from Spain and Portugal, the focus of the threat had simply shifted to the Christian populace and their latent capacity for cohering into an anti-*Bakufu* force.

NOTES

1. Kataoka, *Nihon Kirishitan Junkyōshi*.
2. Takase, *Kirishitan Jidai no Kenkyū*, pp. 75–171.
3. Fujiki, *Oda Toyotomi Seiken* pp. 215–19.
4. Valignano, *Nihon Iezusukaishi Reihō Shishin* is one example.
5. This is point is argued strongly in Murata, 'Kirishitan Kyōgi to Hōkensei'.
6. Ishii, *Kinsei Hōsei Shiryō Sōsho*, p. 206.

7. Shimizu, 'Kirishitan Sonin Hoshōsei ni tsuite', and idem, *Kirishitan Kinseishi*.
8. See, for example, Ishii, *Tokugawa Kinreikō*, vol. 6, p. 376.
9. Ibid., p. 378.
10. Ishii, *Kinsei Hōsei Shiryō Sōsho*, 2, p. 110.
11. Ishii, *Tokugawa Kinreikō*, 4, p. 350.
12. Soejima, *Honkō Kokushi Nikki*, 4, p. 55.
13. That the focus of repression until the Shimabara Rebellion was on *bateren* has already been pointed out by Asao in his *Sakoku*, p. 226, but he interprets the term exclusively to mean Christian missionaries.
14. On the historiographical controversy surrounding this law, see Iwazawa, 'Toyotomi Hideyoshi no Bateren Seihai Shuinjō ni tsuite'.
15. Hirai, ' "Goshuin Shishoku Kokaku" to Yamada Mikata – Toyotomi Hideyoshi no Kirishitan kinrei o megutte', p. 68.
16. Tōkyō Teikoku Daigaku, ed. *Dai Nihon Shiryō*, p. 561.
17. Shimizu, 'Kirishitan Kankei Hōsei Shiryōshū', pp. 280–1.
18. The reader is referred to the list of Shimabara and Amakusa martyrs in Morejon, *Nihon Junkyōroku*.
19. The only martyr given by Morejon for Amakusa is Adam Arakawa. This is not to be taken to mean that no further martyrdoms took place, but the numbers were fewer than in Shimabara, and the methods of persecution employed milder.
20. Translator's note: The translation of these articles is Elison's (*Deus Destroyed*, pp. 117–18).
21. Murai, *Bakuhansei Seiritsu to Kirishitan Kinsei*, pp. 14–16.
22. It is to be noted that by this time warriors of higher status, such as the *daimyō*, had with the exception of a small number of men like Takayama Ukon, apostatised as the prohibition bit more deeply (Ebisawa, *Nihon Kirishitanshi*, pp. 142–3).
23. Fukaya, *Zōho Kaiteiban Hyakushō Ikki no Rekishiteki Kōzō*, pp. 156–79.
24. Kyoto is something of an exception to the general tendency, however. The rewards as published there in Kan'ei 12 (1635) in the name of the *Shoshidai*, Sakakura Shigemune, actually do set out rewards for denouncing Christian members of the general populace (Shimizu, 'Kirishitan Sonin Hoshōsei ni tsuite', pp. 274–5). Kyoto's local conditions, namely, the absence of a class of entrenched Christian gentry, and the presence there of the power of the court, are key. (See also Murai, 'Kirishitan Kinsei o meguru Tennō to Tōitsu Kenryoku'.)
25. Senmoto, 'Kirishitan Kinsei Kenkyū Nōto'; *Shimabara no Ran*; 'Shimabara no Ran to Kirishitan Ikki'.
26. Senmoto argues that before the Shimabara Rebellion, the local *daimyō* tacitly tolerated the religious practices of the peasantry, because to start a persecution would threaten his income from taxation (*Shimabara no Ran*, pp. 182–6.).
27. [Translator's note: Okamoto Daihachi was a Christian in the service of Ieyasu, bribed by Arima. Okamoto convinced Arima that he was in a position to use his influence with Ieyasu so that Arima might have restored to him territory lost in fighting with the *daimyō* of Hirado domain. Okamoto clearly never intended to use his influence, but the fact that he had received bribes, and had, moreover, forged Ieyasu's letters patent became known to Ieyasu.

Okamoto's punishment was to be burned alive. That Okamoto was a Christian did much to increase Ieyasu's suspicions of the foreign religion.]
28. Hayashi, *Shimabara Hantōshi*, p. 273).
29. On this, see *Kumamotoken Shiryō, (chūsei)*, pp. 65–75.
30. Kazuraki appears to be a mistake for Takagi, the name of an area in Shimabara.
31. *Shintei Zōho Shiseki Shūran*, 21, p. 478.
32. Cited in *Zokuzoku Gunshoruiju*, 12, p. 590.
33. Cited in *Shiseki Zassan*, 2, pp. 200–201.
34. See, for example, Tsuruda's 'Shimabara ni okeru Kasei no Jisshō'.
35. Ishii, *Kinsei Hōsei Shiryō Sōsho*, 2, p. 101.
36. Shimizu, 'Shūmon Aratameyaku Nōto', p. 44. Shimizu makes the important point that while it was in 1640 that the *Ōmetsuke,* Inoue Masashige, was sent to Nagasaki to begin his 'inquisition', it was not until 1657 that his role became *exclusively* that of 'inquisitor'. Shimizu argues that the creation of the inquisitor's office is more properly put as 1657.
37. Ishii, *Tokugawa Kinreikō*, 3, p. 271.
38. Ibid., p. 279.
39. Ibid., p. 273.
40. Yoshimura, 'Kinsei Shoki Kumamotohan ni okeru Kirishitan Kinsei no Tenkai', pp. 17–25.
41. Murai, *Bakuhansei Seiritsu to Kirishitan Kinsei*, pp. 66–128.

# 4 Acculturation among the *Kakure Kirishitan*: Some Conclusions from the *Tenchi Hajimari no Koto*
## Stephen Turnbull

The *Tenchi Hajimari no Koto* (Concerning the Creation of Heaven and Earth) is a work consisting of 16 000 characters divided into 15 chapters. It may be justifiably regarded as the secret Bible of the underground Christians of Japan, who kept the faith alive between the expulsion of foreign priests in 1614 and the granting of religious freedom in 1873. So successful were the *Senpuku Kirishitan* (secret Christians), that when European missionaries returned in 1865 many groups of them chose not to be reconciled with the Catholic church, and stayed both separate and secret. These *Kakure Kirishitan* communities, many of which still exist, effectively constitute a separate Christian denomination in Japan.[1]

The *Tenchi Hajimari* was probably not committed to paper until the 1820s, and as several versions of it were known to exist during the 1860s, we may confidently regard it as representing an important oral tradition shared by several of the *senpuku* communities, as will be discussed. The importance of the *Tenchi Hajimari* lies in its unique contents, providing a rich source of written material on which to base studies of the communities' beliefs, preserved from generation to generation and expressed nowadays in the rituals and traditions of the *Kakure Kirishitan*.[2] The *Tenchi Hajimari* therefore has an important comparative role, providing clues to the beliefs that may lie behind *Kakure* rituals and practices, such as an apparently fervent devotion to the Virgin Mary[3] and the veneration of local martyrs.[4]

In this chapter I shall use the *Tenchi Hajimari* to examine what conclusions are suggested by its contents concerning the question of acculturation. Since the discovery of the underground Christians in 1865 questions have been asked regarding how much of Christian teaching was preserved during the time of persecution, and how much was added to it. Did the faith thus transmitted develop into a genuinely Japanese form of Christianity, or does its present survival among the *Kakure* represent the actual disintegration of Christianity into a syncretism of many beliefs, expressed as a modern form of animism? In asking these questions I shall be particularly concerned with the additions to orthodox gospel accounts found in the text.

The pioneer of the study of the *Kakure Kirishitan* was the scholar Tagita Kōya. He spent 20 years gaining the confidence of various *Kakure* communities, and remains one of the few people ever to have penetrated their secrecy, although many of the groups are now far more ready to accept and cooperate with outsiders genuinely interested in their lives. Tagita's *Shōwa Jidai no Senpuku Kirishitan* was published in 1954, and remains a notable achievement considering the difficulties of communication with the remote islands of Japan until comparatively recent times. To Tagita:

> what was transmitted to the *Kakure* inspired them with faith which is evident in their lives even today. Furthermore it was accultured. It was made into the stuff of their everyday lives.[5]

Quite early on in his research Tagita took an interest in the *Tenchi Hajimari*, and published the text twice.[6] He obtained his copies from the *Kakure Kirishitan* he was studying, and of the first seven copies of the *Tenchi Hajimari* discovered by Tagita in the 1930s, four were from Sotome (on the Sonogi peninsula to the north-west of Nagasaki), two from the Gotō, to which many *Kakure* from Sotome emigrated in the 1790s[7] and one from Nagasaki itself.[8] The document appears to have been unknown among the *Kakure* groups further to the north, who are concentrated mainly on the islands of Hirado and Ikitsuki. They had very different religious traditions and, according to Tagita, 'nothing in writing';[9] 'the people of Sotome and Gotō on the other hand have books of several kinds'.[10]

Tagita had known of the existence of the *Tenchi Hajimari* from comments in the diary of Father Bernard Petitjean, the French missionary priest to whom the Hidden Christians of Urakami had revealed themselves in March 1865.[11] Petitjean's own copy of the work was lost, but he had noted in his diary that it was 'written from memory in 1822 or 1823'. This tallies with the date of 1827 on the oldest copy Tagita was able to acquire,[12] but an unbroken succession of preserved written copies cannot entirely be ruled out. Whatever its mode of transmission we may therefore justifiably regard the commitment to writing of the *Tenchi Hajimari* as the fortunate act that preserved, for at least one of the *Kakure* groups, some record of what must have been a fairly common oral tradition.

Having regard for the obvious importance of the *Tenchi Hajimari* as a source, it is strange to record the neglect which it has received from theologians and even from scholars of Japanese Christian history.[13] This may be due simply to the fact that it has only once been translated into English. This was by Tagita himself, who published privately.[14] There is also a

German translation by Bohner.[15] But neglect of the text goes back to the occasion when the first known copy of the *Tenchi Hajimari* was given to Father Petitjean by a certain Domingo Mataichi, who held the position of baptiser among the group who revealed themselves to him:

> I asked Bishop Urakawa in 1931 if he knew the whereabouts of Mataichi's book, but all he could tell me was that some years previously Father Salmon of Nagasaki had examined it and declared it worthless.[16]

It is important to note that this dismissive attitude was by no means held by Petitjean himself, and in fact a dispute arose among the French priests as to the use of catechisms for the former Hidden Christians who desired to re-enter the Catholic Church. The church hierarchy favoured a catechism based on those used successfully in China and written in a traditional style. Petitjean disagreed, and argued that the best model to use was one in the style of the *Tenchi Hajimari* because of the Christians' familiarity with it.[17] His initial comments, as recorded in his diary, included the words, 'We have found in it some errors, but they are of little importance'.[18]

There are indeed many 'errors' in the *Tenchi Hajimari*, and while it is clear that changes and distortions did take place, I shall argue in this essay that this is by no means the whole story. Far from acting solely as a distorting mirror, this book can be shown to have acted also as a time capsule, wherein are preserved many features of doctrine which were taught to the Christians in the sixteenth and early seventeenth centuries. Our study of it will therefore be as much concerned with what has been preserved of the original Jesuit teachings, as with what has been added to it.

A summary of the contents of the *Tenchi Hajimari* is as follows. The work begins, as its title implies, with the creation of heaven and earth, an account which follows the sequence in Genesis quite closely. Adam and Eve are created, and there is an elaborate account of the temptation by the Devil. Evil enters the world, and the story of Noah's Ark is blended with similar oriental legends. There is then an abrupt jump from Genesis to the New Testament, omitting the whole of Old Testament history and with no reference to Jesus' Jewish ancestry. Instead we have the Annunciation, into which is inserted an elaborate tale whereby the King of Luzon falls in love with Mary, who spurns him because of her greater duty to give birth to the Saviour. Mary conceives Jesus, and pays a visit to her cousin Elizabeth, who is pregnant with John the Baptist. Jesus is born, and is visited by the Three Kings, who tell their story to King Herod. Herod plans the Massacre of the Innocents, but the Holy Family escape by the Flight into Egypt. The finding of Jesus in the temple becomes a debate between Jesus and a Buddhist teacher. We hear nothing of the teachings of Jesus. Instead the story moves directly to the betrayal of Judas and Jesus' arrest. There is a long Passion narrative, followed by the Resurrection and Ascension. One version ends here.[19] The longer version[20] continues with the Communion of Saints, the End of the World and the Last Judgement, at which the narrative ends with the words, 'Amen, Jesus'. Tagita also includes a short appendix which refers to a legend connected with Purgatory.[21]

Much of the narrative was no doubt derived from the various catechisms used by the Jesuits during the late sixteenth century, such as the first one to be printed in Japan, the *Doctrina Cristan* of 1592.[22] The *Tenchi Hajimari* can, however, also be identified as an elaborate version of the Rosary. As the 15 prayers of the Rosary follow the life of Christ in chronological order, it is not surprising that we can identify them through the events related in the *Tenchi Hajimari*, but it is no doubt significant that the passages from the New Testament in the *Tenchi Hajimari* match almost exactly the selected passages which make up the meditations on the first ten sets of prayers of the Rosary, known as the Joyful Mysteries and the Sorrowful Mysteries. What is less easy to explain is the cursory treatment given to the last five, the Glorious Mysteries. However, the connection with the Rosary is undoubtedly strong, because a direct association is made on three occasions in the text, though the word Rosary is not used, and we are dependent upon Tagita's identification. So we have reference at (49)[23] to the prayers of the Five Articles of the Morning (The Joyful Mysteries); the Daytime Five Articles (The Sorrowful Mysteries) (58) and the Five Articles of the Evening (The Glorious Mysteries) at (75).[24] Tagita's conclusions are supported by Miyazaki, who sees an important role for the Rosary.[25]

Whereas the above points summarise the Christian sources for the narrative, there are many additions to the story which reinforce the picture of a church totally isolated from the rest of the Christian communion. This comes over most strikingly in an apparent confusion over names and titles, and a bizarre geography, as in the example which follows, which deals with the arrest of Jesus:

> Meanwhile *Yorōtetsu* (Herod) of *Beren* (Bethlehem) sent *Ponsha Piroto* (Pontius Pilate) with a large force to Rome. (63)

Elsewhere *Sagaramento* (the sacraments) becomes a person sent from God to teach Jesus (48). A stranger confusion of names occurs in (42), where Pontius Pilate becomes Pontius and Pilate, the two *karō*, or chief retainers, of King Herod! The use of the term *karō* is one among many obvious Japanese additions. For another, note the use of bamboo in the following section dealing with the scourging of Christ:

They tied him up as they had been ordered and flogged him hard enough to break his bones until the bamboo rods split into pieces. They pushed various things that were bitter and hot into his mouth, and pressed an iron crown onto his head. Blood ran down from his body like a waterfall. (65)

A well-established piece of Japanese folklore comes into the description of Satan's angels, at the time of his Fall, and Judas Iscariot, after he has betrayed Jesus, for all become *tengu*, the curious goblins, half man and half crow, that occupy a popular place in Japanese mythology. There are two varieties, the bird-like *karasu-tengu* with a strong beak, and the more human *konoha tengu*, characterised particularly by a long nose,[26] Tagita notes that among the *Kakure* of the Kurosaki area of Sotome *tengu* is commonly used as a word meaning devil.[27] For Satan himself, 'his nose grew long, his mouth widened, scales grew on his hands and feet, and horns on his head' (11), the latter aberration going beyond that required for the description of a *tengu*, and probably added from the conventional Christian description of the Devil. Judas is more like the usual *konoha tengu*:

on his way home he suddenly changed; his nose grew long and his tongue increased in size ... Judas ... threw the money away by the side of the temple, ran into the depths of the forest and hung himself to death. That is the reason for the traditional saying about the money mound by the temple of *Santa Ekirenjiya*. (62)

According to Tagita's note, *Santa Ekirenjiya* is to be read as *Santa Ecclesia*, the Holy Church, which has been identified earlier in the text as having been built by Jesus in Rome to spread salvation throughout the world (50), but the textual variants (it also occurs as *Santa Ekirejiya*) indicate that it is probably another example of the confusion of a place with a person. The reference to a money mound probably recalls some folk memory of a supposedly inexhaustible supply of funds for the missions. Almost every paragraph contains similar material inviting comment and speculation. Mary conceives Jesus when a butterfly flies into her mouth (29). The Three Kings are stated respectively as being the monarchs of Turkey, Mexico and France (38). At the conclusion of the Noah's Ark story we find the comment that 'the custom of married women shaving their eyebrows and blackening their teeth originated at this time' (19).

Other additions derive from Japanese religion, and as the underground Christians were forced to live openly as Buddhists, it is not surprising to see Buddhist elements within the *Tenchi Hajimari*. However, the work clearly does not accept Buddhism as an equal partner. The greatness and the majesty of God, and His superiority to Buddha, are apparent right from the beginning of the narrative. God is 'the maker of heaven and earth and the Father of men and all created things' (1). He has 'two hundred *sō* and forty-two *sugata* (forms)' compared with the only 32 *sō*, or marks of the competent character, of Buddha. The debate between Jesus and a Buddhist teacher (50–56), which is ten times longer than the account of the Resurrection, ends with Jesus victorious and the opponent becoming his disciple.

At first sight, therefore, the *Tenchi Hajimari* consists of a blend of Christian catechetical materials and prayers with a rich mixture of native tradition and belief, and appears as a classic example of acculturation, whereby the Christian message has taken Japanese roots, and flowered as an exotic bloom. But can it, therefore, be regarded simply as a Christian catechism adapted, whether deliberately or accidentally, for Japanese taste? This is Tagita's view, which he uses to support his argument that the *Kakure Kirishitan* of today represent the acculturation of Christianity within the Japanese milieu. But I feel there is more to it than that, for many of the additions are not quite what they seem to be. For example, in the section dealing with the Flight into Egypt, the Holy Family pass a group of farmers sowing grain, and make a request:

> 'We have one thing to ask of you. We have pursuers after us. If they come here and ask about us, please tell them that we passed here when you were sowing.' The farmers laughed and said, 'We are sowing now, so it is a strange thing to say that it happened when we were sowing. How ridiculous!' It is said that this grain never ripened. (59)

The story goes on to say how the Holy Family met a further group of farmers who agreed to their request, and told their pursuers that the fugitives had passed by long ago when they were sowing their grain, which had now miraculously ripened. This story has its origins in a Christian legend from Ōe on the Amakusa islands, and relates to a fugitive missionary priest of the seventeenth century.[28]

There are also additions from unexpected sources. I suggested earlier that the *Tenchi Hajimari* is more than just a Japanese corruption of a Christian catechism, but a time capsule, and it is in these additions to the story that we see the *Tenchi Hajimari* preserving elements of what the earlier Christians were taught by the Jesuit missionaries. The *Tenchi Hajimari* therefore becomes valuable on two counts. First, it reveals elements of Jesuit teaching, recorded nowhere else, which passed into *Kakure* theology, and second, it sheds light on the mode of instruction used by the Jesuits, and their attitude towards the converts. To illustrate the first point we may note, during the account of the Passion, the familiar story of Veronica's veil:

However, on the way he met a woman named Veronica who was carrying water, and she felt pity for the Holy One and wanted to comfort Him. She wiped away the sweat of blood and offered him water. He took it and drank it gladly. What a kind thing it was to do! He would save her one day. As his image appeared on the cloth, the woman considered it precious and offered it to the temple of *Santa Ekirenjiya*. (67)

This legend is so hallowed in Catholic tradition that it is celebrated as one of the Stations of the Cross. Yet how many Catholics realise that the story does not appear in the Bible, and forms no part of the Gospel accounts of Christ's passion? Its origin appears to be the book known either as the *Gospel of Nicodemus*, or the *Acts of Pilate*.[29] Farmer notes that the devotions of the Stations of the Cross only became standardised (with Veronica in it) in the eighteenth to nineteenth centuries, yet here we see it in precisely the correct place in the Passion narrative in the *Tenchi Hajimari*, evidence of its early importance in at least the beginning of the seventeenth century.[30]

However, whatever its origin, the Veronica legend is firmly within tradition, and nothing remarkable need be concluded from the discovery that it was used as part of a programme of catechetical instruction by the Jesuits in Japan. However, a more extraordinary inclusion from the *Gospel of Nicodemus* occurs in the story of the Nativity. In the *Tenchi Hajimari* account, Mary gives birth to Jesus in the stable, and then the wife of the innkeeper (or houseowner) takes pity on them and invites them into her house:

> When three days had passed, Mary asked for a bath. Then she recommended that the son of the house, take a bath in the same hot water. The housewife said, 'Although I appreciate your thoughtfulness, our son is suffering from the pox, and in danger of his life. Please forgive me.' But Mary insisted: he took a bath, and was suddenly cured of the pox and lived, to the great thanks of all. (36)

At first sight this looks like a charming Japanese addition to the story. The sharing of the bathwater suggests the well-established Japanese custom of washing outside the bathtub, and using the bathwater for successive bathers. However, an almost identical story is found in the *Arabic Infancy Gospel*:

> the woman took sweet-smelling water to wash the Lord Jesus; when she had washed him, she kept that water with which she had done that, and poured some of it upon a girl who lived there, and whose body was white with leprosy, and washed her with it. Immediately the girl was cleansed of the leprosy.[31]

Later in the *Tenchi Hajimari* we find a remarkable association being made between this apocryphal nativity story and the Passion narrative. A straightforward account is given of the two criminals sentenced to be crucified with Jesus, one on his right, the other on his left. The conversation follows the Gospel story quite closely, then:

> The criminal was, after detailed investigation, found to be the child who had been cured of the pox by bathing in the water left over from the Lord's first bath at His birth. At that time the child had almost died with the pox. He had been miraculously cured by the Lord's bath, and yet this fellow became wicked after he grew up and was condemned to death and in the end followed the Lord hanging on the cross. How wonderful are the ways of God! (69)

This is not an addition put in by the underground Christians, but one version of the legend of Saint Dismas (Demas or Dysmas), the Good Thief. He, together with Gestas, the unrepentant thief, is named in the Passion account in the *Acts of Pilate*. In the *Arabic Infancy Gospel*, which, as we noted above, contains the story of a girl being cured, there is no such connection, only a prophecy by Jesus himself, after the Holy Family have been accosted by robbers on the road:

> And the Lord Jesus answered and said to his mother: 'In thirty years, mother, the Jews will crucify me in Jerusalem, and those two robbers will be fastened to the cross with me.[32]

However, in the Greek Recension B of the *Acts of Pilate*, which James regards as a later working-over of the original text,[33] we find a story similar to that of the *Tenchi Hajimari*, only in this case the child who is healed of leprosy is the son of Dysmas rather than Dysmas himself, and the context is the flight into Egypt.[34] There is one other apocryphal addition within the Nativity story, which again is so traditional that few realised that it is absent from the canonical Gospel account:

> Now as it was winter the Holy Body was in danger of freezing, but the cows and horses on his left and right warmed him with their breath and He withstood the cold. (34)

Again this may be found in an apocryphal Infancy Gospel, this time the one attributed to St. Matthew.[35]

In addition to the above literary and oral sources for the *Tenchi Hajimari*, we can also recognise possible pictorial origins of certain passages, no doubt derived from memories of holy pictures. These are most noticeable in sections dealing with the Virgin Mary, who would have been the subject of many such artistic works. For example, the description of the Descent from the Cross suggests the memory of some holy picture of a *Pietà* brought by the missionaries, and we noted earlier that Mary conceives Jesus when a butterfly flies into her mouth (29). Tagita merely notes that Toyotomi Hideyoshi is said to have been conceived when the sun jumped into his mother's mouth, which is a possible source.[36] But is it not more likely that the compiler of the *Tenchi Hajimari* had in mind a picture of the Annunciation, long since destroyed or confiscated, that he had once seen, copied time after time until the conventional image of the dove took on such a vague appearance that it became a butterfly? (I have made the personal observation that Japanese butterflies can be much larger than European ones!)[37]

The *Tenchi Hajimari* therefore proves that the Jesuits were not above using apocryphal and non-canonical material to spread the Gospel, but it also reveals something of their style of teaching, and their attitude to the catechists. The inclusion of these stories, and the use of holy pictures, suggests an approach that favoured a simple theology, working through uncomplicated Bible stories, and supported by anything which would reinforce the central truth, providing of course that it was not actually contrary to the catechism. In conclusion, therefore, a study of the contents of the *Tenchi Hajimari* does not lend much support to the theory that the faith of the *Kakure Kirishitan* represents the acculturation of Christianity within the Japanese milieu, because many of the supposed Japanese additions can be shown to have a European origin, and must therefore have been deliberately introduced by the Jesuit missionaries before persecution began.[38] Furthermore, if the Jesuits were so assiduous in this regard, might it not be the case that those sections which have an obvious Japanese origin could also have been added by the missionaries as a way of making the Christian message more acceptable to their Japanese converts?

The *Tenchi Hajimari* therefore points us towards seeing *Kakure* theology not merely as the result of what was taken away by persecution and isolation, but of what had been deliberately and firmly implanted long before persecution began. The Jesuits taught them a peasant's simple faith, transferred from the fields of Europe and well-rooted into the rice paddies of Japan, and this is what we see preserved in the time capsule of the *Tenchi Hajimari*. Whatever its sources, the *Tenchi Hajimari* illustrates how an isolated, persecuted and faithful group could transmit orally over two centuries the central truths of what their ancestors had been taught. The sheer achievement of this makes any apparent distortion of the faith appear of little concern when set beside the persecutions they faced. The 'Hidden Christians' are still with us, and so is this rare gift to Christian literature, the *Tenchi Hajimari*. Their own survival was their greatest achievement, and that such a moving and fascinating account of their beliefs should have survived along with them must be regarded as an additional triumph.

## NOTES

1. I am here using the expressions *senpuku* and *kakure* in the manner which is now accepted by most scholars, whereby *senpuku* refers to the communities prior to 1873, and *kakure* to those of the present-day, whose ancestors made the decision not to rejoin the Catholic church. For a useful discussion on nomenclature see Miyazaki, 'Kakure Kirishitan', p. 3.
2. It is important to note that the *Tenchi Hajimari* appears no longer to be a living tradition among the *Kakure*. On the island of Naru, I interviewed a prominent member of the *Kakure Kirishitan* community, aged 93. In preparation for my visit I had written to him, mentioning my interest in the *Tenchi Hajimari*. During the course of the interview I brought up the subject, and he replied that until receiving my letter he had never heard of the *Tenchi Hajimari*, but he had now obtained a copy from a friend, had read it, and was prepared to answer any questions I might care to ask.
3. See Turnbull, *Devotion to Mary*.
4. See Turnbull, 'The Veneration of the Martyrs of Ikitsuki', and Turnbull, 'From Catechist to Kami'.
5. Tagita, *Study of Acculturation*, p. 126.
6. Tagita, *Shōwa*, pp. 76f.; Ebisawa et al., *Kirishitansho*, pp. 382f.
7. Kataoka, *Kakure Kirishitan*, p. 184.
8. Tagita, *Study of Acculturation*, p. 136.
9. Tagita, *Study of Acculturation*, p. 129. This however contradicts Laures, (*Kirishitan Bunko*, p. 115) who states that there was an Ikitsuki version of *Tenchi Hajimari*, which Laures compares unfavourably with the virtually error-free version of Urakami. Laures however associates the Ikitsuki version with the three versions Tagita used for his published edition, but in *Shōwa*, p. 76, Tagita lists the sources for the eight copies he possessed, none of which is Ikitsuki. In the absence of any other reference to an Ikitsuki *Tenchi Hajimari*, I am inclined to agree with Tagita.
10. Tagita, *Study of Acculturation*, p. 130.
11. Cary, *History of Christianity*, p. 282; Marnas, *La Religion de Jésus*, p. 488.
12. Tagita, *Study of Acculturation*, p. 135.
13. Tagita remains the only Japanese scholar to have given the *Tenchi Hajimari* detailed treatment. Kataoka devotes only one page of his book *Kakure Kirishitan* (p. 174) to the topic, and Furuno does not discuss it at all in his *Kakure Kirishitan*. More recent, yet still brief, discussions are by Hayashi, *Nihonjin*, pp. 74–7, and Miyazaki, 'Tenchi Hajimari no Koto Kō'.
14. It is contained within Tagita, *Study of Acculturation*.
15. Bohner, *Tenchi Hajimari*.
16. Tagita, *Study of Acculturation*, p. 136.
17. Laures, *Kirishitan Bunko*, p. 128.

18. Tagita, *Study of Acculturation*, p. 135. As noted earlier, this copy was unfortunately lost, probably in the fire which destroyed the Catholic mission in Yokohama in 1874 (Laures, *Kirishitan Bunko*, p. 115).
19. This is the version translated by Bohner, *Tenchi Hajimari*.
20. Tagita, *Shōwa*; Ebisawa et al., *Kirishitansho*.
21. Tagita, *Shōwa*, p.162.
22. Ebisawa et al., *Kirishitansho*, p. 14. Laures' summary of the contents of the copy preserved at Sophia University, Tokyo, is as follows: 1. What Christian doctrine is; 2. The Sign of the Cross; 3. The Our Father; 4. The Hail Mary; 5. The *Salve Regina*; 6. The Apostles' Creed; 7. The Ten Commandments; 8. (Chapter missing); 9. The Precepts of the Church; 10. The Seven Capital Sins; 11. The Sacraments; 12. Other necessary things; the corporal and spiritual works of mercy, the theological and cardinal virtues, the gifts of the Holy Ghost, the Eight Beatitudes, the Confiteor, prayers before and after meals. There is also an appendix of 'various matters which a Christian must know' in ten short articles, and a glossary (*Kirishitan Bunko*, p. 42). For an earlier example, Lopez-Gay notes the following for the *daimyō* of Ōmura in 1563, which parallel the chapter headings of the *Tenchi Hajimari*: The creation of the world; The Most Holy Trinity; The fall of Lucifer, and the explanation of sin and the world; The sins of Adam and Eve; Jesus Christ and Redemption; Final judgement, hell and glory (*El Catecumenado*, p. 2).
23. The translations of passages from the *Tenchi Hajimari* are taken from Tagita *Study of Acculturation* with some editing and correction. Tagita numbers the paragraphs, which I have retained for convenience in my quotations as '( )', but I have put nearly all the Portuguese and Latin names into English along with the Japanese ones, except where the context requires comment.
24. Tagita, *Study of Acculturation*, p. 36.
25. Miyazaki, 'Tenchi Hajimari', p. 2.
26. De Visser, 'The Tengu', p. 25.
27. Tagita, *Study of Acculturation*, p. 42.
28. The story of the *Kirishitan no Hatake* or the 'Christian field', is told on a display card in the Rosariokan, the museum of Christian history in Ōe. The field itself is now a wood of pine and bamboo, but the terraces that indicate the sites of former Christian habitation can clearly be seen, and nearby is the well-attested site of the original church of Ōe, destroyed during the persecutions.
29. James, *Apocryphal New Testament*, pp. 94f.
30. Farmer, *Oxford Dictionary of Saints*, p. 422. It is interesting that the earliest version of the Veronica legend has no connection with the Passion (James *Apocryphal New Testament*, p.102). Having first identified Veronica as the woman healed from an issue of blood (Mark 5,25f), the *Acts of Pilate* records the legend as follows:

> The Emperor Tiberius, being sorely diseased, heard that there was a wonderful physician in Jerusalem, named Jesus, who healed all sicknesses. He sent an officer of his named Volusianus to Pilate to bid him send the physician to him. Pilate was terrified, knowing that Jesus had been crucified ... On the way back to his inn, Volusianus met a matron called

Veronica and asked her about Jesus. She told him the truth, to his great grief, and, to console him added that when our Lord was away teaching she had desired to have a picture of him always by her, and went to carry a linen cloth to a painter for that purpose. Jesus met her, and on hearing what she wished, took the cloth from her and imprinted the features of his face upon it. This cloth, she said, will cure your lord: I cannot sell it, but I will go with you to him. (James *Apocryphal New Testament*, p. 157).

31. Hennecke, *New Testament Apocrypha*, p. 408.
32. Hennecke, *New Testament Apocrypha*, p. 408.
33. James, *Apocryphal New Testament*, p. 115.
34. The story continues to find that Dysmas is struck by the beauty of Mary, and says 'If God had a mother I would have said that thou art she'. He receives the Holy Family into this house, and after the miraculous healing, 'he was accounted worthy through the grace of the merciful God and his Mother ... to bear witness upon the cross together with Christ'. (James, *Apocryphal New Testament*, p. 117). James also notes a variation on the story in the *Vita Rhythmica* (which draws on later Greek sources), where the Holy Family are accosted by robbers, and wounded robbers are healed by the water in which Jesus is washed, a neat development of the theme. (James, *Apocryphal New Testament*, p. 117).
35. Hennecke, *New Testament Apocrypha*, p. 375.
36. Tagita, *Study of Acculturation*, p. 53.
37. There is also a slight possibility that the original pictorial image was of a butterfly, because Hall (*Dictionary*, p. 132) notes that 'in Christian art the butterfly is a symbol of the resurrected human soul, either in the hand of the infant Christ or in still life', but in the absence of pictorial evidence of such in an Annunciation context this possibility can no doubt be discarded.
38. The above discussion still begs the question as to the mechanism of transmission of these apocryphal Christian stories. It seems unlikely that the Jesuits would go the lengths of actually recounting them as being of equal worth to the canonical gospels. However, possible clues are provided by the link with Christmas and Easter in all the apocryphal additions. Could it be that they entered the Japanese Christian tradition through Nativity plays and Passion plays, both of which have long been vehicles for popular catechising? In a personal communication to me, Father Diego Yūki has confirmed that such plays were performed in Japan, and that some were written by Brother Paulo Yōhō SJ, though unfortunately none has survived, so no direct comparison can be made between their contents and the stories in the *Tenchi Hajimari*. Paulo Yōhō entered the Society of Jesus in 1580, and was noted for the 'elegance, beauty and gracefulness of his language', according to an account of Frois quoted in Laures, *Kirishitan Bunko*, p. 40. He died in 1596. This is clearly an area where further research is needed.

# 5 Beyond the Prohibition:
## Christianity in Restoration Japan
### John Breen

INTRODUCTION

On 4 May 1868 Kido Kōin, the leader of the Chōshū faction in the new imperial government, heard for the first time about the Christian troubles in Urakami village, Nagasaki.[1] Kido recorded his 'profound concern' in a diary entry for that day and, with Inoue Kaoru, the bearer of tidings from Nagasaki, drew up plans for an imperial conference to discuss the disposition of the incident.[2] The conference, which sought the views of the entire government, duly met in Osaka on 14 May. The motion put to the conference, composed by Kido and Inoue, was based closely upon the missive Inoue had brought with him from Sawa Nobuyoshi, the Nagasaki magistrate.[3] It moved that leaders of the Christian community be summoned for a final interrogation, and those who refused to recant be summarily executed; others would be exiled to select domains. The motion was passed by a significant majority. A compromise was later forced, however, by the vigour of diplomatic protests: deportations would go ahead but, 'owing to the Emperor's especial compassion', there would be no executions in Nagasaki.[4] The deportations subsequently took place in two phases: the first group of a hundred or so Christians was removed from Nagasaki in July 1868 and the second, some 3400, in December 1869.

Kido's decision to hold an 'imperial conference' rendered the local Urakami incident one of national significance; the government's disposition of it transformed it into one of the major diplomatic events of the early Meiji period.[5] But, unlike the March Sakai incident, say, the Urakami incident was to assume much more than diplomatic significance. It will be argued here, in brief, that its eruption thrust upon the Restoration government the entire question of the relationship between the modern state and religion. More precisely, it will be suggested that the Urakami incident, and the fear of foreign religion it inspired, accounts – probably more than any other single factor – for the development of an intimate, and often fraught, relationship between Shinto (and Buddhism) and the early Meiji state. This relationship alone gave the political leadership the confidence to see beyond the Christian prohibition and, indeed, to acquiesce in its removal.

The analysis of government Christian policy that follows proceeds broadly chronologically, and is divided into three sections. The first considers why the Urakami incident assumed the proportions it did; the second examines the beginnings of the government search, under intense diplomatic pressure, for an alternative to traditional counter-Christian methods; the third explores the dynamic creation of Restoration Shinto policy in its relationship to Christianity.

## I   URAKAMI; POLITICS AND IDEOLOGY

The gravity with which the government viewed the Urakami affair is evident in the sanctions to which it had recourse. The question of *why* it acted requires further comment. Most immediately, the Urakami incident touched upon the critical question of political legitimacy: quite simply it proffered an opportunity for enemies internal and external to challenge the Restoration government's right to rule. The government had re-established the ban on Christianity on 7 April as an 'immutable law'.[6] Under fierce pressure from the British minister Sir Harry Parkes, the 'pernicious' adjective was removed, but the proscription itself remained in place until March 1873.[7] It did so partly, at least out of deference to the 'vast majority of people from Kyūshū to the extremes of Ou' who, it was believed, were violently anti-Christian.[8] To have retracted the law, or failed to implement it, out of fear of foreign reaction, would have led to 'internal enemies banding together, joining with the Tokugawa and breathing new life into the enemy forces in Tōhoku'.[9] Given the existence of the law, the government had no choice but to take action. Sawa, in the report Inoue brought to Kido in early May, dwelt on the possibility of *rōnin* mobilising against the Christians if the government were slow to act, and concluded: 'People of this country who break our laws must be punished according to the provisions of the law. There is no question of foreigners having any right, even under International Law, to interfere or protest.'[10] The responses to the May conference motion of men like Iwakura Tomomi, the new government's leading courtier, dwelt similarly on the question of political authority. For Iwakura:

> Those who flout the proscription should be punished with death ... the treaties state explicitly that foreigners shall not convert our people to Christianity ... In my view, therefore, we are fully justified in implementing the proposed [execution and deportation], and should do so without a second thought, even if it leads us to war.[11]

The demands of legitimacy are, of course, often in conflict. Those placed on Japan by the diplomatic community were for a response very different to that advocated by Kido. Parkes told Date on 17 May that the proscription's reference to Christianity as 'pernicious' was the 'greatest insult that foreigners had ever received in Japan', and demanded its removal.[12] A week later, he articulated for the benefit of Kido and others the diplomatic reaction to the proposed deportations:

> Among civilised nations, there is none that does not permit liberty of belief. To have laws punishing people who have done nothing wrong, to erect barriers for shutting out the truth is a shame even for a barbarous country.... You are rejecting the friendship of other lands. You ought to consider the condition of Japan and think of its future.[13]

Despite the bluster, it became clear there was a degree of 'give' in the foreign response, where none could be expected from internal enemies. Parkes, persuaded first by Kido that the anti-Christian proscription had to remain, now – albeit with the greatest reluctance – accepted the arguments of Ōkuma Shigenobu and others at the meeting on 24 May that 'for [the same] reasons connected with the internal affairs of the country' the government had no choice but to act.[14] The diplomatic community made no further protest when on 17 June orders were issued for the deportation of the entire population of Urakami. In other words, irreconcilable though the demands of legitimacy ultimately were, there was some room for manoeuvre on the diplomatic side.

It is clear that where the government saw challenges to its authority, it also saw exploitable opportunities. Kido especially seems to have been mindful of this. By organising the imperial conference, he transformed the local Nagasaki incident into one of *national* importance. The conference motion was a highly emotive text, designed to stir fear. The aim was to identify a common enemy, in the fight against which internal divisions could be encouraged to dissolve, and the government be given a stage on which to demonstrate its initiative and resolve. Kido and Ōkuma knew, too, that legitimacy-enhancing respect in the eyes of both internal enemies and foreign diplomats was the benefit to be had from resisting diplomatic pressures: Ōkuma was right to reflect that the 24 May meeting marked a decisive end to the 'kowtowing' and 'tactical delaying' that had defined Japanese diplomacy since the 1850s.[15] More 'local' interests, too, were being served by the Urakami incident. The Chōshū faction of Kido and Inoue quickly took charge: having set up the imperial conference, and composed the motion, it was they who collated colleagues' responses and determined the next step; representatives from the rival Satsuma clique were not involved now nor at the major diplomatic encounter on 24 May; it was Kido, too, who secured an imperial commission to go to Nagasaki to oversee the deportations; and it was to Chōshū that one party of Christians was exiled in July.

Legitimacy – the demands it made and the opportunities it proffered – is central, then, to an understanding of why the Restoration leadership viewed Urakami with such gravity. But was this all: did the fact that it was a *Christian* incident have no special significance? Did men like Kido not fear foreign religion for what it was? Certainly, in diplomatic negotiations, fears were rarely expressed openly. Ōkuma told Parkes it was not out of loathing for Christianity that action was being taken, but for internal political reasons alone.[16] But this was disingenuous, for it is clear the senior leadership *did* regard foreign religion as a major threat to social stability. Nor is this a cause for wonder. The illegal activities of the French missionaries in Nagasaki, the intransigence and rumoured lawlessness of the Christians, and the bullying of the foreign powers would have been sufficient cause for anxiety alone. But alone they were not. They were in a historical context 'loaded' against Christianity. I refer to the anti-Christian tradition in Japan (the Nagasaki magistrate had warned of the dangers of a reprise of the Shimabara rebellion); but also, though, to more recent events. The Taiping rebellion in China had only finally been put down in 1864, and in 1866 the French had responded with gunboats to attacks on Catholic missionaries in Korea. There is no good reason to doubt the sincerity of Kido when he complained to the British consul in Nagasaki that missionaries were being sent to Japan 'to teach the Japanese to break the laws of their own country'. Kido left the consul in no doubt but that he 'intended by every exertion in his power to stop the progress of Christianity'.[17] Later in July, after the first Christians had been deported, Algernon Mitford heard from senior Chōshū leaders – probably Inoue and Itō Hirobumi – of their fears that Catholic missionaries were 'endeavouring to supplant the government in its functions'.[18] Others expressed anxiety at the news that a French missionary had been appointed 'Bishop of Japan'. 'Who save our Emperor has the right to make such an appointment?'[19] Concerns such as these were undoubtedly exacerbated by the unstable political situation of spring 1868, but they were not entirely occasioned by it. Western religion was feared – with very good reason – for what it was.

One final point here concerns state ideology as a factor in government anti-Christian action. Quite simply, 'ideology' played no obvious causal role in the events so far surveyed. Whatever else motivated the Restoration government, the incompatibility of foreign religion with Shinto offers no satisfying explanation, and those who find in the disposition of the

Urakami incident early evidence of the intolerance of Emperor state ideology confuse *post* with *propter hoc*.[20] For it was, rather, well-founded fears of Christianity that now for the first time prompted Kido and others to look favourably at the proposals of Shinto ideologues in government for the establishment, in some form or other, of Shinto as state creed. In his written response to the imperial conference on the Urakami incident, the *kokugaku* scholar Ōkuni Takamasa, and his disciples Fukuba Bisei and Kamei Koremi argued that the Christian proscription could not survive for ever; that other, long-term measures were urgently demanded. Ōkuni proposed the nation-wide dissemination of Ōkuni Shinto. This alone, he argued, could ensure Christianity was 'overcome'.[21] It is significant then that the list of domains to host the Urakami Christians, issued on 17 June, included Tsuwano, since Tsuwano was the domain of Ōkuni Takamasa; again, when Kido was in Nagasaki overseeing the deportations in July, he told Sawa that Tsuwano held 'the answer to the Christian problem';[22] indeed, it was to the domains of Chōshū, Fukuyama *and* Tsuwano that the first group of Christians was dispatched on 12 July 1868.

## II THE SEARCH FOR LONG-TERM MEASURES

On 6 April 1868, the *Dajōkan* had issued the *saisei itchi gofukoku*, an historic declaration that ritual (*sai*) and government (*sei*) were together embodied (*itchi*) in the imperial office; that the Emperor was, in other words, high priest of state ritual *and* omnipotent political sovereign.[23] The spirit of *saisei itchi* was manifest in a succession of state events after the declaration: the Charter Oath ritual in April 1868; Meiji's enthronement in September; his acts of shrine veneration during the autumn progress to the new capital; his pilgrimage to Higawa shrine on arrival there; his historic veneration at Ise in April 1869; and the state ritual in the new *Jingikan* in August. This latter ritual marked the Emperor's assumption of rule over a new Japan following the surrender of domain registers.[24] Clearly, then, there were those in government who from the start knew the legitimising value inherent in Shinto-rooted symbols. When an expansion of the parameters of *saisei itchi* was proposed in spring 1869 – to include propagation of Shinto teachings and reform of shrines – it would appear to be a natural enough development of the 1868 declaration. In a sense, of course, it was. But on closer examination, a full explanation seems to require that due attention be paid to the perception, greater even than in the previous year, of a threat from Christianity. The end to the civil war on the mainland in November had not solved internal problems; it served rather to bring them into relief. The 'localism' of *daimyō* combined now with the restiveness of anti-foreign, and increasingly anti-government, samurai newly returned from the wars, and these meshed with profound economic problems. Christianity made a major contribution to this enduring sense of crisis.

Christianity had slipped from the government's political agenda following the July deportations, but resurfaced with a vengeance at the end to the civil war. On 21 December 1868, Kido Kōin had approached Parkes in Yokohama to seek approval for the withdrawal of the 'declaration of neutrality'. The civil war was all but over, and defeat for Tokugawa supporters was assured. Parkes agreed in principle, but the meeting was memorable for a fierce exchange on Christianity.[25] Now that political stability had been restored, a more accommodating approach to Christianity could be adopted, insisted Parkes. Kido's response provoked 'very violent language' from Parkes,[26] and the whole episode profoundly affected Kido. It prompted a long diary entry on the conceit of International Law[27] and a letter to a colleague warning that only the most careful handling of the Christian business could prevent war with the Western powers.[28]

But ensuing weeks gave little respite as the diplomatic community kept up pressure for changes to policy. Early in January, Parkes presented Iwakura with allegations of a new persecution in the Gotō Islands off Nagasaki, and had him dispatch a senior Foreign Ministry official there to investigate. Gotō was raised again at a meeting between Parkes and Kido in February, and subsequently, too, in March and April; the first official response to Parkes' allegations was made by Ōkuma in early May. Ōkuma reported that the ministry official, despite exhaustive inquiries, had found evidence of peasant unrest on the Gotō islands, but none whatsoever of Christian persecution.[29] Such was the vigour of the diplomatic response to this that the Foreign Ministry in June was referring to the Gotō incident as 'a major problem that could develop into an unprecedented national disaster'.[30]

Against this background of tension over the unfolding Gotō incident and the smouldering Urakami affair, the *rōnin* took action. On 15 February, ten days after the Emperor had left Kyoto for the new capital, samurai from the Gisentai assassinated the senior councillor Yokoi Shōnan outside the Kyoto palace. Yokoi was targeted for his alleged tolerance of Christianity, and charged by his assassins with 'plotting to spread the pernicious foreign religion throughout Japan'.[31] Conservatives in government, notably those in the *Danjōdai*, petitioned for clemency for the culprits; the French, meanwhile, sent a gunboat to Nagasaki to protest at the government's handling of the Gotō affair. The leadership was once more in an intolerable position, caught between violent extremists on the one hand and belligerent foreign powers on the other. If all of this taught Iwakura that Christianity must never be permitted in Japan 'even if it means opening hostilities',[32] it provoked a more considered response in Kido. 'The evils of the day,' he wrote to Ōkubo Toshimichi at the end of May, 'are the Christian problem ... the currency problem ... and the masterless samurai problem. In my view, the very survival of the nation depends to a great extent on the successful solution to these three challenges. Unless long-term measures are established for each of these, and people forced to abide by them, the future for the imperial nation is truly bleak.'[33] Work on long-term measures for countering Christianity had, in fact, as Kido well knew, already begun. The nature of those measures we need now to consider.

In early April 1869, the government had set up within the Dajōkan a bureau for propaganda research, the *Kyōdōkyoku*. A contemporary diarist reveals that a petition from Ono Jusshin, a Chōshū Confucianist, was behind its creation.[34] Ono had been in charge of the Urakami Christians in Chōshū since their deportation there in July 1868. The gist of his petition was that the Christian ban could not endure forever in the new international era; that it was imperative that preparations for the lifting of that ban be started; that the key was to revive what he called 'Japanese teachings'. These, which he omitted to define, would protect Japan and prevent people from 'longing for foreign religion'.[35]

In early June, after Iwakura and Ōkubo arrived in Tokyo for the Tokyo Conference,[36] new appointments were made to the bureau and two new 'commissioner' posts were created: '*saisei itchi* commissioners' and 'Christian commissioners'. It is of particular interest that Ōkuni Takamasa's disciples, Fukuba and Kamei, and Ono jointly occupied all three posts. This is clear evidence that, in early summer 1869, the countering of Christianity and the development and dissemination of Shinto had come to be seen by the new government as a single whole. State-sponsored attempts to *persuade* people away from Christianity (toward Shinto) would begin to replace more violent persecution. Whatever additional political benefits Shinto propagation might have – these do not appear to have been discussed openly in spring 1869 – such a policy promised at least to deflect increasingly fierce diplomatic challenges.

It was partly to seek a broad base of approval for the new approach, and partly, too, to offer reassurances that the commitment to opposing Christianity was unchanged that the leadership now called upon domain representatives in the *Kōgisho* to debate a motion styled 'Expelling the Religion of the Lord of Heaven'. The debate took place on 26 June, and resulted in the motion being carried, advocating the expulsion of Christianity by non-violent means. The vast majority of representatives declared themselves in favour of expulsion by means of 'the Way of the Emperors', 'Japan's national creed' or 'the Great Way'.[37] None of these terms are defined in *Kōgisho* records – nor perhaps in the debates themselves – but the *principle* of implementing nationally an ideological counter to Christianity had found favour. The next step was to seek the support of prefectural governors and senior courtiers. This the government did at the Tokyo Conference, which opened in the imperial palace four days later. Top of the agenda was an item styled 'The Revival of the Way of the Emperor'.[38]

> My rule has yet to extend throughout the realm; ethical teachings have yet to spread. Now, then, is the time to revive *saisei itchi*, the way of the Emperors since the age of the first Emperor Jinmu. It is my wish that you, my subjects, display gratitude to the ancestors, and not be enticed by foreign temptations. May ethical teachings be disseminated throughout the realm.[39]

The reference, in this concluding paragraph, to 'foreign temptations' was undoubtedly a veiled reference to Christianity, and it can anyway be demonstrated that the subsequent construction of the 'Great Way' was intimately linked to government concern to counter Western religion.

Whilst there may have been an element of appeasing the conservative court in the Shinto policies that now unfolded, the enthusiasm for them amongst senior leaders anxious about Christianity is striking. The most striking of many examples is the insistence of the Tosa leader Gotō Shōjirō that the government now 'establish a religion', 'the central feature of which will be the Emperor and the entire government venerating the deities':

> For the millions of people to believe in this creed, it is essential that the government conducts itself in the manner of priests of state ritual. There can be no other way to stop the flood of the foreign religion. Executing tens of thousands of Christians will simply not work.[40]

## III  CONSTRUCTING THE 'GREAT WAY'

### The Nagasaki experiment

The 'Great Way', or the *Daikyō Senpu Undō* as it came to be known, was launched at a state ceremony in the *Jingikan* on the 3rd day of the New Year of Meiji 3. Masterminded by Fukuba Bisei, the senior official in the resurrected *Jingikan*,[41] Ono Jusshin, who ran the *Senkyōshi* or Missionary Office sited within the *Jingikan*,[42] and, from summer 1870, Kadowaki Shigeaya, a Watarai Shintoist,[43] it comprised three interlocking components: (1) the *Senkyōshi* office of state-appointed missionaries, charged with the development and dissemination of 'propaganda';[44] (2) national and local shrines, to be organised into a national network capped by the Ise shrines, where registration would be enforced and veneration encouraged to 'anchor' the missionaries' 'message'; (3) imperial ritual, to be redefined in order to provide a model for local shrine ritual.

The historic importance of the events of New Year 1870 is beyond doubt, notwithstanding the disagreements over detail already emerging within the political leadership. These were appearing not only along the Chōshū–Satsuma divide but also between the leadership and the Ōkuni faction, and between the Ōkuni faction and the followers of Hirata Atsutane, who occupied subordinate *Jingikan* and *Senkyōshi* posts. After the summer Tokyo Conference, dissent had surfaced over the *Senkyōshi*: the substance of the message to be propagated, its *modus operandi* and its position relative to the *Jingikan* and the *Dajōkan* were all vigorously debated. But it remains that New Year marked the start of some five years of active propagation by the Meiji state.[45] There were disagreements, too, over the role and status of shrines, national and provincial, but the legacy of the policies gradually now implemented is beyond doubt. There had been argument furthermore over the site and symbolism of state ritual – even over the very existence of the *Jingikan*. However, the ritual symbolism now developed survived numerous cosmetic changes and remained intact until 1945.

The symbolism I refer to was spelt out in the first of two imperial rescripts published in New Year of Meiji 3. In it, Emperor Meiji proclaimed that Jinmu's act of state foundation, his veneration of the deities and his compassion for his people, constituted the *saisei itchi* ideal. He declared at the same time his intention to emulate the ideal in his own veneration of the myriad deities of heaven and earth, the Eight Deities and the spirits of the deceased Emperors, 'in order to display my filial piety'.[46] The *locus classicus* for this 'Jinmu archetype' is, of course, the *Nihon Shoki*, where Jinmu is to be found performing sacrifice to the heavenly deities 'therewith to develop my filial piety'.[47] It is the 'display of filial piety' in the manner of Jinmu that constitutes the new, strictly ethical symbolism of modern Japanese state ritual. In the New Year ritual itself, styled the *Shindensai*, the Emperor, in the presence of the most senior members of his government, made offerings in person to the *Jingikan* shrine dedicated to the heavenly and earthly deities, the Eight Deities and the imperial ancestors. It was the presence of the last of these, the shrine to the imperial ancestors, that above all gave the event its *filial* symbolism, transforming Meiji into a paragon of filial virtue.

This question of ritual symbols was at the heart of the *Jingikan* disputes referred to above. The Hirata group and their courtier supporters insisted the Meiji *Jingikan* be a replica of the 8th century original, whose shrine was dedicated to the Eight Deities; it had housed no shrine to imperial ancestors, and the Hirata faction was hostile to its inclusion now. Fukuba, by contrast, opposed the Emperor venerating the Eight Deities shrine, and it emerges that he opposed the very existence of the *Jingikan* itself: Jinmu had worshipped neither before the Eight Dieties nor within an office called the *Jingikan*; for Emperor Meiji to do so was to blur the core symbolism of state ritual. A compromise had to be struck and, very much at the last minute, a shrine to the Eight Deities was built within the *Jingikan*.[48]

The *Shindensai* was the first in an annual cycle now inaugurated that had three notable features. First, it was an admixture of ancient rituals like the *Toshigoisai* and *Niinamematsuri* and rituals newly designed by Fukuba. Second, the new rituals all carried the same filial symbolism as the *Shindensai* commemorating Emperor Ninkō, Meiji's grandfather, in the first month, Jinmu himself in the third month, and Emperor Kōmei, Meiji's father, in the twelfth month. Third, there ran parallel to this cycle of *Jingikan* state ritual another, based largely on T'ang precedent, performed privately by the Emperor within the imperial palace.[49] Fukuba's objective in coming months was, quite simply, to have *all* imperial ritual, new and old, transferred to the imperial palace, replacing that performed there now, the better to emulate the Jinmu archetype.

A second rescript issued on the same New Year's day, 1870, announced the dispatch of missionaries 'throughout the realm' to disseminate the 'Great Way of the Gods'. It promised that the Emperor's clarification of ethical teachings, through his performance of ritual, would render 'resplendent' the 'customs of the people' as in ancient times.[50] The reason for the launch of this *Senkyōshi* mission is clear enough. At a meeting in the *Dajōkan* ten days earlier, Tokudaiji Sanenori had explained: 'Christianity is now rampant and has led the people into a state of confusion; it is for this reason that the Great Way must now be disseminated'.[51] Indeed, when the first mission, headed by Ono and comprising five other *Senkyōshi*, left Tokyo in April, it headed straight for Nagasaki. It must be said, however, that the rescript gives an entirely false impression of *Senkyōshi* capacity and prospects. There was, to begin with, the unsolved problem of what precisely the missionaries should propagate. Clearly, it was to be an ethical message inspired by the Emperor's performance of state ritual, but there was no agreed corpus of texts, no single text even, for the *Senkyōshi* to work from. In August 1869, Ono Jusshin had given a lecture to the Emperor on Shinto teachings called *Shinkyō Yōshi*.[52] Of its two sections, the latter, 'On Clarifying Ethics', expounded the five ethical virtues commonly associated with Confucianism, while the former, 'Venerating the Deities', treated Amaterasu. Amaterasu was 'the deity who rules heaven and earth' and 'who gives to men their souls which, when they die, return to Takamagahara'; local shrine deities were 'servants of Amaterasu' who merited veneration as they determined the fate of the soul in the afterlife. The emphasis on Amaterasu as creator and on Takamagahara as a place of eternal rest are new additions to the pre-Meiji theology of Ōkuni Takamasa, and they may well reflect Ono's personal experience in Chōshū with the Urakami Christians. But if this was to become 'orthodoxy', and be disseminated throughout the realm, it needed the approval of the Hirata faction. Their support in the provinces amongst shrine priests and *kokugakusha* was far greater than that for Ōkuni Takamasa. The Hirata group, however, dismissed the new theology as 'Ono's Confucian creation' and refused to cooperate.[53]

The question of *Senkyōshi* staffing, too, had by no means been resolved in New Year of Meiji 3, when the rescript was issued. The Hirata faction advocated training Shinto priests and provincial *kokugakusha* as *Senkyōshi*, but the Ōkuni faction favoured domain and prefectural officials: the *Senkyōshi* had to be seen to derive their authority from central, or at least local, government. In April 1869, the Ōkuni faction scored an initial victory when all domains were ordered to nominate officials for *Senkyōshi* training in the capital, but it was to be another full year before all domains had made nominations and training was begun. The *Senkyōshi* mission only ever functioned effectively in Nagasaki; it soon became clear the office could not survive in its present form. Within 18 months of its launch, major adjustments were being discussed.[54]

A final problem for the *Senkyōshi*, and the third of the interlocking components of the Great Way, concerned shrines. For the Ōkuni faction the institutional 'anchor' of shrine registration was essential to the success of the mission. Government interest in shrines, apparent in the 1868 *saisei itchi gofukoku*, was revived in the autumn of 1869 owing largely, it appears, to pressure from the Foreign Ministry. In November, Sawa Nobuyoshi, recently transferred to the ministry from Nagasaki, submitted a petition on shrine registration that appears to have been a major catalyst. In his preamble, Sawa acknowledged the urgent need to provide a counter to Christianity and continued:

> If by chance [native Christians] choose to ignore the regulations for shrine registration [outlined below] and insist on sticking to their old religion, their refusal to register will constitute a breach of our [civil] law ... We can then mete out suitable punishments for the crime of not registering without fear of being accused [by foreigners] of insulting their religion.[55]

Sawa made two concrete proposals that concern us here. The first was for all Japanese to register new births at local shrines 'since all Japanese are descended from the deities'.[56] The second was that the proven counter-Christian skills of Buddhists should be employed and the Buddhist monopoly over funerals be retained.[57] With Shinto shrines monitoring births and Buddist temples monitoring deaths, Christianity could never take root, he argued. Sawa's document was subsequently passed to the *Minbushō*, and emerged in April 1870 as the 'Temporary Shrine Registration Laws for Nagasaki'.[58] That the Nagasaki mission was a success clearly owed much to the fact that *Senkyōshi* were able to time their sermons to coincide with mass registration at local shrines.[59] In its notice to the Nagasaki governor, the *Minbushō* stressed that shrine registration was a temporary measure, taken because of the Christian problem in Nagasaki, and that national regulations on family registration would follow in due course.[60] It was, in other words, an 'experiment' and, not yet anyway, a commitment to Ōkuni faction plans for nationwide shrine registration.

A new sense of crisis over Christianity is evident in government discussions on rituals, shrines and missionaries at the end of 1869 and through 1870, and it owes much to the vigorous diplomatic response to the action taken against the remaining Urakami Christians. On 6 January, just three weeks before the *Jingikan* ceremony and the launch of the mission, the second 'round-up' of thousands of Nagasaki Christians had begun; deportations followed over the next few days. The symbolism was obvious: foreign Christianity was being uprooted from Nagasaki and the seeds sown in its place of 'indigenous teachings'. Deportations went ahead despite protests from Parkes, who happened to be in Nagasaki at the time. He hurried to Osaka and then Tokyo to stir the diplomatic community to action. Such was the intensity of the diplomatic exchanges that ensued, the government believed the Western powers would sever relations,[61] but it nonetheless stood firm.

We should note here that, even after the intense diplomacy of January, there was not another month until 1872, when the first of the Urakami villagers were released, in which Christianity was not being discussed within some government office or across the diplomatic table. Summer of 1870, moreover, brought news of the Tientsin massacre – which Kido blamed on the 'French insistence on religion';[62] early in 1871 reports arrived of the illegal activities of Protestant missionaries like Hepburn; later in the year a diplomatic storm broke over the arrest of the Protestant convert Ichikawa Einosuke;[63] and then, on three occasions in 1871, Parkes had teams sent to investigate allegations of cruelty against the exiled Christians. This relentless diplomatic pressure is one crucial factor explaining the subsequent development of the 'Great Way'. More immediately, though, it was debates within government on political reform in the summer of 1870 that provided the Ōkuni faction with the opportunity to turn the Nagasaki experiment into national policy.

## A Policy for Nation Building

In September 1870, Iwakura, Kido, Ōkubo, Ōkuma, Hirozawa, Etō Shinpei and others wrote proposals on political reform, the shared objective of which was to suggest how the power of the centre over the periphery might be enhanced. These proposals were subsequently reworked by Iwakura into a discussion document called *Kenkokusaku* or 'A Policy for Nation Building'.

The first of its 15 articles defined Japan's unique polity as consisting in the Emperor's special relationship with his people. He, ordained to rule by Amaterasu, serves heaven by bestowing harmony on his people; the people, in turn, serve him by devoting themselves to work. The article urged those charged with reform to ensure the institutional clarification of this 'founding principle'.[64] The *Jingikan* responded to this with a series of suggestions. First, Kadowaki made it clear that it was essential that the government consider how '*saisei itchi* in fact as well as name' could be achieved, and the 'great foundation of the sacred realm' be made clear.[65] What made this so pressing was 'the pernicious creed'. A subsequent petition, signed also by Fukuba provided more concrete proposals: the *Jingikan* was a copy of a copy of a T'ang Chinese institution; the restoration of the Emperor had been inspired by the example of Jinmu; its long-term success or failure depended on adhering to the Jinmu archetype of *saisei itchi*. In other words, (1) performance of all imperial ritual must be transferred from the *Jingikan* to the imperial palace; (2) state ritualists must be moved to the *Dajōkan*, the *Jingikan* abolished, and ritual moved to the imperial court; (3) the *Senkyōshi* must be attached directly to the *Dajōkan*, in order that their authority be seen to derive from the political centre.

A few weeks later came new proposals: the *Senkyōshi* should concentrate for the present on tackling the Urakami Christians in exile, but a 'flexible approach' (to the future of the *Senkyōshi* programme?) was needed; regarding shrines, prefectural governors and their staff should attend local shrines on the occasion of major state rituals.[66] In November, as a result of this last petition, Iwakura met Fukuba and Kadowaki. They are known to have discussed *Senkyōshi* as well as *saisei itchi*. Two weeks after the meeting, Fukuba submitted a new proposal on shrines, stressing the need for 'shrine registration to be implemented throughout the nation if *saisei itchi* is to reach the extremes of provincial society'.[67] The *Dajōkan* in response ordered the *Jingikan* to draft a national ranking system for shrines and their priests, and a programme for shrine rites too.

Space does not permit a detailed analysis of the political processes that now unfolded; suffice it to say that, within a year, Ōkuni faction proposals on state ritual and shrines had been implemented in most of their details. The *Senkyōshi*, as we shall see, proved more intractable.

The reform of state ritual began after the abolition of the domains. On 22 September, the *Jingikan* was abolished and replaced by a *Jingishō*, the top posts being assumed by Fukuba and Kadowaki.[68] With the *Jingikan* now removed, the *Dajōkan* became the supreme organ of state; the Emperor, as both political sovereign and priest of state ritual, presided now *directly* over the *Dajōkan*. Within the *Dajōkan* a new Ritualist Bureau was created, charged with supervising state ritual. A month later on 27 October, the building of a new shrine to the ancestral deities in the imperial palace was announced by rescript.[69] Two weeks later, the ancestral spirits were transferred there in a solemn procession joined by all senior government officials. Six months later, the other shrines in the old *Jingikan*, those dedicated to the Eight Deities, and the Myriad Deities of Heaven and Earth, were also solemnly transferred to the palace. Hereby, the site for modern Japanese state ritual was established; thus it has remained with only minimum change to the present day. T'ang-influenced ritual that had till now been performed in the palace was banished, and a new cycle of palace-based ritual, derived from that performed in the *Jingikan* since New Year of Meiji 3, was activated.[70]

Shrine reforms predated these on ritual by several months. On 1 July 1871, a new system of shrine ranking was published; the Ise shrines were placed in a class of their own, and 'reformed': the inner shrine to Amaterasu and its attendant priests being accorded new status higher than that of the outer shrine to Toyouke. A second piece of legislation declared all shrines to be 'sites for the performance of state ritual'; priests at Ise and all other shrines thus became 'state appointees'.[71] National shrine registration, fundamentally the same as that operating in Nagasaki, was introduced on 19 August.[72] There were subsequently major adjustments to these laws, but the definition, now established, of all shrines as 'sites of state ritual' remained until 1945.

Final comments are reserved for the *Senkyōshi*. Much remains unclear about the operations of the office through 1870 and 1871, but 19 August saw the publication of the *Daikyō Goshui*, an outline of Shinto doctrine for the *Senkyōshi*.[73] The *Goshui* offers a striking contrast with Ono's *Shinkyō Yōshi*: Gone is all reference to creation and the soul; it speaks more generally, rather, of veneration for 'deities', of the way of loyalty and filial piety; of the virtue of abiding by the decrees of the Emperor. The *Goshui* was clearly an attempt to establish theological common ground between conflicting factions in the *Jingikan* and *Senkyōshi* offices. It did not, however, mean the end to theological dispute; nor was it sufficient to secure the long-term survival of the *Senkyōshi* who were now ordered to leave Tokyo and return to their domains to begin propagation.

Sometime in September 1871, there was a major dispute in the *Seiin* over the pros and cons of ending the Christian prohibition. Imminent negotiations on treaty revision were probably the trigger. Gotō Shōjirō and Yamagata Aritomo thought the time was right; Iwakura and Etō Shinpei did not.[74] Iwakura did, however, commission a 'feasibility study'. Styled *Ishū Bōgyo ni tsuki Mikomi* or 'Defence against Alien Creeds: Prospects for the Future', it acknowledged the possibility of ending the proscription on three conditions: that (1) shrine registration strictly be enforced throughout Japan; (2) Buddhist and Confucianists be recruited to *Senkyōshi* ranks; (3) anti-Christian spies be dispatched to all ports.[75] The *Seiin* did its own study, and like Iwakura, argued for the deployment of Buddhists in the defence against Christianity.[76] As the counter-Christianity needs of the modern state beckoned the establishment of a new formal relationship with Buddhism, the Buddhist priest Shimaji Mokurai submitted a petition to government suggesting the form that that relationship might take. The long title of his petition discloses its main point: 'That the government replace the *Senkyōshi* with an official organ to supervise all religions, oversee Buddhist priests and monitor their propaganda activities in order that foreign religion might be countered'.[77] Shimaji's idea, effectively for a ministry of religions to replace the *Senkyōshi*, was subsequently discussed by Kido, Etō and Fukuba on 4 November. Etō then produced a series of more concrete proposals for the mobilising of Buddhist resources. Buddhists would be bound to 'revere the deities', 'expound the great ethic of loyalty' and 'protect the state', but they would be given a major counter-Christian role to play.[78]

In April 1872, four months after Iwakura and his embassy had left Japan for the United States, the *Kyōbushō*, a new ministry of religions, was established along the lines suggested by Shimaji and refined by Etō. Etō and Fukuba were charged with policy formulation. The establishment of the *Kyōbushō* was acknowledgement that the capacity of the exclusively Shinto *Senkyōshi* was limited; that without active Buddhist help, the state was defenceless against Christianity.

CONCLUSION

The Meiji proscription against Christianity, proclaimed on noticeboards throughout Japan since April 1868, was finally withdrawn in February

1873; the last Urakami Christians were released from years of exile in March of that year. These events stemmed mainly from official and unofficial protests encountered by Iwakura and his embassy first in the USA and then in Europe. The message received was that negotiations over treaty revision were unthinkable with a nation that persecuted Christians and banned the religion of the civilised world.

This study has shown, however, that preparations for this inevitability had begun long before the Iwakura embassy arrived in America: the Ōkuni faction petitions to the Osaka conference in May 1868, the exile of Christians to Tsuwano, Ono's petition of spring 1869 and the creation it inspired of the *Kyōdōkyoku*, the launch of the Great Way in New Year 1870 and ensuing developments in state ritual, shrine reform and the dissemination of propaganda – and the *Kyōbushō*, too – all of these were part of a search for counter Christian measures that would endure beyond the end of the prohibition. Christianity was clearly not a problem confined to the immediate present; it was one that would endure.

It is not suggested here that Christianity *alone* accounts for the forging of a relationship between the early Meiji state and Shinto, but it has been shown to constitute a factor of the utmost importance. The leadership knew that Christianity could not be banned; it had, in some form or other, to be contained and accommodated. The erection of Shinto structures and the dissemination of Shinto, and later Buddhist, teachings were part and parcel of this process of accommodation.

Finally, if it is acknowledged that the process we have examined was, indeed, one of 'accommodation' – albeit reluctant – then perhaps that process is best understood, after all, not as characteristic of the intolerance of the so-called Emperor state, but rather as an initial stage in the long and painful process that accompanies the accommodation of alien religions within any culture, a process not entirely unfamiliar to students of Japan's earlier cultural history.

## NOTES

The author acknowledges with gratitude a generous grant for research received from the Daiwa Anglo-Japanese Foundation. Gratitude for assistance provided goes, too, to Professor Sakamoto Koremaru and Dr Takeda Hideaki.

1. The discovery of the hidden Christians of Urakami was made in 1865 by French missionaries in Nagasaki. The Tokugawa handling of the affair is examined in Urakawa, *Urakami Kirishitanshi*, pp. 122–226. The problem resurfaced after the Restoration government appointed a new magistrate to Nagasaki in early March.
2. Kido, *The Diary*, vol. 1, pp. 8–9.

3. Kido, *The Diary*, pp. 16–17. Sawa's report is in *Higohan Kokuji Shiryō*, vol. 8, pp. 863–4.
4. Miyachi comp. 'Shūkyō Kankei Hōrei Ichiran' (hereafter 'Hōrei'), p. 426.
5. Katsu, *Kaishū Zadan*, p. 136. Despite Katsu's estimation, neither Beasley, *The Meiji Restoration* nor any other standard texts on political or diplomatic history makes even passing reference to the Urakami incident.
6. Hōrei, p. 425.
7. The revised proscription was issued on 25 May ('Hōrei', p. 426).
8. Ōkuma, *Sekijitsudan*, p. 279.
9. Ibid.
10. *Higohan Kokuji Shiryō*, vol. 8, pp. 464.
11. *Dajōkan Jinmon Kirishitan Shūto Shobun Mondai ni kansuru Tōshin narabi ni Kankei Monjo*, (Tōkyō Daigaku Shiryō Hensanjo).
12. *Date Munenari Shuki* (not paginated) (Shiryō Hensanjo).
13. Cary, *A History of Christianity*, p. 310.
14. Ibid., p. 311.
15. *Ōkuma Sekijitsudan*, p. 280.
16. Cary, *A History of Christianity*, p. 310.
17. Paske Smith, *Japanese Traditions of Christianity*, pp. 119–20.
18. Cortazzi, ed., *Mitford's Japan*, p. 138.
19. Ibid.
20. Those who argue in this way include Kataoka, *Urakami Yonban Kuzure*, and Haga Shōji, 'Shinto Kokkyōsei no Keisei'. Suzuki argues, as I do, that 'ideology' played no part in the early persecution, but she does not acknowledge the importance of Shinto policy as a counter-Christian device (Suzuki, 'Meiji Seifu no Kirisutokyō Seisaku'.)
21. I have explored Ōkuni Takamasa's views on Christianity elsewhere. See especially, Breen, 'Accommodating the Alien'.
22. Sawa, *Kyūshū Jiken* (not paginated).
23. 'Hōrei', p. 425.
24. On these and other political rituals in Restoration Japan, see Haga, 'Meiji Jingikansei no Kakuritsu', Takeda, 'Kindai Tennō saishi', and Breen, 'Emperor, State and Religion', chapter 2.
25. The declaration of neutrality was formally retracted on 9 February 1869.
26. Satow, *A Diplomat*, p. 389–90.
27. Kido, *The Diary*, p. 148.
28. *Kido Kōin Monjo*, vol. 3, p. 185.
29. *Nihon Gaikō Monjo* (hereafter *NGM*), vol. 2, 1, Doc. 133, pp. 533–4.
30. Ibid., vol. 2, 1, Doc. 198, pp.787–8.
31. See Miyachi, 'Haihan Chiken no Seiji Katei', pp. 39–40.
32. *Iwakura Tomomi Kankei Monjo*, vol. 1, pp. 882–6.
33. *Kido Kōin Monjo*, vol. 3, p. 318. Kido wrote to Iwakura in a similar vein two days later.
34. Tokoyo, *Shinkyō Soshiki*, p. 363. It was the sponsorship of Hirozawa Saneomi, the senior Chōshū councillor, that guaranteed the petition a favourable hearing. (Ibid.)
35. Ibid.
36. The convening of a major conference in Tokyo was first announced in February. See Adams, *A History of Japan*, p. 170. The official title of the conference was the *Jōkyoku Kaigi*.

37. *Meiji Bunka Zenshū*, vol. 1, pp. 69–98.
38. Other conference items were the appointment of '*daimyō* governors', and the development of the island of Hokkaidō.
39. *Meiji Tennōki*, vol. 2, pp. 125–6.
40. *Iwakura Tomomi Kankei Monjo*, vol. 3, pp. 473–4.
41. The *Jingikan* was 'resurrected' as part of the institutional reforms on 15 August.
42. The *Senkyōshi* replaced the *Kyōdōkyoku* at the end of July.
43. These men form the core of what we shall refer to as the 'Ōkuni faction', to distinguish them from the followers of Hirata Atsutane in government.
44. *Senkyōshi* was the name given to the office as well as those who worked for it.
45. See Hardacre, *Shinto and the State*, for the impact of state propaganda on popular religious.
46. *Meiji Tennōki*, vol. 2, p. 248.
47. *Nihongi*, pp. 132–4.
48. See Haga, 'Meiji Jingikansei', and Breen, 'Emperor, State and Religion', chapter 2.
49. See on this, and Fukuba's activities in general, Takeda, 'Kindai Tennō Saishi' and Sakamoto, *Meiji Ishin to Kokugakusha*, pp. 52–72.
50. *Meiji Tennōki*, vol. 2, p. 248.
51. *Saga Sanenaru Nikki*, vol. 3, p. 183.
52. *Shinkyō Yōshi* has been discussed from differing perspectives in Fujii, 'Daikyō Yōshi', and Haga, 'Shinto Kokkyōsei'.
53. Tokoyo, *Shinkyō Soshiki*, p. 364.
54. On the *Senkyōshi* see Fujii, 'Senkyōshi no kenkyū', and Sakamoto, *Meiji Ishin to Kokugakusha*, pp. 82–100.
55. *NGM*, 2, 3, Doc. 672, p. 630.
56. Ibid., p. 631.
57. Ibid., 631–2.
58. 'Hōrei', p. 432. See also Sakamoto, *Kokka Shintō*, pp. 172–80.
59. See, for example, the accounts of Nishikawa Yoshinosuke, one of the *Senkyōshi* sent to Nagasaki, in Fujii, 'Senkyōshi no Nagasaki Kaikō', pp. 25–6.
60. These other regulations were the Family Registration Laws of May 1871. See Sakamoto, *Kokka Shintō*, pp. 172–80.
61. *Gaikō Jirui Zenshi*, p. 146 (Tōkyō Daigaku Shiryō Hensanjo) *NGM*, vol. 2, 3, contains diplomatic and other records.
62. *Kido Kōin Monjo*, vol. 4, p. 111.
63. Ozawa, *Bakumatsu Meiji Yasokyōshi*, pp. 83–107.
64. *Iwakurakō Jikki*, vol. 2, p. 826.
65. *Kadowaki Shigeaya Ikō Shiryō* (Shiryō Hensanjo).
66. Ibid.
67. *Hōki Bunrui Taizen*, vol. 1, pp. 105–6.
68. *Meiji Tennōki*, vol. 2, pp. 521–2.
69. Ibid., pp. 540, 545–6.
70. On these rituals, see Takeda, 'Meiji Jingikan', and Breen, 'Emperor, State and Religion', chapter 2.
71. 'Hōrei', pp. 437–8.

72. 'Hōrei', pp. 839–41. These regulations differed simply in that provision was made for the performance of Shinto funerals for those who wished; and that sole responsibility for birth registration was not to rest with shrines. Their brief was to support local government which, as stipulated under the Family Registration Laws of May, was to assume the key administrative role. See on this point Sakamoto, *Kokka Shintō,* pp. 172–90.
73. 'Hōrei', p. 441.
74. Sasaki, *Hogo Hiroi*, vol. 5, p. 173.
75. *Iwakura Tomomi Kankei Monjo*, vol. 8, pp. 269–76.
76. The *Sein* study, known as the *Yasokyō Bōatsu Tejun Mikomisho*, is in the *Kōbunroku*, Kokuritsu Kōmonjokan.
77. *Shimaji Mokurai Zenshū*, vol.1, pp. 6–11.
78. *Kōbunroku*, Kokuritsu Kōmonjokan. The document reads in part: 'We strictly forbade Christianity, and, indeed, put to death hundreds of thousands of their number, and yet their descendants exist in the neighbourhood of Nagasaki to this day. Thus we can know how difficult a task we face in defending Japan against Christianity.'

# 6 Christianity Encounters Buddhism in Japan:
## A Historical Perspective
### Notto R. Thelle

There seems to be a consensus among Buddhists and Christians that the present interfaith dialogue represents a unique and decisive breakthrough. Protestants talk of the World Council of Churches and its dialogue programmes, which have developed since the 1950s, Roman Catholics emphasise the new attitudes introduced by the Second Vatican Council in the 1960s, and Japanese Buddhists readily respond to the challenges, engaging in exciting encounters with Christians.

There is no reason to underestimate the importance of recent developments in Buddhist–Christian relations. The literature concerned with dialogue has increased dramatically. A few decades ago only a few concerned individuals published their views in books and articles; now there is an abundance of scholarly and popular books, articles and reports. The many opportunities for organised dialogue facilitate encounters at various levels: academic discussions on theological and philosophical themes; conferences concerned with peace, environment and social issues; cooperation on the practical levels of social protest and political action; and encounters on the level of spirituality, including meditation, prayer and sharing of religious experiences.

An additional factor is the internationalisation of the encounter between the two religions. Particularly since the 1960s an increasing number of Western theologians and other scholars have visited Japan in order to become acquainted with Buddhist philosophy and practice. Many of them have been impelled not only to change their view on Buddhism, but even to reformulate their own theological understanding. The fact that many works of the leading representatives of the Kyoto School of Philosophy, such as Nishida Kitarō, Nishitani Keiji, Tanabe Hajime and others have been translated has contributed to this trend. The direct contact between Buddhist and Christian theologians and thinkers on the international level has also intensified and sharpened the dialogue.

My own interest in the development of Buddhist–Christian relations in Japan stems from perception of a need for a historical perspective on the present dialogue. The lack of historical consciousness among those involved in dialogue challenged me to engage in a further investigation of the earlier stages of Buddhist–Christian contact. My final conclusion was that the real transformation of the relationship between the two religions took place a hundred years ago, in the 1890s. Although it was a decade of bitter hostility and conflict, characterised by extreme nationalistic sentiments, anti-Western and anti-Christian, those same years were decisive for the formation of a creative dialogue between Buddhists and Christians. The development in the 1890s was, of course, part of a much longer history which, in spite of conflict and suspicion, had prepared the way for mutual respect and understanding. But it was during the 1890s that radical change took place.

In the present study I shall first consider major developments since the opening of Japan in the mid-nineteenth century, with the radical transformation in the 1890s as the focal point, and then analyse certain developments and trends in our own century. A few additional remarks on the contemporary dialogue will conclude the essay. The Roman Catholic encounter with Buddhism in the sixteenth and seventeenth centuries, and the related history of oppression and persecution of Christianity cannot be included here, but are to be taken as an important background for the religious conflict after the opening of Japan. Similarly, the role of Shinto is also beyond the scope of this paper.[1]

## INITIAL CONFLICT: BUDDHIST PREOCCUPATION WITH CHRISTIANITY

The initial contact between Buddhists and Christians after the forced reopening of Japan in 1854 presented no basis for peaceful encounter. From the Buddhist point of view, dialogue was impossible. Christianity was regarded as a fatal enemy and there was no room for concessions. From the Christian point of view, dialogue was superfluous. According to missionaries and Western observers, Buddhism posed no threat and there was no need for contact. The relationship was thus extremely unbalanced: a onesided preoccupation with Christianity on the part of the Buddhists, characterised by exaggerated fear and suspicion; and an almost total neglect of Buddhism on the part of the Christians. The tension was exacerbated in the mid-nineteenth century by the moves, interpreted by the Buddhists as Christian-inspired, to reopen the country, and, in a characteristic combination of slogans, they combined 'defence of the state' (*gokoku*) with 'defence of Buddhism' (*gohō*) and 'opposition to the pernicious religion' (*bōja*). A characteristic example is the warning of the Buddhist priest Gesshō in 1856:

> If the Land of the Gods is held by the barbarians and the [Christian] heresy prospers, how can we protect Buddhism from decay? ... I am really afraid that the present trend will finally result in fraternisation between the foreigners and the ignorant coastal population ... They will be led astray by the heresy and become a [rebellious] band of brutes. Hence, as for the urgent need of coastal defence, today nothing compares to resisting religion [Christianity] with religion [Buddhism].[2]

The anti-Christian sentiment was further stimulated by the fact that Japanese Buddhism was in serious crisis in the mid-nineteenth century. Among various aspects of this crisis historians often mention the inner corruption of the Buddhist priesthood, two hundred years of government protection and control, intellectual trends of anti-Buddhist thought among both Confucian and Shinto scholars, and numerous waves of anti-Buddhist riots and local attempts to eradicate Buddhism. According to Tsuji Zennosuke, by this time Buddhism had become entirely formalistic, alienated from the people, and almost paralysed: 'Because of inertia, temples and priests barely managed to protect their social position.'[3] Soon after the Meiji Restoration (1868) attempts were made to establish Shinto as a national religion at the cost of Buddhism.

In such a situation it is little wonder that Japanese Buddhists found no room for concessions. Buddhism was threatened from all sides, and the renewed encounter with a vigorous Christian church was seen as a possible death-blow. The most easily available method of defence was to appeal to the deep-rooted fear of the foreign faith. Buddhists reprinted the old anti-Christian literature which had been used in the early Tokugawa period, including that written in Chinese and pamphlets produced by Japanese propagators.

The old anti-Christian writings, however, had been produced in order to face a different political situation and a different Christian denomination (Roman Catholicism), and were in many ways inadequate. The need for renewed study of Christianity resulted in fervent activity organised by several Buddhist head temples. Just as the government sent spies to keep the activities of the missionaries under surveillance, the Buddhist head temples dispatched priests disguised as religious seekers in order to monitor the advances of the missionaries. The spies made detailed reports on the activities of the missionaries, wrote summaries of their teachings, registered differences between various denominations, and even compiled lists of the books found on their shelves. Some of the spies were even baptised in their attempt at concealing their intentions, and some apparently converted to Christianity.

A further consequence of such apologetical work was the introduction of Christian studies and Western learning into the Buddhist seminaries. In order to oppose the attack of the 'evil religion', the Buddhist leadership had to study its teachings and activities.

The missionaries, for their part, were aware of the Buddhists' activities and made their observations. Guido F. Verbeck, missionary from the Dutch Reformed Church in America, reported from Nagasaki:

> They [the Buddhist priests] are certainly a strange set of men, if my suspicions are founded; for they have bought whole boxes of Chinese Bibles and Christian books and tracts, and all, as they said, for the purpose of teaching their scholars. These books, perhaps gotten for bad purposes only, may yet turn out a blessing to many, quite contrary to the wicked intention.[4]

Apart from such observations, and in contrast to the Buddhists who engaged in fervent attacks on Christianity, the Christian communities showed no interest in Buddhism, which was generally regarded as so dated and corrupted that it was doomed to fade away. 'The kingdom of Satan is already divided against itself', commented the American missionary O.H. Gulick. 'The people still favour Buddhism, the government favours Shintoism, while many, at least not a few who are destined to be the leading minds, think that Christianity is better than either.'[5]

It is appropriate to mention here that even though the missionaries had their prejudices, including a quite triumphalistic understanding of the situation, their disregard of Buddhism was not based on a particular bias against Buddhism as such. It was rather a reflection of the predominant sentiment of Japanese intellectuals and politicians, who also tended to ignore or even despise Buddhism. In addition, other challenges seemed more relevant, such as Confucian philosophy with its ambivalent attitude to religion; and the increasing influence of what the missionaries called 'Western infidelity', that is, religious indifference, atheism, materialism, and trends in philosophy and science. Compared to such challenges, Buddhism was not regarded as a serious rival.

## MUTUAL CONCERN AND MUTUAL STUDY

Buddhist–Christian relations entered a new stage in the 1870s and 1880s. In 1873 the Japanese government ordered the removal of the notice boards proscribing Christianity and introduced a policy of tacit recognition of Christianity. The change initiated a period of increasing missionary activity. But, as Christianity gradually expanded beyond the narrow boundaries of the treaty ports, with evangelistic campaigns and church planting in the countryside, the deep-rooted influence and power of Buddhism also became more obvious. One of the first missionaries to acknowledge the power of Buddhism, the American missionary D.C. Green, observed in the early 1870s that Buddhism had a 'far stronger hold upon the people than the Sintooism (*sic*) which the rulers wish to uphold and strengthen', and that 'whatever a Japanese may be while he lives, he is Buddhist when he dies.' Hence, he encouraged the study of Buddhism, for 'our great fight in Japan, it becomes more and more clear every day, is to be with B(uddhism) ...'[6]

What happened, then, particularly in the 1880s, was the development of a mutual concern in the relationship. The apologetical concern was obvious, clearly motivated by the need of preparing oneself for effective propagation and defence. This antagonistic relationship, however, gradually led to more penetrating studies and direct acquaintance. Several missionaries were invited to lecture on Christianity in Buddhist seminaries, while Buddhist priests lectured or gave private instruction to Christian missionaries. The result was in many cases development of courteous friendships between the antagonists.

A number of missionaries, and in turn also Japanese Christians, engaged in further Buddhist studies. In spite of quite arbitrary evaluations, one can discern among the Christians a growing admiration for the learning and personal integrity of the Buddhist scholars and leaders. The Congregational missionary J. H. DeForest, who was active in Japan in the 1870s and 1880s, is a characteristic example of such a change of attitude. He began his career in Japan with successful campaigns against idol worship, denouncing and ridiculing 'the evil of worshipping dried wood'. Acquaintance with Buddhists, however, gradually convinced him that it was wrong to call the native religions false or to call the Japanese heathen. Instead he regarded Buddhism and Confucianism as part of God's preparatory work, Buddha and Confucius being 'the moral prophets to fit the East for Christ'.[7]

As regards the Buddhists, the study of Christianity continued, but gradually led to new insights. The leading head temples sent delegations to Europe and America in order to acquaint themselves with the spiritual base of Christianity. Everything was studied: philosophy, theology, the relationships between church and state, cultural trends, education, political systems and, most importantly, the new science of religion. The Buddhist observers realised that Western Christianity was weakened by theological unrest and happily introduced the writings of critical theologians to Japan, such as Ernest Renan's *Vie de Jesus* (The Life of Jesus, 1863). They also discovered that Christianity was threatened by anti-Christian trends in the intellectual world. They introduced, and in some cases even facilitated, the translation of literature they regarded as anti-Christian. It was argued that 'science has laid the Christian religion captive at its feet', thanks to such noble men as Darwin, Huxley, Spencer and Mill, who had 'striven to shake off this horrible religion'.[8]

Such aggressively apologetical attitudes were, on the other hand, balanced by a number of scholars who went beyond apologetics and apparently had a sympathetic understanding of the Christian faith. It is significant that the Buddhists referred to above belonged to the progressive parties of their respective sects. They were painfully aware of the crisis in Buddhism, and saw the Christian expansion as a real threat. But as zealous reformers they were also stimulated by the challenge from Christianity and believed that the situation would change as soon as their reforms were adopted. This combination of reform zeal and increasing confidence *vis-à-vis* Christianity contributed to more friendly attitudes and in various ways prepared the ground for open dialogue.

DIALOGUE AND COOPERATION

While the 1880s had been characterised by enthusiasm for the West, with waves of Westernisation and a favourable climate for Christian expansion, the 1890s were characterised by a nationalistic reaction, strongly anti-Western and anti-Christian. It is no exaggeration to say that Buddhism rode on this nationalistic wave, making every effort to defame and stigmatise Christianity as anti-national, dangerous, and incompatible with the national polity. Especially in the years from 1889 to 1893 the Buddhists engaged in fervent anti-Christian propaganda, including even violent persecution and destruction of church buildings in the districts. Christian work was systematically obstructed, and Christian families were ostracised. The opposition was so strong that even Buddhist observers sometimes pitied the Christians for their extreme hardships.

Given this background, it is significant to note that the decade of the 1890s, for all its nationalistic and anti-Christian sentiments, was also the period during which the first peaceful encounter between Buddhists and Christians was prepared and reached a decisive breakthrough. The dynamics behind this development cannot be described sufficiently here, but a few elements should be noticed.

First, the Japanese Christians finally managed to convince their critics that it was possible to combine Christian faith and patriotism. Throughout the Meiji era Christians had claimed that their faith enabled them to serve the nation as true patriots, but conservative Japanese – including the Buddhist establishment – had consistently suspected their motives. Nothing proved their patriotism more eloquently than the Sino-Japanese War (1894–5), when they were finally able to demonstrate in action what they had maintained all the time. With reference to the patriotic spirit of the Christian college, Dōshisha, it was commented that 'if there existed any real doubt of the entire compatibility of Christianity and patriotism, all semblance of ground for doubt had been swept away by the enthusiasm shown at every stage of the Chino-Japanese (*sic*) war'.[9] It is somewhat ironic that a war was necessary to prove that Christians were loyal citizens who could live in peace with fellow Japanese.

Second, along with the new emphasis on patriotism, the churches developed a theology which systematically advocated the need for Japanisation of church life and theology. Expressed in the words of representative church leader and theologian, Yokoi Tokio, Christians 'should believe in Christianity as Japanese, study theology as Japanese, propagate Christianity as Japanese … . We should hold up Christianity with the right hand and stretch down the left hand to grasp the forty million [Japanese] brethren'.[10] Such a new emphasis on Japanese traditions – slightly anti-Western and anti-denominational, but also influenced by Western liberal theology – naturally led to a renewed interest in Japanese indigenous traditions, including Buddhism.

On the part of the Buddhists, several reform movements advocated the need for a *new* Buddhism, *shin Bukkyō*. A reformed Buddhism had to be new in terms of a progressive grappling with social and political issues, and new in terms of a radical reformation of the formalistic and hierarchical *old* Buddhism. The concern for reform led to contact with Christian communities, which to a great extent provided models for practical reform, social work, missionary activity, and for the whole problem of coming to terms with modernity. The very concept of a new Buddhism confronting the old establishment was actually borrowed direct from Christianity, where the Protestant Reformation in Japanese was understood as the conflict between the old religion (*kyūkyō*) of Roman Catholicism versus the new religion (*shinkyō*) of the Reformation.

Among other factors that facilitated more formal contacts were the establishment of a Chair of Comparative Religion at the Imperial University in 1889, an example soon followed by other places of learning, and the World Parliament of Religions in Chicago in 1893. A number of

Japanese Buddhists attended the latter and established contacts in the West, and it provided the model for a similar Japanese small-scale parliament of religions in 1896, the so-called Buddhist–Christian Conference.

The Conference, convened in September 1896, was officially called the Conference of Religionists (*Shūkyōsha Kondankai*). Since most of the 42 representatives were Buddhists and Christians, however, it was generally referred to as a Buddhist–Christian encounter (*Butsu-Ya Ryōkyō Kondankai*). The meeting was held in the villa of Viscount Matsudaira in Tokyo, and was organised as a social gathering for the exchange of opinions. Critics denounced the meeting, or ignored it as a gathering of liberal Buddhists and Christians. Nevertheless, it was significant both as a friendly encounter of former enemies, and as a manifestation of a new relationship with symbolic meaning far beyond the actual event.

A Buddhist participant described the encounter in dramatic terms. Many of the leading figures of the religious communities were linked up on the tatami floor, facing each other in formal positions, the Christians on the left side, the Buddhists on the right. 'The time had come when the former enemies were sitting side by side in the same hall.'[11] The simple fact that people who for years had been involved in mutual struggle now for the first time met each other face to face seemed almost miraculous, and created a very peculiar atmosphere.

The meeting only lasted a few hours, but a number of leading Buddhists and Christians delivered their messages, advocating toleration, friendly relations, and even cooperation. Patriotic sentiment dominated the talks; all seemed to agree that religious leaders needed to join hands for the sake of the country, for the sake of the Emperor. Another dominant feature was the concern for social problems. But doctrinal issues were also discussed, and a number of speakers suggested ways to find common points or to build bridges of understanding.

Probably the phenomenon itself was more significant than the actual content of the talks. As a Christian journal commented, the Conference signified that 'the age of blind obedience and suppression has already passed, and the age of gentleman-like criticism and study is about to come. How can gentlemen who already once have talked cheerfully with each other in the same hall, and, moreover, had a photo taken together, once more start to abuse and slander each other?'[12]

The Buddhist–Christian Conference and the discussions in its connection of course did not reach a sophisticated level of mutual understanding. It is, however, possible to discern, already at this early stage of dialogue, most of the recurrent themes of later dialogues, and even the basic models of the relationship between the two religions.

In the years 1898–9 Buddhist communities again engaged in anti-Christian campaigns, this time in connection with opposition against the new legislation which would allow foreigners freely to reside in the interior of Japan, the so-called 'mixed residence'. But the anti-Christian agitation soon lost its momentum.

## DEVELOPMENTS IN THE TWENTIETH CENTURY

I have elsewhere compared the development of relations between Christianity and Buddhism in the 1890s, particularly manifested in the Buddhist–Christian Conference in 1896, to a railway junction where lines from different places come together and then spread out again in many directions.[13] It was a meeting point where earlier developments in Buddhist–Christian relations were brought together and made manifest, positively or negatively, and then developed further in various directions.

A rough sketch must suffice to indicate a few of these directions. For the sake of clarity and convenience, I will indicate three characteristic trends, well aware that the various types of relationships were often combined. These are (1) various types of dialogues at the official level between representatives of the established religious communities: what one might call the 'establishment dialogue'; (2) the dialogue between outsiders and reformers critical of the religious establishment: what one might call the 'anti-establishment dialogue'; and (3) various types of spiritual search and encounter.

### The establishment of dialogue

I have already suggested that even though the first Buddhist–Christian Conference in 1896 was planned and carried out by liberal Buddhists and Christians and criticised by conservatives, it expressed a concern that was also rapidly gaining support in conservative circles. The establishment of dialogue represents the contact and cooperation that developed among influential leaders in the mainstream of the Buddhist and Christian establishments.

As already noted, it was nationalism more than anything else that broke down the barriers between Buddhists and Christians in the 1890s, enabling them to cooperate for the sake of patriotism. As the Sino-Japanese War prepared the way for the recognition of Christian patriotism in the mid-1890s, the Russo-Japanese War (1904–5) brought religious leaders together in a common effort to support the government and strengthen the unity of the Japanese people. A 'Wartime Conference of Religionists' was convened in 1904, gathering more than a thousand Buddhists, Shintoists and Christians, and justifying the war as a means of protecting the security of the Japanese Empire and the lasting peace of the Far East.

In the following years several other conferences and associations were organised, supported by the religious establishments and often by the government. The general aim of such conferences was to nurture the patriotic spirit, strengthen the power of religion, and create a religious front against such 'dangerous ideas' as socialism, Marxism and anarchism.

Developments in the 1930s and during the war years were, of course, dominated by patriotic and Shinto indoctrination, and religious leaders had to adapt themselves to the circumstances. Further research is necessary to elucidate the religious cooperation and the trend of patriotic Christianity in those years. In general, however, it can be said that the establishment dialogue failed to make religious leaders aware of the inherent dangers of identification with the patriotic spirit.

**The anti-establishment dialogue**

We have already registered that various Buddhist reform movements dissociated themselves from the Buddhist establishment. They denounced the old Buddhism, and advocated a new Buddhism which could overcome the inherited formalism and the inertia and thus face the challenges of modern society. These efforts brought Buddhist reformers into close contact with Christian groups, mainly liberal Christians, Unitarians and Christian socialists. They were not only in conflict with their own religious establishments, but often critical of what they regarded as the political opportunism of the establishment dialogue and its naive support of nationalistic policies.

A similar expression of anti-establishment contact was evidenced in the years around 1930, when socially concerned Buddhists and Christians stimulated one another and engaged in various types of cooperation. The relationship between Buddhist socialism and social Christianity in those years needs further exploration, but there are interesting areas of ideological closeness. While the Christians anticipated the establishment of the Kingdom of God, the Buddhists advocated the establishment of the Buddha-Land, not as a state of mind, but as an actual social reality.

Compared to the establishment dialogue, the contact between the small groups that were critical of established religion and nationalistic values may seem insignificant. Nevertheless, they stand for a trend that deserves due consideration, particularly because of their critical function in the predominantly conservative religious world of Japan. A vestige of such a critical contact may perhaps be seen in recent efforts of various religious groups to coordinate campaigns against the nationalisation of the Yasukuni Shrine, and attempts to oppose militarism and nationalism, race and sex discrimination.

## Spiritual encounter

The above-mentioned types of dialogue were certainly expressions of a spiritual encounter, but the term is here used in a narrower sense to characterise various types of contact resulting from a spiritual search on the individual level.

The most common expression of spiritual encounter might be characterised as spiritual pilgrimages. Numerous Japanese have experienced the attraction of both religions. Buddhists who were challenged by Christianity and converted to the new faith, discovered later that Buddhism was still a part of their spiritual history, and somehow had to reconcile the two faiths. Or, perhaps more often, Buddhists who were attracted to Christianity without leaving their faith, somehow had to integrate Christian insights into their Buddhist understanding. A number of Christians went the other way, leaving the church and becoming Buddhists, but without abandoning their faith in Christ. Such spiritual pilgrims live in a constant dialogue with the other faith, their own hearts being the place of encounter. There are numerous such Buddhist-Christians or Christian-Buddhists in Japan. They are more or less committed to the traditional religious life in one tradition, but also show affection for the other tradition or maintain elements of its religious beliefs or practices. Such quiet spiritual search leading to a hyphenated religious life is perhaps the most characteristic expression of the Buddhist-Christian encounter in Japan.

Spiritual search has often been combined with the study of comparative religion. The two founders of comparative religion in Japan, Kishimoto Nobuta (1866–1928) and Anesaki Masaharu (1873–1949), were devoted to Christianity and Buddhism respectively. They were both engaged in the initial stage of the interfaith encounter in the 1890s, and regarded the study of religion as a vital part of their spiritual search. Of the numerous comparative studies published in Japan, a surprising number deal with Buddhist–Christian studies. The quality varies a lot, but as a phenomenon they are symptoms of a spiritual climate and reveal how many Japanese feel the need of coming to terms with both religions.

The philosophical dialogue between Buddhists and Christians can be traced back to the initial contact, but did not reach any depth until Nishida Kitarō prepared the ground for a more penetrating search. The present dialogue would be inconceivable without the influence of Nishida and his disciples, who in various ways have dealt with such issues as theism and atheism, the personal and impersonal character of the Ultimate (God), transcendence and immanence, the selfhood and selflessness of the human person. Such discussions took place in the 1930s, and are still vital issues in the dialogue, both in Japan and in international fora between Buddhists and Christians.

Christian mission is often regarded as incompatible with the spirit of dialogue. It is, nevertheless, a fact that missionary and apologetical concerns have been among the decisive forces that brought Christians into direct contact and dialogue with Buddhists. Since the more systematic and serious study of Buddhism among Christians in Japan began in the 1880s, a number of missionaries have contributed to such studies, often in a paradoxical combination of missionary commitment, spiritual search, and admiration for Buddhist thought and experience. Such a commitment to dialogue and mission is characteristic of a number of Christian study centres, such as the NCC Centre for the Study of Japanese Religions in Kyoto and the Roman Catholic Nanzan Institute for Religion and Culture in Nagoya. The latter has in recent years contributed to a renewed international dialogue by publishing works of philosophers related to the Kyoto School of Philosophy and by organising spiritual encounters between European and Japanese monks.

## CONCLUSION

There are several enthusiasts who describe the Buddhist–Christian encounter as the most important event in our century. Such an exaggeration is hardly warranted, but can be understood as an expression of the excitement and joy of sharing with others in the search for truth. A similar excitement was also found among those who pioneered the dialogue in the 1890s, when the rapprochement was regarded as the beginning of a new age in religion. There is, however, no doubt that the encounter between Buddhists and Christians is important and will continue to play a vital role. An increasing number of Western theologians realise that Buddhism may become one of the most important factors in theological reflection in years to come. And not a few Buddhists have received strong impressions from their study of Christianity.

There are still a number of problems to be overcome. In the Japanese context the dialogue is still onesidedly concerned with Zen Buddhism, and to some extent Pure Land traditions, while, for example, Esoteric

Buddhism, Nichiren Buddhism, and other traditions have only been involved to a limited degree. The Buddhist participants are also characterised by a somewhat eclectic understanding of Christianity. With few exceptions, they have been exposed to one theological tradition or to a few modern theologians; they engage in a philosophical discussion entirely moulded by Buddhist presuppositions; or they have a superficial understanding of Christianity based on random observations and readings. In spite of such limitations, there is no doubt that the encounter between the two religions will develop and perhaps contribute to a mutual transformation in the years to come.

## NOTES

1. This chapter is based on research first presented as a doctoral thesis and published in limited edition, and later published as *Buddhism and Christianity in Japan: From Conflict to Dialogue, 1854–1899*. Apart from reference to direct quotations from other sources, I refer to this study.
2. Quoted from Kashiwabara and Fujii, eds., *Kinsei Bukkyō no Shisō*, p. 546.
3. Tsuji, *Nihon Bukkyōshi*, pp. 493–4.
4. Quoted from Griffis, *Verbeck of Japan*, pp. 134–5.
5. *The Missionary Herald* (July 1871), p. 207.
6. Greene, *A New Englander in Japan*, p. 120.
7. De Forest, *The Evolution of a Missionary*, pp. 230, 239, 244–45. See also Thelle, *Buddhism and Christianity in Japan*, pp. 62–6.
8. From an anti-Christian tract by Hirai Kinzō, translated in *The Missionary Herald* (September 1883), p. 353.
9. Pettee, *A Chapter of Mission History*, p. 99.
10. *Rikugō Zasshi* 114 (June 1890), p. 5.
11. Hirota, *Kirisutokyō to Bukkyō*, pp. 98–9.
12. *Rikugō Zasshi* 190 (October 1896), p. 492.
13. Thelle, *Buddhism and Christianity in Japan*, p. 246.

1  *Mater Dolorosa*, oil on canvas, 52.5 x 40 cm. Nanban Bunkakan, Osaka

2  *Our Lady of the Rosary*, colour on paper, 75 × 63 cm. Kyoto University

3   *St Francis Xavier*, colour on paper, 61 x 49 cm. Kobe City Museum

4  Nobukata, *Woman Playing the Lute*, colour on paper, 55.5 x 37.3 cm. Yamato Bunkakan, Nara

5 'Two Figures in a Pastoral Scene', colour on paper; detail from a pair of six-panel screens, 93 x 302 cm. Private collection

6 'The King of Rome', colour on paper; detail from *The Battle of Lepanto*, one of a pair of six-panel screens, 153 x 362.5 cm. Kōsetsu Art Museum, Kobe

*Four Mounted Western Warriors*, colour on paper, four-panel screen, 166.2 x 460.4 cm. Kobe City Museum

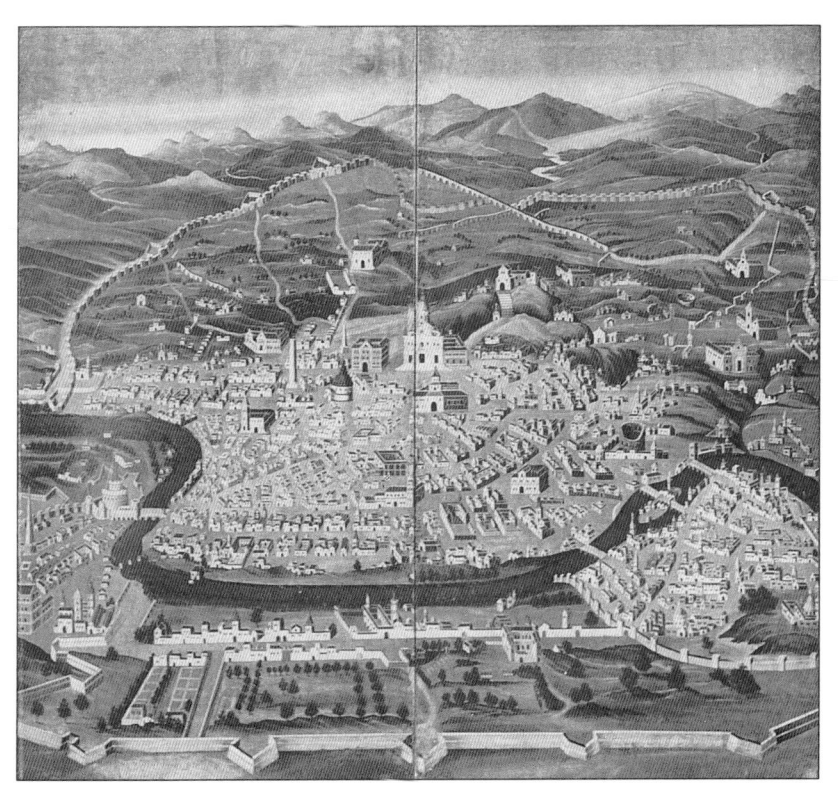

8 'The City of Rome', colour on paper, detail from *Four Great Cities of the West* (Rome, Lisbon, Seville and Constantinople), one of a pair of eight-panel screens, 158.7 x 477.7 cm. Kobe City Museum

9 *Map of the World*, colour on paper, detail from one of a pair of six-panel screens, 153 × 362.6 cm. Kōsetsu Art Museum, Kobe

# 7 The Religion of the West versus the Science of the West:
## The Evolution Controversy in Late Nineteenth Century Japan
### Helen Ballhatchet

1859, the year when the first Protestant missionaries arrived in Japan, was also the year in which Darwin's *Origin of Species* was first published in Britain. By the mid-1870s, when the first groups of Protestant converts were appearing in Japan, Darwin's theory of evolution had become the focus of an anguished and sometimes heated debate over the relationship between Christianity and science in both Europe and the United States. While some prominent Christian scientists and theologians had accepted the theory either in the original form or with modifications, others had rejected it. Journalistic reporting of the debate, including the activities of that ardent pro-Darwinist Thomas Huxley, had encouraged the idea of an eternal war between the forces of enlightened – or blasphemous – science, and those of reactionary – or revealed – religion.[1] The purpose of this chapter is to examine how this mythic controversy developed when it reached Meiji Japan, and in particular to look at its effect on Japanese Protestants.

The early Protestant missionaries to Japan did not necessarily have any knowledge of science beyond a grounding in natural theology and the very argument for design in the universe which Darwin's theory had put under threat. They were convinced that Christianity was the basis of Western civilisation, this conviction being of great importance in giving them the confidence to become missionaries and the hope that their labours might be successful. They therefore assumed that as knowledge of, and borrowing from, the West advanced, traditional Japanese beliefs would be progressively weakened and the Japanese would gradually become more and more receptive to Christianity. The overtly Western orientation of the Meiji government therefore gave them optimism, and they tended to interpret any adoption of Western customs as an advance in the direction of

Christianity, since 'the rapidly rising tide of civilisation can hardly fail to sweep in Religious Toleration along with itself'.[2]

This attitude also meant that most missionaries were willing to respond to (or exploit) the Japanese desire for secular Western learning. They taught English (through the medium of the Bible), particularly in the years before 1873 when direct evangelisation was impossible, and became involved in setting up schools such as (the) Dōshisha, where a Western education was given in a Christian setting. A significant proportion of the foreign teachers employed in early Meiji Japan also seem to have been committed Christians, prominent examples being Captain L. L. Janes of the Kumamoto Yōgakkō, and W. S. Clark of the Sapporo Nōgakkō, While Janes hoped to convert his students from the start, Clark appears to have become more enthusiastic about his Christianity while in Japan.[3]

The exploitation was mutual, since the Japanese themselves were willing to use missionaries as repositories of Western expertise. Guido Verbeck of the Dutch Reformed Mission was employed by the early Meiji government as an adviser on educational and other matters. On an individual level, ambitious but impoverished young ex-samurai were willing to learn English from missionary teachers, even if it meant reading the Bible, and missionaries often seem to have been approached with questions about secular matters, to the extent that one enquirer was even dubbed 'the scientific questioner'.[4]

Hostility to Christianity remained, however. This was basically caused by fear of its subversive potential, but neo-Confucian attitudes to religion ensured that explicit attacks frequently pointed to illogicalities in the Bible, and particularly in the Genesis account – for example the creation of light before the creation of the sun and moon, and the reason for the Fall if God was really the omnipotent and omniscient creator of mankind. Rationalist arguments about Christianity of Western origin were quickly picked up. Although many of the first foreign textbooks used in Meiji Japan presented a Christian world-view, the works of Draper, Paine, and John Stuart Mill were also read in many educational establishments. Some of these works were also translated at a very early date: for example Paine's *Age of Reason* was published in Japanese in 1876. Japanese writers of anti-Christian tracts also drew on their authority, and in 1875 a contributor to *Meiroku Zasshi*, the famous journal of a group of enlightenment intellectuals, was able to mention how 'Westerners have noted that their religion obstructs science'. Two years later, Yatabe Ryōkichi, Professor of Botany at the Kaisei Gakkō, who had studied at Cornell University, gave a lecture on Buddhism and Christianity. To an audience which included the British Minister he declared that the Japanese would never accept Christianity, partly because of the licentious and rude behaviour of foreign residents and the luxurious way of life of missionaries, but also because its dogmas were too superstitious for the philosophical Japanese.[5]

The young ex-samurai converts who became the leaders of early Japanese Protestantism shared in this neo-Confucian background. They first came into contact with Christianity not for religious reasons, but as a result of their search for Western learning, which they saw as a medium of social and political advancement. The Kumamoto, Yokohama and Sapporo 'bands', the three groups of converts which respectively produced such leaders as Ebina Danjō, Uemura Masahisa and Uchimura Kanzō, were all formed under the influence of charismatic American teachers (Janes, the Dutch Reformed missionaries Samuel Brown and James Ballagh, and Clark respectively). The idea that Christianity was the religion of civilisation and the basis of Western technological superiority played a crucial role in both motivating and justifying their transfer to a spiritual allegiance alien to Japan. The idea of an essential unity between Christianity and Western science was therefore of great importance to them, as both an external and an internal justification of their beliefs. Any challenge to this unity was equally double-edged, becoming a subject for discussion and sometimes a cause of spiritual torment.[6]

The opening article of *Rikugō Zasshi*, a periodical which a group of these early-Meiji Christians launched in Tokyo in 1880, gives a good picture of the confident view of the relationship between Christianity and Western strength which they presented to Japanese society. The article argued that Japan was only experiencing a superficial enlightenment, since moral progress was not occurring at the same rate as material progress. Japan needed a religion suited to the changing nature of its society. This was obviously Christianity, the force behind the more progressive and patriotic countries of the world. In other words, Christianity was the only religion suited to the new Japan that was in the making.[7]

However, their confidence did not have very deep roots, particularly where the relationship between Christianity and science was concerned. The main evidence for this lies in the description of the early religious experiences of members of the Kumamoto and Sapporo bands, as recalled by Ebina Danjō and Uchimura Kanzō respectively.

Ebina identified natural science as one of the elements which led him to believe in Christianity. This was partly because of the influence of *jitsugaku*, the particular brand of Confucianism in which he had been trained, but also partly because the biology and chemistry textbooks which Captain Janes used at the Kumamoto Yōgakkō worked on the premises of natural theology. In describing his conversion, Ebina even used an extended scientific simile:

> Up till then my way of thinking had resembled the theory that the earth was at the centre of the universe. The sun was revolving around the earth's perimeter. I had thought that God was revolving around me, but now God was at the centre and I was like a planet revolving around the perimeter of the sun ...[8]

He also gave the following description of the state of mind in which he and most of his colleagues were when they left the school and entered (the) Dōshisha:

> We were convinced that God was in control of the universe, that His was the Divine government which guided both individuals and states using moral laws, and ruled sovereigns using rewards and punishments. ... We believed that this God was the creator of everything. This we had been able to learn from the Bible. The world of this God was not the same cosmos of Confucianism or of the Bible. We had been able to learn from natural science that it was in fact the great and infinite universe.[9]

As the last sentences of that quotation suggest, however, Ebina and his companions already felt that the scientific world-view both conflicted with and was superior to, that of the Bible. Ebina felt respect for the Bible as a whole, but some aspects of the gospels, such as the resurrection, made him very uneasy, and he felt that miracles were a hindrance rather than an aid to faith in Christ's divinity. Another member of the Kumamoto band, Kozaki Hiromichi, apparently had an eighteen-month struggle between his spiritual longing for Christianity and his intellectual doubts over such issues. Ebina concluded that they never accepted that the whole of the Bible was revealed, but 'wanted to exclude anything which could not be explained scientifically'.[10]

The members of the Sapporo band were actually being trained in agricultural science. Uchimura Kanzō's love of nature from the start played an important role in his understanding of God, but he records how he and his companions were all troubled by rationalistic doubts. Nitobe Inazō, in particular, 'could doubt all things, could manufacture new doubts, and must test and prove everything before he could accept it'. In mid-1879 they decided to hold discussion meetings in preparation for the 'infidels' (unbelievers) they would be sure to meet after graduation. Dividing into Christians and infidels on an alternate basis, the 'members of the infidel side were to ask all manner of questions which infidels might ask, and those of the Christian side were to answer them'. However, they abandoned the plan after the first session, concluding that 'we found that we ourselves had more doubts than we could answer'.[11]

It was against this background of outward confidence and internal vulnerability that Japanese Christians became exposed to the controversy over the theory of evolution.

The first reference to the theory in Japan was probably made in a Shinto tract published in 1874, but this seems to have had little impact.[12] Japanese such as Yatabe Ryōkichi who studied abroad in the 1870s were likely to have learnt of the idea of evolution there, but it was an American biologist, Edward Morse, who first made a conscious effort to publicise the theory, and its supposed anti-Christian implications.

Morse arrived in Japan in 1877 and was offered a post by Tokyo Imperial University, which he held until the end of 1879. He spread knowledge of evolution among both staff and students, but also among the wider public through open lecture meetings. He emphasised the incompatibility of the scientific and religious viewpoints, and claimed that the Christian establishment was opposed to evolution, indoctrinating believers so that they accepted the rival theory of special creation unquestioningly.[13]

Morse's version of the theory was Spencerian or neo-Lamarckian rather than Darwinian, since he clearly accepted that acquired characteristics could be inherited. This was very important in terms of the Japanese response to evolution, since even if not possible in genetic terms, the inheritance of acquired characteristics is clearly applicable to the evolution of human knowledge and behaviour, and essential if the theory is to be transferred from the study of biology to the study of society. In Japan, as in China, it was the Spencerian interpretation which attracted interest; it was also the writings of Spencer rather than of Darwin which tended to be translated.[14]

Japanese intellectuals did not argue over the geological record or discuss whether the theory of evolution was true or false, nor did they investigate its implications for the Japanese claim of descent from the gods and the divinity of the Emperor. Instead they tended to accept the theory and wonder how best to apply its laws to the case of Japan. Thus there was considerable concern over the possibility that higher levels of civilisation might make it harder for natural selection to work, and that the weak, for example, would therefore be more likely to survive and give birth to equally weak children. Most important was the fact that the theory seemed to offer a practical way of working out how to achieve the basic goal of development on which everyone was agreed: a strong and independent Japan which was recognised as an equal by the Western powers.[15]

As in the West, however, Japanese thinkers of a variety of political persuasions were able to interpret evolution so that it lent support to their particular views. Those who gave priority to strengthening Japan in military terms laid great emphasis on the concept of the survival of the fittest, which fitted in with their understanding of the overseas behaviour of the Western powers. Where Japan's political future was concerned, the theory was used both by conservatives such as Katō Hiroyuki, to deny the concept of natural human rights, and by liberals such as Baba Tatsui, who argued that to prevent the growth of democratic forms of government was to impede evolution's inevitable onward march and therefore to invite violent revolution. So popular did evolution become that a satirical work of the mid-1880s has one of its characters, *Yōgaku Shinshi* (the Gentleman of Western Learning), sing out a paean of praise to the 'God of Evolution'.[16]

The anti-Christian implications of evolution, which Morse had made so obvious in his presentation, were also noted and exploited, most interestingly by Inoue Enryō, a Buddhist writer who was working to revive Japanese Buddhism, largely by injecting the insights of Western philosophy. Like some missionaries and Japanese Christians, he argued that the question of scientific plausibility could be used as an objective criterion against which to measure the relative truth of Buddhism and Christianity. Unlike them, however, he went on to claim that attempts to accommodate Christianity to new scientific theories only resulted in a gradual reduction of the power which God was seen to have over the universe. Buddhism, by contrast, did not have to be adapted, since concepts such as the law of cause and effect already fitted in beautifully with the scientific worldview. He suggested that Buddhism was in fact the religion which Western scholars such as Hegel, Spencer and Darwin had been looking for, and proposed a Buddhist mission to the West.[17]

Inoue's argument, while ingenious, did contain flaws. The most serious, perhaps, was the lack of any attempt to explain why the scientific worldview which Buddhism supported had developed in the Christian West rather than in Buddhist Japan; the most interesting was the fact that Inoue saw no need to try to reconcile traditional Buddhist views of the cosmos with modern Western explanations. Western science could apparently be used to attack only beliefs of Western origin. Moreover, it seemed to offer better weapons for this purpose than the actual Japanese beliefs which Inoue was championing.

Neither missionaries nor Japanese Christians could ignore the challenge which an anti-Christian presentation of evolution offered to their image of the harmonious relationship between Western civilisation and the religion at its base. Missionaries realised reluctantly that enthusiasm for Western knowledge and techniques would not necessarily work in Christianity's favour, and even came to think that they formed a more serious challenge than indigenous Japanese beliefs.

In fact, they had been aware of this possibility even before Morse's arrival. To quote from a missionary stationed in Nagasaki, writing in 1875:

> one grieves over the too evident tendency of 'Young Japan' to allow modern scepticism and so-called Philosophy to take the place of the old systems of religion which he finds incompatible with his increased knowledge.[18]

In the period following Morse's arrival, however, the tone became more pessimistic. Many young Japanese might come to reject traditional Japanese religions but there was no guarantee that they would become Christians instead. The next generation of Japanese might prove to be 'proud and godless young men, opposed to all religion, ... and contenting themselves with the idea ... that science & art ... will enable a man to fulfil all that his Creator requires of him ...'. It was admitted that: 'the Japanese want all the benefits and blessings possessed by Christians nations, but they do not want the Gospel. They want the effect without the cause.'[19]

Some missionaries and committed foreign Christians in Japan rejected the idea of evolution entirely, denying that man had descended from the ape and advising the Japanese with whom they came into contact not to take the theory seriously. Their remarks attracted ridicule at the time and have often been referred to in later secondary works, achieving a symbolic status similar to that held by the famous debate between Huxley and Bishop Wilberforce.[20] Others, including probably the majority of missionaries engaged in direct evangelistic work, seem to have believed that simple Gospel preaching was the best method of defence. They felt themselves justified in laying emphasis on the spiritual and emotional aspects of belief rather than the rational:

> experience shows what a mistake it is to suppose that if only the truths of Christianity be known, its reasonableness and superiority in point of morality as compared with other religions be admitted, a man *must* become a Christian. Many here do know and admit all this and yet go no further.[21]

However, a few missionaries and committed foreign Christians were prepared to argue about evolution in public, and had enough knowledge to be able to do so. In general they took a moderate line and criticised both scientists and theologians for polarising the debate. Evolution was only a hypothesis, and even if proven it was not necessarily incompatible with

Christianity. If properly understood, both religious and scientific truth must ultimately unite. At least two missionaries, Henry Faulds of the Scottish United Presbyterian Church, a qualified doctor who enjoyed controversy, and the more retiring John Gulick of the American Board, who was a gifted amateur scientist, were able to offer scientific arguments similar to those used in the West to support Christian interpretations of evolution, as a process controlled by God.[22]

Japanese Christians were clearly influenced by the way in which those such as Faulds dealt with evolution, and indeed became involved in organising for them to speak, and in translating and printing their words. But there was an important difference between the foreign and Japanese Christians in their attitudes to the theory. The foreigners had not come to believe in Christianity because of its claims to scientific plausibility; they were ready to argue against attacks on these claims, but did not see such attacks as a threat to their own beliefs. However, the Japanese Christians were in a very vulnerable position. As mentioned earlier, the scientific argument for Christianity as the basis of Western civilisation had played an important part both in their conversion itself and in justifying this conversion, both to themselves and to the outside world. Unlike non-Christians such as Inoue Enryō, they could not compartmentalise their beliefs from the implications of Western science.

There is evidence that some of them at least actually found evolution a threat to their beliefs, as George Romanes, for example, had experienced in Britain. Matsumura Kaiseki had links with the Yokohama band and had received a more orthodox introduction to Christianity than the members of the Kumamoto and Sapporo bands. The theory came to him as a terrible shock, and for four or five days he felt that he had lost his faith. At first he had found the theory too ridiculous to believe, but when he actually read Darwin and the explanations and proofs which he gave, '[he] was truly stupefied and hardly knew what to do'. Uchimura Kanzō later recalled:

> At times I was finally defeated by the theory of evolution and thought of giving up Christianity; at other times the weak points in Darwin's theory became clear to me. My mind wavered from one side to the other, and I was extremely perplexed.[23]

The response of Japanese Christians to anti-Christian interpretations of the theory of evolution therefore represented a defence of their act of conversion, again perhaps as much for their own benefit as for the benefit of the outside world. There does not seem to have been any effort to reject Darwin's findings; rather, all their energy was put into finding ways of demonstrating that Christianity and science were compatible. They supported those missionaries who defended Christianity in public, but also developed their own defences.

By the late 1870s, a number of able young Japanese Christians had gathered in Tokyo. While forming their own churches, they also came together to organise Christian lecture meetings (*enzetsukai*) in which both foreigners and Japanese were involved. Meetings of this kind were a popular way of exchanging new ideas and encouraging intellectual debates at the time.[24] Since Morse was involved in *enzetsukai* to spread scientific knowledge, evolution was naturally one of the issues which the Japanese Christians wished to cover.

The meetings were well attended, partly because of their novelty, but also because of their liveliness. As Tamura Naoomi, one of the Christians involved, later recalled:

> The lecture meetings were like battlefields. It was so competitive, that if one side gathered an audience of 500, the other would do the same. Both the speakers and the audiences felt as if they were going to war.[25]

A peak was reached in Tokyo with the open-air meetings held on two successive days at Ueno in October 1880, when at one point there were five to ten speakers active in different areas at the same time and a total audience of around 10 000 was attracted. Similar meetings seem to have been organised in Kyoto by Dōshisha students, with the encouragement of the school authorities.[26]

A few months before the gathering at Ueno, in May, a young men's association (Tōkyō Seinenkai) had been formed in the capital, with Kozaki and Uemura as presidents and Tamura as treasurer. Like the foreign-dominated Tokyo Christian Association, it held meetings for both members and non-members, but both Kozaki and Uemura at this time were far better at writing than at public speaking. It was only natural, therefore, that they should decide to organise a periodical which would both spread and defend Christianity, and form an outlet for theological research. This was *Rikugō Zasshi*, already mentioned above. Its scope was broad, and its impact was not confined to Christian circles.[27]

*Rikugō Zasshi* devoted many pages to arguments about the nature of the theory of evolution and its religions implications. In fact, a comparison of the coverage of evolution by *Rikugō Zasshi* and two secular journals of the period which had a much more obvious interest in the sciences, *Tōyō Gakugei Zasshi* and *Gakugei Shirin,* has shown that it was *Rikugō Zasshi* which dealt most thoroughly with the issue. While all three journals were giving more space to evolution than Western periodicals such as *Science* and *Nature* were at the time, it is significant that *Rikugō Zasshi* showed the most interest and concentrated on analysing evolution as a scientific theory rather than accepting it and moving on to investigation of its social applications, as was the tendency of *Tōyō Gakugei Zasshi*.[28]

Contributors to *Rikugō Zasshi* on the theme of evolution sometimes invoked the argument from design, which Darwin had discredited, but also showed familiarity with the ways in which Western Christians had actually accommodated themselves to the idea of evolution. Ebina Danjō, who was later to come under the influence of Higher Criticism of the Bible and Unitarianism, defended the biblical record by explaining that God had displayed what one might call a *laissez-faire* attitude to the Creation, not creating Adam directly, for example, but allowing him to evolve from an animal physiologically near to him. On the other hand, Ebina at this time accepted the general Old Testament outline of human history and, for example, the Flood as an actual event. Ukita Kazutami (also of the Kumamoto band) exploited the fact that Darwin had used language such as 'natural selection' which was embedded in the natural theology tradition to argue that the theory presupposed the existence of something outside man which gave purpose and function to human life.[29]

In general, contributors to *Rikugō Zasshi* adopted a critical view of scientific method not found in professional Japanese scientists at the time, exploiting the various ambiguities of Darwinian theory. They pointed out that the origin of both life and the universe had yet to be explained in purely materialistic terms. They upheld the idea that the universe was originally designed by God even though his control may have been not direct, but indirect, through the laws of evolution. Knowledge of Christianity was therefore essential to the correct understanding of Western science. Indeed, it was the monotheism of Christianity which made the scientific endeavour possible, through producing the idea of a universe which was united under one being and therefore working according to one set of laws.[30]

While those in Japan who used evolution to attack Christianity had denied the existence of absolute moral standards, on the grounds that morality was relative and determined by the exigencies of evolution, *Rikugō Zasshi* placed morality outside evolution and treated the degree to which Christian morals were accepted and observed in any society as an important marker for the stage of evolution which had been attained. Thus religious development towards Christianity became an integral part of the evolution process, and the adoption of Christianity essential if Japan was to continue to evolve successfully.[31]

Two Japanese Christians who had been associated with *Rikugō Zasshi* in its initial stages went on to reconcile Christianity and evolution in a slightly different way. Uemura and Uchimura concentrated on the religious significance of evolution rather than on the evolutionary role of Christianity. In his highly-acclaimed *Shinri Ippan* (An outline of the truth) (1884), Uemura Masahisa stressed that rational enquiry alone could not produce belief, nor could it prove the existence of God. On the other hand, he argued, all the available evidence made a theistic explanation of the universe more plausible than a non-theistic one. He was also unusual in explicitly criticising the idea that the world was governed by brute force, as the theory of natural selection supposed. The usual suggestion of both missionaries and Japanese converts that God was in control of the workings of Darwinian evolution implied a very harsh deity indeed; Uemura, however, saw evolution as a process of intellectual and moral advance, with morality as the controlling factor. He further claimed that a fundamental principle of Darwin's theory was the emergence of a variation superior to the rest of a species which in due course became the ancestor of a new species. The whole universe could thus be seen as leading towards the development of something infinitely good and beautiful. This did not mean that man was the end product of evolution; it was Christ, the Son of Man, who was the focus of history and the true goal of evolution.[32]

The Meiji Christian who most tirelessly pursued the problem of the relationship between religion and science was Uchimura Kanzō. He too insisted that science in no way contradicted religion, and pointed out that religious belief had provided much of the impetus for scientific research. He went even further, however, declaring: 'science is the handmaid of religion, no ... religion is a type of science'. Despite inconsistencies and ambiguities, Uchimura's treatment of Genesis was both more uncompromisingly orthodox and more confident than the explanations offered by foreign Christians in Japan and by other Japanese Christians. On the other hand, like Uemura, he was willing to admit that there were limits to rationality in matters of faith. He went further than Uemura in tackling the problems which the struggle for survival posed for belief in a benevolent God by pointing out the survival of apparently weak species. The rabbit, for example, had developed reproductive facilities rather than the ability to kill. He also emphasised the role of mutual aid in Nature. Ingeniously, he suggested that 'Man sees competition as the main force in Nature because he is observing Nature with a mind steeped in sin'. Like Uemura, he saw Christ as the central figure in evolution.[33]

Meiji Christians thus responded to the theory of evolution in two broadly different ways, according to the relative emphasis which they gave to faith and rationality in religious belief. On the one side were those like Ebina and Kozaki, whose primary concern was to maintain the rational, scientific reputation of Christianity. In the late 1880s and early 1890s they became strongly attracted to liberal theology, and many were prepared to rationalise their beliefs, denying for example the divinity of Christ. Their vision of evolution was this-worldly and involved the gradual development of a rational Christianity. For them, the main justification of Christianity was that it was the religion of progress and civilisation.

For their part, Uemura and Uchimura did not deny the link between all that was true in both Christianity and science, but their faith had a strong extra-scientific base. Rather than incorporating Christianity into the evolution process, they incorporated the evolution process into Christianity. Evolution was the course through which man's development was being worked out; Christ stood at the apex of the process and was the goal of human development.[34]

Such differences apart, both sides were more sophisticated in their understanding of evolution and its implications than either foreign Christians or non-Christian Japanese. They were also far more concerned to reconcile Christianity with evolution than were the former. They were able to overcome the challenge of the theory, and to use it to support their conviction that Christianity was essential to further Japanese development, by arguing that the evolution of religion must keep pace with that of technology. The theory also enabled them to see Japan's non-Christian religions in a constructive way, as an evolutionary preparation of the Japanese for Christianity, and for a Christianity which, in its Japanese form, might well be spiritually superior to that of the materialistic West.[35]

Missionaries and Japanese Christians were, of course, united in their refusal to accept that evolution might disprove Christianity. But there is an interesting similarity between missionaries and non-Christian Japanese in the ability of both to draw barriers between the possible implications of evolution and their own world outlook, with its secure cultural base. For missionaries it was evolution which needed to be tested and proved, not Christianity; for non-Christian Japanese there was not really any need to assess their own world outlook according to alien scientific criteria. Whether Christian or non-Christian, however, Meiji Japanese were much more positive in their response to the idea of evolution than were the missionaries. Non-Christians might emphasize the inevitability of progress or draw attention to the struggle for survival in which Japan itself was engaged; Christians might emphasise the evolutionary role of Christianity. For both, however, evolution provided a framework against which they could understand the changes which Japan was undergoing and link the past with the future, salving cultural pride. Japan, they could claim, was not so much copying the West as taking part in the evolutionary development of the world, towards a stage beyond that which the West had achieved so far.

NOTES

1. See in particular Moore, *The Post-Darwinian Controversies*.
2. Fyson to Fenn, ?1875, Church Missionary Society Archives (CMS) C J/0 12/10. (The archives have been moved to Birmingham University since I consulted them, and the cataloguing system may have been changed); Dōi, *Nihon Purotesutanto Kirisutokyōshi*, p. 32.
3. See, for example, Burnstein, *The American Movement to Develop Protestant Colleges*; Watanabe, *O-yatoi Beikokujin Kagaku Kyōshi*; Notehelfer, *American Samurai* (esp. pp. 107–10); Ōta, *Kurāku no Ichinen* (esp. pp. 167–9).
4. Dōi, *Nihon Purotesutanto Kirisutokyōshi*, pp. 42–3; Griffis, *Verbeck of Japan*; Saba, *Uemura Masahisa to sono Jidai 1*, p. 264; Evington, Diary, May 1876, CMS C J/0 11/18.
5. See, for example, Sakaguchi, 'Bakumatsu-ishinki no Hajaron', pp. 133–52; Ikeda, 'Eigo Kyōkasho', p. 363; Schwantes, 'Christianity versus Science', p. 124; Sakatani, 'On Nurturing the Human Spirit', p. 494; *Tokio Times*, 31 March 1877, (also cited in Schwantes, 'Christianity versus Science', p. 125).
6. For English language accounts of these early conversions, see, for example, Notehelfer, 'Ebina Danjō', pp. 1–56; Howes, 'Japan's Enigma', pp. 34–59.
7. '*Rikugō Zasshi* Hakkō no Shui', pp. 1–13.
8. Quoted in Watase, *Ebina Danjō-sensei*, p. 97 and also translated by Notehelfer, 'Ebina Danjō', pp. 46–7; see also Yoshinare, *Ebina Danjō no Seiji Shisō*, especially pp. 14–18.
9. Watase, *Ebina Danjō-sensei*, p. 92.
10. Kozaki, *Reminiscences of Seventy Years*, pp. 36–7; Watase, *Ebina Danjō-sensei*, pp. 94, 130, 131.
11. Uchimura, *How I Became a Christian*, pp. 29, 36–7, 50–2.
12. Aoikawa, *Hokkyōdan*, briefly analysed in Murakami, 'Seibutsu Shinkaron', pp. 151–2.
13. For evidence of Morse's hostility to Christianity, see Wayman, *Edward Sylvester Morse*, e.g., pp. 225, 250, 301; Morse, *Dōbutsu Shinkaron*, pp. 323, 330, 334, 353, 362; Morse, 'What American Zoologists have done for Evolution', pp. 496–7. For a different interpretation, however, see Ōta, *E.S. Mōsu*, pp. 42–52.
14. Morse, *Dōbutsu Shinkaron*, p. 324; Peel, *Herbert Spencer*, pp. 142–3. For the influence of Spencer in Japan, see Yamashita, *Supensā to Nihon Kindai*; for China, see Schwartz, *In Search of Wealth and Power*.
15. In English, see Watanabe, *The Japanese and Western Science*, pp. 70–5; in Japanese, see Watanabe, 'Katō Hiroyuki no iwayuru "Tenkō"', pp. 27–30 and articles on evolution in *Tōyō Gakugei Zasshi*, including the debate on the role of natural selection in human society initiated by Katō Hiroyuki in 1884, most of which is reprinted in *Meiji Bunka Zenshū*, 5 (1927), pp. 559–76.

16. See, for example, Funayama, *Zōho Meiji Tetsugakushi Kenkyū*, pp. 294–349; Nakae, *Sansuijin Keirin Mondō*, esp. pp. 185, 213–14. This work is available in English as *A Discourse by Three Drunkards on Government*, trans. Nobuko Tsukui (New York, Weatherhill, 1984), esp. pp. 52–3, 80–1.
17. See, for example, Inoue Enryō, *Shinri Kinshin*, pp. 309–75. (This work was originally published in 1885); for an English-language survey of Inoue's career, see Staggs, 'Defend the Nation', pp. 251–81.
18. Maundrell to Fenn, 13 December 1875, CMS C J/0 14/25; also, for example, Davis, 'A Mission Problem in Japan', pp. 131–5.
19. Evington, 'Education as a Missionary Agency in Japan', CMS C J/0 1/1C; Williams to Fenn, 'Annual Letter', ?1878, CMS C J/0 17/12; Greene, 'The Influence of Modern Anti-Christian Literature', p. 122.
20. See, for example, the case of Jerome D. Davis at Dōshisha as described in Watase, *Ebina Danjō-sensei*, pp. 137–79; also Ishikawa describing D.W. MacCartee at Tokyo Imperial University in 'Mōsu-sensei to Shinkaron', p. 59 and 'Mōsu-sensei', in Ishikawa, *Ningen Fumetsu*, p. 441. Ishikawa is quoted in Ozawa, *Nihon Purotesutantoshi Kenkyū*, pp. 177–8, and Murakami, 'Seibutsu Shinkaron', pp. 152–3; he is also referred to by Ōuchi in 'Nihon Kirisutokyōshi', p. 6.
21. Fyson to Fenn, 26 December 1877, CMS C J/0 12/12; Hopper, Report for Quarter ending December 1881, Archives of the United Society for the Propagation of the Gospel LR 1881. (The archives have been moved to Oxford University (Rhodes Library) since I consulted them and the cataloguing system may have changed). See also the discussion following Greene's paper at the Osaka Conference, *General Conference of Protestant Missionaries of Japan*, pp. 129–53.
22. See, for example, Faulds, *Hensenron*. For contemporary Japanese (Christian) appreciation of Faulds and Gulick, see, for example, Kozaki, *Nihon Kirisutokyōshi*, p. 64.
23. Matsumura, *Shinkō Gojūnen*, pp. 46–7, 52; Uchimura, 'Yo no Shūkyōteki Shōgai', pp. 261–2.
24. For the origin and popularity of *enzetsukai* see, in English, Oxford, *The Speeches of Fukuzawa*, pp. viii–xiii.
25. Tamura, *Shinkō Gojūnenshi*, pp. 88–9. This passage is also cited in Scheiner, *Christian Converts*, p. 111, but Scheiner mistranslates, and indeed seems to misunderstand the whole paragraph.
26. Tamura, *Shinkō Gojūnenshi*, p. 90; Saba, *Uemura Masahisa to sono Jidai 2*, pp. 527–9; Abe, *Shakaishugisha to naru made*, pp. 67–72.
27. For example, Kozaki, *Reminiscences of Seventy Years*, pp. 61–4; Tamura, *Shinkō Gojūnenshi*, pp. 83–7; Sugii, 'Kozaki Hiromichi no Tōkyō Dendō', pp. 131–66 and 'Tōkyō Seinenkai no Seiritsu', pp. 13–55; Takeda, 'Nihon no Shisō Zasshi', pp. 109–20. For the role of the Tokyo Christian Association, see Sugii, 'Tōkyō Seinenkai no Seiritsu', p. 23.
28. Watanabe and Ose, 'Meiji shoki no Gakujutsu Zasshi', pp. 186–93; findings presented in an abbreviated form in Watanabe, *The Japanese and Western Science*, pp. 68–9, 79–80.
29. Ebina, 'Seisho Shinkasetsu', pp. 220–330; Ukita, 'Shinkaron to Yūshinron', pp. 178–87.

30. For example, Ukita, 'Shinkaron to Yūshinron', pp. 180–2. For a general survey and analysis of Ukita's writings in *Rikugō Zasshi*, see Ozaki, '*Rikugō Zasshi* ni okeru Ukita Kazutami', pp. 205–19.
31. For a particularly good example of this approach, see Kozaki, 'Kirisutokyō to Shinpo', pp. 500–7. For a very positive appraisal of Kozaki's role in *Rikugō Zasshi*, see Imanaka, '*Rikugō Zasshi* ni okeru Kozaki Hiromichi', pp. 139–60.
32. See Uemura, *Shinri Ippan*, pp. 9–188.
33. See, for example, Uchimura, 'Shūkyō to Kagaku', pp. 95–8; Uchimura, 'Sōseiki Daiichi-sho', vol. 1, pp. 37–42 and vol. 3, pp. 189–94; Uchimura, 'War in Nature', pp. 126–9; Uchimura, 'Kirisutokyō to Shinka', pp. 184–8. For a scientist's analysis of Uchimura's scientific views, see Kawakita, 'Uchimura Kanzō no "Tennen"-kan', pp. 1–27.
34. For another analysis of the differences between these two groups, see Chō, 'Shinkaron no Yuyō Hōhō', pp. 198–208.
35. I have pursued this issue with particular regard to Kozaki Hiromichi in my article, 'Confucianism and Christianity in Meiji Japan', especially pp. 360–9.

# 8 Written and Unwritten Texts of the *Kakure Kirishitan*
Christal Whelan

## CHARACTERISTICS

The term *Kakure* refers to a group of Japanese people who share a common history of persecution and discrimination. Even after the lifting of the ban on Christianity in 1873, they continued to refer to themselves by a host of names designed to distinguish them from others who had willingly rejoined the newly implanted Church: *kotchi, motochō, furuchō, kyū-Kirishitan*, and *Kakure Kirishitan*. Adherents of Buddhism and Shinto would refer to them pejoratively as *hirakimon, itsukimon* or *gedō*.[1] Contemporary scholars differ in their choice of which term is most appropriate. Among the choices are: *senpuku* (secret), *hanare* (separate), and *Kakure* (hidden). Even where *Kakure* is preferred, one scholar opts for writing the word in *katakana* (the syllabary used for foreign or empathic words) in order to emphasise the fact that this group of people is undergoing a rapid transformation both socially and economically. In view of these changes, even the term *Kakure* appears anachronistic, but it is used here since it is the term favoured by the adherents of the religion today.

The greatest concentration of *Kakure* is still to be found in Nagasaki Prefecture: from Sotome, north to Hirado and the Ikitsuki islands, and offshore west from Nagasaki on the Gotō Islands, congregating mostly on Fukue. The *Kakure* communities are clearly, then, a rural and not an urban phenomenon. Both their geographical isolation from mainland Japan and their intra-island segregation have greatly limited their social sphere and contact with the majority population. Without the catalyst of constant confrontation, decisive political action, such as the unification of *Kakure* groups on any given island, was not to be expected. Again, the social structure of the islands with its traditional preference for endogamy both among the *Kakure* and non-*Kakure*, has minimised the frequency of contact and social involvement.

Acceptance of this marginal status has been the rule, and the attempts of the *Kakure* at political organisation have all ended in failure. The notion of standardisation of religious practice will always be resisted by groups whose identity and ancestral fidelity is intricately bound to long-cherished local practices and not to others. Given this lack of success in political organisation on the local level, it follows that no attempts have been made on a national scale. The *Kakure*, then, remain the most invisible and silent of Japan's minority groups. Their numbers are ever dwindling, too, as many of the children of *Kakure* have relocated permanently to Japan's cities, and have effectively cut themselves off from their past and assumed a new identity. *Kakure* elders have reported that their children do not return to Gotō even for *O-shōgatsu* or *O-bon*, the two national holidays when most Japanese return home.

Given the rural and secluded environment of the *Kakure*, their religious life inevitably exists in symbiotic relation to the fishing and agricultural activities which characterise their daily life. These lives are thus transformed through ritual from the mundane to the sacred. The installation of a guardian spirit into a new boat, the yearly blessing of a fishing boat at the New Year, and the feast of San Jiwansama (St John), which coincides with the completion of the yearly rice planting, all of these are examples of the transformation of the mundane to the sacred. For the *Kakure* then, religion and daily rural life are a single whole and, divorced from their rural environment, their faith cannot survive. This state of affairs is supported by research I have conducted among *Kakure* youth emigrated to Fukuoka. None reported any *Kakure* religious activity among peers from Gotō, or indeed affiliation with any other religion, including the so-called 'new new religions' that enjoy a popularity cutting across class lines in urban areas.

It has been rumoured that in addition to Nagasaki Prefecture, *Kakure* still exist to this day in Tōhoku[2] and elsewhere in Japan, but no concrete evidence seems to bear this out. Given the anti-Christian edict of 1868 and subsequent forced deportation of Christians (approximately 4000) from the Nagasaki area to various fiefs throughout Western Japan,[3] it certainly seems possible that the remains of such diasporic communities might exist elsewhere. However, if such pockets of *Kakure* do exist elsewhere in Japan, they would probably consist of Gotō-type non-organised *Kakure*, faithful to their own highly idiosyncratic Christian traditions on a personal or familial level but not forming part of a larger community of organised believers. The Gotō *Kakure* continue to transmit highly codified traditions: prayers in Latin or an old form of Japanese with sprinklings of Portuguese which they do not themselves understand, and ceremonies performed within a family as a group or as a single member in which the symbolic meaning of gestures has been forgotten. The *Kakure* who transmit such formal traditions do so more as a duty to, and out of reverence toward, their ancestors' religion rather than as an affirmation and expression of a living and personal faith. This ancestor-pleasing activity brings solace to the faithful, too, even if no community exists to reinforce or even define belief. These unorganised *Kakure* comprise the great majority of those who are known today as *Kakure*.

In his study of Japanese folk religion, Hori Ichirō admonished those who wished to understand Japanese religion by discouraging a religion-by-religion approach; he favoured viewing Japanese religion as a single entity with many manifestations, all sharing some common elements. The same theme is shared by Ian Reader, who accounts for the success of the new religions on the basis that they are renovations of traditional Japanese ideas within a more modern and relevant urban framework. Reader suggests that religions in Japan prosper in proportion to how much they adhere to a basic orientation shared by all Japanese religions. Two elements common to all Japanese religions are filial piety and ancestor veneration. These are binding, inviolable elements to the *Kakure*, at least to the eldest son, to whom the responsibility for maintaining the ancestral tablets falls. Out of respect to his *Kakure* ancestors, he must continue to observe their death anniversaries by inviting the *san'yaku* to his home to officiate at the proper *Kakure* ceremonies.[4] The *san'yaku* will then recite the prescribed *orashio* (L. *oratio*, prayer) depending on the gender of the deceased, and thereby perpetuate the tradition.

The first exposure of the Gotō islanders to Christianity was as early as 1562. The missionary whose name is best known in Gotō today is the evangelising Portuguese Jesuit, Luis de Almeida who, together with his Japanese companion Br. Lourenço, travelled to Fukue, the southernmost of the Gotō Islands. By 1592 the Christians of Gotō numbered 2000.[5] Although martyrdoms and apostasy put an end to this early phase of Christianity in the region, recent research reveals the likelihood that some communities survived those persecutions and were later joined by, and merged with, the *Kakure* settlers who came from Ōmura in the late eighteenth century. In this way, the earliest Christians lost their distinct identity as the oldest Christians of Gotō.[6] Fukue became the springboard of the second wave of Christianity in Gotō in 1797 when the *daimyō* of Ōmura (Ōmura Sumiyasu) began sending settlers to Gotō from his allegedly overcrowded domain.

Most documentation favours the image of a predominantly homogeneous *Kakure* community, oppressed in their communities and hopeful of a more congenial future. Interviewed about his ancestry, however, an 86-year-old *chōkata* of Fukue suggested that the groups who came to Gotō from the mainland were not altogether homogeneous but also contained samurai who were sent to escort the *Kakure* settlers and perhaps remain with them. Equally, it may have been that Christian samurai of Ōmura too wished to leave the oppressive domain. As the *chōkata* insisted:

> My ancestors came from Ōmura, right? There's a place called Kurosaki right? Well, they came from there. Mie, Shikimi, almost all from the Ōmura lands. They were samurai, all right. Samurai who carried two swords, and they came to this place, long ago, samurai from Ōmura; but what could they do here? There were no retainers here. They were samurai all right, my ancestors were.[7]

While this statement should not be accepted uncritically since oppressed peoples everywhere have a tendency to create compensatory legends of noble or exalted ancestry, it ought not to be ignored either. It suggests the possibility of a more heterogeneous group of settlers, hence a less monotone history than previously documented.

Descriptions of these immigrants generally are similar to the following one written by the critic Furuno:

> The *Kirishitan* of Gotō were a swarm of poor immigrants. The original inhabitants called them *itsuki* [appendages], *gedō* [heretics], and at least in the early days they were despised in the manner of *eta* or *hinin* [outcast groups]. Owing to the low cultural level of the *Kakure* seen in their odd way of dressing, they were often held in contempt as *gedō-batchi* [damned heretics]. The long-standing residents called *jige* [original inhabitants] by the *Kirishitan* would neither marry nor form friendships with the *Kirishitan*. And as they wielded the power of life and death for a long time, they were proud.[8]

Because the era of persecutions discouraged a written tradition and the *Kakure* were mostly illiterate, there are no first-hand accounts by *Kakure* people themselves of this migration. This leads one to ask if such historical accounts, like the one the *chōkata* related, are not part of an oral rather than a written tradition.

This essay deals with the problems of transmission in the *Kakure* tradition. It draws heavily on information gathered from *Kakure* informants. This methodology seems most apt since both oral and written traditions exist, and illiteracy and secrecy have, in their own ways, conditioned the modes of transmission. Through the discussion of the origin and contents of a text written by a *Kakure* official who later converted to Catholicism, it is hoped that the problems of religious dialogue for the *Kakure* will be better understood.

## PROBLEMS OF TRANSMISSION

### Written Texts

The issue of textuality is a very complex one, as anyone who has struggled with *Kakure* manuscripts will testify. One feature of the *Kakure* tradition is that all written texts were previously oral ones. Today, four types of written texts can be found:

(1) *orashio* notebooks, usually written in the simple *katakana* script and including either all the prayers of the village of origin or at least the most essential.

(2) *Tenchi Hajimari no Koto* (Concerning the Creation of Heaven and Earth), written in a mixture of the cursive *hiragana* script and *kanji* (Chinese characters), which is sometimes referred to as the *Kakure* Bible.[9] It is a collection of biblical legends mixed with popular Japanese folktales, and re-renderings of significant moments in *Kakure* history. This is not a standardised text and several versions have been found. As a written text, the *Tenchi Hajimari no Koto* is almost unknown to all living *Kakure* in Gotō today, although in the Sotome peninsula some continuity with that tradition still exists. When asked if the *Kakure* in his village had read the *Tenchi Hajimari*, the *chōkata* of Fukue responded:

> The people around here haven't read it. Hmmm ... maybe some, but not many. But in one day or two days you can't read a thing like that because you can't understand it. You know, it takes several years, otherwise you can't understand anything.[10]

*Kakure* who had never heard of the text, were nevertheless perfectly capable of narrating some of the stories found in it.

(3) Ceremony books, slender volumes bearing titles such as *Our Religion*. Extremely practical 'how-to' books, they explain what to offer and how to make offerings, when to bow and just how far, the numbers of prayers to be said for every *Kakure* occasion; they often include the texts of those prayers as well. While these books explain the format and formulae, they never explicate meaning, and are now usually found in the hands of *Kakure* who have inherited them; often enough they do not use them, nor do they even understand their contents.

(4) Bastian Calendar, or the *Kakure* liturgical calendar. This lists the feast days celebrated throughout the year as well as the *sashiaibi* (unlucky days) on which all work defined as ritually impure, such as the mixing of fertiliser, or needlework, is prohibited. This calendar is rewritten yearly. What makes the Bastian Calendar so special is its mystical origin that

places it in the tradition of sacred or prophetic texts. The name Bastian refers to Sebastian, a catechist living during the era of persecutions. He worked underground for 23 years in various parts of Kyushu, teaching other Japanese *Kirishitan* how to determine the holy days in order that they could perpetuate them secretly in the absence of the foreign priests. Bastian himself came upon this detailed knowledge after the martyrdom of his beloved foreign teacher. According to the legend, while Bastian lay asleep, his mentor visited him in a dream and dictated the entire contents of the calendar. Later, Bastian was captured, tortured and beheaded and is said to have uttered four prophecies before his death. One of these was the coming of the Black Ships.[11]

Clearly, ranking of the four types of texts is not something the *Kakure* themselves are wont to do; indeed, given the current state of the religion, such ranking is impossible. The two most important texts, however, in the current practice and state of the *Kakure* religion are the Bastian Calendar and the *orashio* notebooks. As for the Ceremony books, they seem to have been created wtih a sense of urgency for an increasingly ignorant posterity, but their importance is minimal today. Said the same *chōkata* of Fukue:

> Nowadays children come home in the evenings and have their own homework to do. Then they usually leave the island when they grow up. They don't understand anything about what Lent is or on what day it begins and what we do. They understand nothing.

This image contrasts markedly with the way in which this man assimilated the traditions of the *Kakure* people. When asked at what age he had learned the *orashio*, he answered:

> When I was in primary school, old man Sutegorō taught me prayers in Latin at the *irori* [pit hearth]. Now I've completely forgotten them because they were so long. One of the *orashio* took a whole hour to recite. But they were in Latin, so I didn't understand.

The *Kakure* settlers who came to Gotō from the mainland in the late eighteenth century and those who remained behind in the Sotome area were limited to two occupations in these rural areas – fishing and farming. Education was almost non-existent for these heavily taxed and poor farmers. This basic illiteracy, rather than the penchant for secrecy which is so often cited, is perhaps the single most important factor in the long perpetuation of an oral tradition. The need for secrecy was certainly real during periods of aggressive persecution and close surveillance, but the choice to write or not to write did not exist for unlettered farmers. Given the texts extant today, most of the *orashio* collections were composed in the Shōwa period (1926–1989) in what is considered to be the simpler of the two Japanese syllabaries – *katakana*. But, as education became more widespread, the option to write down what had once necessarily been of an exclusively oral tradition became available. As the *chōkata* of Fukue said:

> Way back, with the persecution, we couldn't learn by any written means the *orashio* or other books. You might get your head cut off if these things were found. So texts could never be shown. Some person with evil designs would always come, but during other times a person could write things to pass on to future generations.
>
> If you can't write down, you can't pass on either, and because we didn't have any educational opportunities we quickly and totally lost things. Because we didn't have books. Really, if you don't have books to teach you and you don't have education, it will never last long. There's the problem of not being able even to judge for yourself if you haven't learned. Because there was no education to write books to pass down to posterity. In the evening everyone used to gather in my home and I would lecture to them and they would listen. But no one was able to take notes ... It was difficult.

**Unwritten to written texts**

One of the early uses of the written word, which fed directly back into the oral tradition, consisted of writing down the *orashio* as an aid to their memorisation for later recitation. A 91-year-old *chōkata* of Narushima reported that, as a young boy, although he was neither the eldest son nor the youngest one (who, in the former pattern of *Kakure* families, was the inheriting son) the responsibility fell upon him to learn the *orashio*. He claimed that the method of learning *orashio* was to retreat into the hills surrounding his home, armed with a small notebook of *orashio* written in *katakana*, and commit them to memory. This method and the instruction received in the home from a father, a grandfather, or some village elder, comprised the two ways of learning – one written and one oral. But in neither case does the learner appear to have understood the content or meaning of what he committed to memory. This lack of understanding affirmed by all *Kakure* interviewed has not caused undue perturbation, but seems rather to have enhanced both the mystery and the remoteness of the ancestral religion. This is an important point given the next transition within the written tradition. As educational opportunities increased, so also the use of *kanji* spread among the *Kakure* in the Taishō and Shōwa periods. This was a decisive moment in the tradition and was to have far-reaching implications.

The transcription from a *katakana* tradition to one employing *kanji* marks a shift from a strictly phonetic system to a system in which understanding is essential for an accurate transcription. The chance, too, for the introduction of conceptual errors at this stage is as great as the number of possible readings of a single or compound *kanji*. Furthermore, once such errors have been transmitted, they, too, are incorporated into the holy space of tradition and become inviolable because they were handed down from ancestors deserving of loyalty and respect. Once such errors have been committed to writing they will be jealously protected, out of a combination of fear and respect – even in the face of later contradictory evidence. Invariably, some justification will be offered to sustain transmitted errors for fear of rupturing the supposed purity of the *Kakure* family tradition.

One example of such a case, with the potential for significant error, is to be found in the ceremony book from Narushima entitled *Our Religion*. A full page is devoted to a ceremony that is called *Kūkai* in the book. The *kanji* of this name is the same as that used for the name of the great Heian founder of the Shingon sect of Buddhism in Japan. This is of interest given the popularity of the Shingon sect on Narushima; the conversion of numerous *Kakure* women not so much to Shingon as to a cult of *Kūkai*; and the active participation in Shingon rituals of one of the most esteemed *Kakure* priests on the island. For these reasons, the *Kūkai* ceremony seemed to constitute written evidence of syncretism within the *Kakure* religion, and a positive clue as to why so many *Kakure* have embraced the sect in one form or another. Instructions followed which advised the use of the *Kūkai* prayer, and proceeded to name the deities to whom the prayer should be addressed. Among these were *Onmenyosusama* (Amen Jesus), *Anatasama* (Christ) and *Otobansama* (an intermediary messenger deity).

Was this *Kūkai* ceremony a special veneration of the Buddhist saint within the *Kakure* community where the book was found? As the family of this *Kakure* man had completely ceased to practise their religion, the owner of the book did not himself understand the meaning of the ceremony. However, when the text in question was shown to a *Kakure mizukata* of the same village, he offered a probable solution to the riddle. The contents of the prayer were familiar to this *mizukata*, and he immediately recognised *Kūkai* as a simple error in *kanji*. The correct word was *kokkai* or *kurikya*, meaning confession. The Buddhist saint was not implicated at all, according to this official, yet the error would remain in the tradition of the family to which the book belonged. This was perhaps not a serious problem for a family which had quit the religion, yet, for an interested extra-familial researcher, such confusion could lead to bizarre misinterpretations and should serve as a warning to those who study *Kakure* texts.

Thus the transition from a *katakana* syllabary to *kanji* was a critical turning point in terms of meaning within the tradition. At this stage many errors were introduced that would become part of a tradition of diminishing meaning passed on to an ever more perplexed *Kakure* posterity that would attempt to justify, make sense of, or show blind respect for significant errors such as the one mentioned above. This state of perplexity was to have yet another more creative effect. It disposed the vulnerable *Kakure* to other religious currents in their search for clues to their own tradition's baffling loss of meaning. They turned for answers to those religious systems most readily available, Buddhism, Catholicism, Shinto and shamanistic folk religion.

Parallel to this problem of meaning within the *Kakure* religion was a frustration that some *Kakure* officials began to feel, resulting from the loss of recognition or appreciation for their services. The *chōkata* quoted previously expressed it during an interview in the following manner: 'I have kept my religious office for 60 years. It was a serious matter. If I were a soldier, I would have received a big medal for such service, wouldn't I?'

This itch for recognition for services rendered constitutes a backdrop in the efforts of some *Kakure* of Fukue to unify, and thus compensate for the perpetual outflow of the population. Some talk of electing a *Kakure* bishop had transpired, or, failing that, at least a unification of the eight then-remaining *Kakure* communities on the island of Fukue. *Kakure* leaders called a meeting which proposed a system whereby the groups would gather in a specified village each year on a rotational basis. Not all the *Kakure* groups wished to participate in this conference, and ironically, the group that refused remains the only active *Kakure* group on the island today.

*Orashio no Shiori*
Possibly an outcome of this conference or yet another meeting, a small handwritten text entitled *Kakure Kirishitan Orashio no Shiori* (*Kakure Kirishitan*, Guide to the *Orashio*), was published in Nagasaki in 1954 by the *Kirishitan* Research Society. The last page of the text lists the authorship as eleven *Kakure* officials – eight *chōkata*, one *mizukata*, and two *toritsugikata*. The text is loosely compiled, with long sentences, mixed metaphors and is structurally reminiscent of the *Doctrina Cristan* (1592), a catechism first published in Amakusa by the early Jesuits, that contained all the essentials of the Catholic faith. Likewise, the *Orashio no Shiori* explains the Ten Commandements, the Seven Deadly Sins, the regulations of the Church, the sacraments, and also includes a version of the *Konchirisan* (Contrition). Whatever its flaws, however, it is still precious for what it reveals of the history of the *Kakure* religion in the postwar period.

This slim text of 68 pages also includes the *orashio* of the Fukue *Kakure* tradition, its liturgical calendar, and 16 pages that deal with two important topics: 'What is Religion?' and 'An Outline of Japanese *Kirishitan* History'. As the text seems to be the only evidence of a public attempt at self-definition, what, we may ask, was the impetus for writing it at that time? Was the intended readership *Kakure*? Or was the text perhaps written to the edification of Catholics or Buddhists or some other group? How was the selection of contents determined?

The stated purpose of the meeting at the *Kakure* officials and the production of the text is expressed early in its preface:

> To what religion does our daily belief belong? How many of us believers can answer the question? We lead our lives believing day and night without paying much attention to this question. This book is a summary of *orashio* and a few thoughts to pass on to younger people.[12]

The narrator also claims that the contents have been agreed upon unanimously by the leaders of the seven villages who, together, constitute the true authorship of the text. The text was presumably intracultural, that is, destined for people such as the authors themselves who already knew or had been exposed to the *Kakure* religion to some extent. Such a self-conscious attempt at the forging of a communal voice would be a political action of immense importance in the history of any minority group, particularly one as habitually silent and theologically reticent as the *Kakure*.

The narrator of the text openly expresses his debt to Urakawa Wasaburō (Bishop of Nagasaki), and his book, *Kirishitan no Fukkatsu* (Revival of the Catholic Church in Japan). The tone is apologetic, claiming that the *Kakure* book is but a first attempt, a temporary gesture. It is clear that the act of writing was intended to be the first fruit of an ongoing study group that would bring forth better and more thorough works. In this declared first effort, the author takes care to warn the reader that he or she will not find full answers to the questions provoked.

Closer analysis of this text raises interesting questions about its communal authorship and whether the promised future texts had ever been realised. As the narrator is no longer living, I consulted another *Kakure* official mentioned. When shown the text, this *chōkata* claimed he had never seen it before, although he was not surprised by it. In fact, he offered essential background information that allowed for a whole new interpretation. Around the time of the book's publication, the narrator, along with his entire *kuruwa* of Fukue, had met with members of the Catholic Church and, at their leader's instigation, the entire group converted to Catholicism.[13] This former *Kakure* official had suggested to all eight *kuruwa* of Fukue that they meet regularly twice a year – for *O-bon* and *O-shōgatsu*. I suspect that, given the narrator's own subsequent conversion and the crisis the *Kakure* religion was facing, he wished all eight *kuruwa* to follow his example. A clash of opinions ensued, however, and my informant believes that the narrator wrote the book together with the Catholics and not with the consent of the whole body of *Kakure* who, like him, probably did not know of the existence of the text either. Despite his imminent conversion, the narrator refers to himself and his religion throughout as '*Kakure Kirishitan*'.

After publication, the text was not put on sale to the general public but was distributed among the people involved. The text, therefore, cannot be considered a communal attempt to abandon secrecy and assume a public identity, but rather an attempt on the part of one village to merge with Catholicism. The book, then, has a comparative scope and can be interpreted as an exercise in drawing parallels between the *Kakure* and the Catholic religion. As mentioned earlier, the alleged purpose of the book was to pass on something to younger people, but the real purpose seems to be quite other than the one stated in the preface. The narrator is a *Kakure* who is attempting to depart from his natal religion and convert to another. His action in writing the text, then, if not overt propaganda for his new religion, is at least a highly political gesture in which he attempts to minimise the difference between the two religions. He attempts to bridge the gap by affirming a remote yet common history before the banishment of all foreigners and the closing of the country in 1640.

The book is of great interest because it illustrates the psychology of a man at the crossroads, trying to embrace Catholicism through learning its doctrine; and in the light of this newly acquired knowledge he attempts to review the *Kakure* religion. Thus the text is an exercise in illuminating the old religion in light of the new, a kind of interior dialogue between the *Kakure* and the Catholic religion. It is the testimony of a person gradually and willingly converting to Catholicism.

In the section 'What is religion?', the narrator is quite explicit in his use of Catholic theology, and throughout the text one can find both the old Portuguese and Latin lexicon and later Meiji-era usage. Both *anima* and *reikon* can be found to denote the idea of the soul, for example. This section also addresses one of the issues that perplexes many – the use of the term *Kakure Kirishitan*. The term implies that the faithful are hiding, but in an age when freedom of religion is permitted by law, such a stance appears to have outlived its functionality. In speaking of the *Kakure*, the narrator says:

What a splendid religion we have! Is it Buddhism, where we decorate the Buddhist family altar, offer incense, and worship Buddhist images? No, it is never like that! Is it Shinto, where we offer branches of *sakaki* and *gohei* at the Shinto household altar to purify our souls? Certainly not! Is it the Catholic Church wherein we enshrine images of *Kirisuto* and *Santa Maria* on the altar and worship and serve *Deusu* morning and night and hold Mass every Sunday? Considering words such as *Deusu*, *Zezususama* and *Santa Maria*, which are part of our daily conversation, our religion undoubtedly resembles the Catholic faith. However, the authors of the text themselves are not sure what name would be good to use for our religion. So for the time being, until we find a better name, we will call this religion *Kakure Kirishitan*.[14]

Although in this quotation, and elsewhere in the text, the narrator denies any true affinity with Buddhism or Shinto, no such denial occurs regarding the Catholic faith. But he himself still seems unprepared to answer the fundamental question he has raised: just what does distinguish the *Kakure* from the Catholic religion? Elsewhere in the text, the Buddhist altar is referred to as 'a disguise', and the Shinto household altar as 'meaningless'. But, instead of addressing these problematic areas, the narrator asserts that the historical section will reveal the causes for the current state. The only cause he mentions are those well documented in standard Japanese history texts, such as the strict government surveillance and controls designed to suppress all Christian activity. As he concludes:

> Even so, the *Kirishitan* tried to maintain their faith in every possible way: in the guise of *Maria Kannon*, a Shinto shrine in which a cross is installed, and so on. The government officials ordered the investigation of shrines to check the images; or at the time of *O-bon* in July, they would go on rounds to check the Buddhist altars of believers. So effective were they at oppressing the *Kirishitan* that the *Kirishitan* group was thinning out. Just like fallen leaves from a condition in which they had once appeared like the rising sun.[15]

*Religious practices*
The sense of sin played a central role in *Kakure* theology, however lacking in nuance it may have been. In fact, the function of religion was to provide a way to save oneself from the effects of sin. The definition of the function of religion in the text is stated as follows:

> The soul of a good person will go to heaven and the soul of a bad person will go to hell. The rest will go to purgatory. Everyone must go to one of

these three places. The soul of a dead person, once separated from its body, cannot do anything to save itself. It is absolutely necessary therefore that we mortal humans do our utmost to save our souls while in this world. The teaching of how to accomplish this goal of saving oneself is religion.[16]

Closely bound to the notion of sin and ritual purification were the penitential practices observed by Fukue's *Kakure Kirishitan*. Remnants of these can be found only in fasts two or three days a week now practised by very few *Kakure*. In former times, one of the chief penitential practices originated in response to the annual *fumie* ceremony that took place in the New Year's celebrations. All persons were required to report to the temples where their families were registered and tread on a plaque bearing a sacred image, most often of Christ or Mary. This treading was done wearing shoes – or rather with straw sandals. Japanese culture attaches strong symbolic value to the removal of shoes, especially before entering a building. To leave their shoes on would in itself be a defiling act. Not being permitted to remove the shoes served to heighten the sense of profanation during the *fumie* ceremony. Refusal to tread was a sure indication of being Christian, an offence punishable by death. Upon returning home from such a demoralising event, some *Kakure* groups of Fukue would first burn the straw sandals. Then, placing the ashes in a porcelain bowl, they would mix them with water and drink the mixture while begging *Deusu* for forgiveness for this most necessary of sins.

In this and other practices, the *Kakure* religion shows a marked tendency toward concrete expressions of religious emotion. Kawaguchi's text describes what had long been the way of celebrating the most important event in the annual cycle of the *Kakure* religious life. Called *Natara* in parts of Fukue this feast commemorates the birth of Christ. The preparations involved and the expectations thereby induced make for a highly emotional event:

> The feast of *Natara* is the most warmly celebrated feast day of the year. Two or three weeks before *Natara* we gather wood from the mountains and every home has a big feast on the eve of *Natara*. If we own cows, we clean them because this night the infant will be born. Cleaning them we say, 'Tonight the infant will be born in the stable'. We spread ample straw, wash the manger, and afterwards fill it with water and place it in front of the stable. When the baby is born, he will be bathed in it, so we have prepared a fire beforehand to keep the infant warm. We spend the night together that evening, young and old, with each person reciting the *Garasusa orashio* 150 times. Parents must take the place of the children who do not yet know the *orashio* or cannot attend the gathering.[17]

## IN CONCLUSION

The description of *Natara* captures more than any other in all the literature on the *Kakure*, the spirit of the *Kakure* religion. With its emphasis on simplicity, gentleness, and the need to concretise religious feeling, this ritual brings what is distant and remote into the family sphere and is celebrated in a highly communal fashion with the entire group spending the night together. This contrasts markedly with a rational theological approach to the faith.

This need to dramatise devotion is significant when we recall the return of the Catholic missionaries to Japan in the 1860s. During the years of national isolation, the descendants of the early *Kirishitan* had found their own internal compromise, indigenising all they had absorbed from the early contact with the European Christians. The long period of isolation had produced a new version or 'denomination' of Christianity, a tribute to the powerful digestive energy of native Japanese religious sensibilities.

The re-entry of the Catholic missionaries from the 1860s with their insistence on absolute fidelity produced no unanimous response. Depending on the individual's perspective, some converted; others, however, remained indifferent to the missionary presence. There was a further response: others withdrew still further. The Catholic missionaries with their emphasis on exclusive fidelity to an absolute God threatened to undermine the very essence of *Kakure* religiosity with its polytheistic and multi-religious orientation. As a *Kakure* woman converted to Catholicism recently confided, she was unable to give up her Shinto household altar. A Catholic priest had not allowed her to keep it, and this brought her near to quitting the religion, for she had promised her mother prior to her death that she would honour her mother's memory each morning by placing a chalice of rice wine and a dish of rice before the household altar. Her peace of mind depended on keeping this promise. Had this Catholic convert not met another priest who viewed her daily obeisance favourably, remaining a Catholic might not have been possible.

For the *Kakure*, conversion to Catholicism is always fraught with difficulty. The history of the *Kakure* constitutes an immensely important case-study in the history of Japanese religions as they are the only continuous living remnant of that initial contact between Japan and the West. More, though, the *Kakure's* very existence is testimony to the real complexities of the very contemporary issue of inter-religious dialogue.

This point seems to be borne out in one of my discussions with the leader of the only active *Kakure* community on Fukue today. Categorically refusing to answer all questions that touched on belief, he would only say, 'My father told me I was not to speak about such things with anyone'. This was the same *Kakure* leader who had refused to gather with the seven other *kuruwa* of Fukue when they attempted some sort of unification. However, when asking him what he thought the future held for the *Kakure* religion, he did have an answer. 'It's a sad, lonely one', he said. 'It will die. The faith is not complete.'

NOTES

I should first like to thank the *Kakure* people, without whose cooperation this research would not have been possible. I am grateful for the expert assistance of Ishii Tsutomu of Tokyo in the translation of the *Kakure* text, to Tanaka Misako, native of Nagasaki, for her generous help in the transcription of the taped interviews, and to Nagaya Katsuyuki of Fukue, whose resourcefulness and moral support were greatly appreciated during my research on the islands.

1. The term *kotchi* ('here'), dialectal variant of the standard *kochi*) contrasts with *atchi* ('over there'). The first refers to the *Kakure* and the latter to Catholic. The terms *motochō* and *furuchō* refer to the *Kakure* calendar in which are recorded the feast days to be observed. *Kyū-kirishitan* means old Christian or those who refused to join the Meiji Catholic church. The terms *hirakimon* (opening [the ground] person), *itsukimon* (appendage person) and *gedō* (heretic) have been used by the majority population to refer to the *Kakure*.
2. The residents of Shingo, a small town in Aomori prefecture, cherish an unusual legend which claims that Christ escaped the crucifixion and came to Japan, settling in Shingo where he died a natural death at the age of 106. A large white cross stands above his tomb on a hilltop in the village.
3. Kataoka, *Urakami Yonban Kuzure*.
4. The *san'yaku* consists of three *Kakure* officials who together form the necessary unit for officiating at ceremonies. The highest member is the *chōkata* or calendar-keeper, next is the *mizukata* or baptiser; last is the *toritsugikata* who used to report the *Kakure* news of events to the village community but now functions as an assistant to the other two.
5. Schütte, *Introductio*, p. 431.
6. Yūki, 'Fukusha Machado Shinpu'.
7. Interview with the *chōkata* on 28 June 1992.
8. Furuno, *Kakure Kirishitan*, p. 198.
9. See the discussion of this work by Turnbull in this volume.
10. Interview with the *chōkata* on 28 June 1992. All subsequent comments attributed to the *chōkata* are taken from this interview.

11. Volpe, *I Kakure*, pp. 43–4.
12. Kawaguchi, *Kakure Kirishitan Orashio no Shiori*, preface.
13. The term *kuruwa* is peculiar to the *Kakure* of Fukue where it means a group of *Kakure* pertaining to a particular village.
14. Kawaguchi, *Kakure Kirishitan Orashio no Shiori*, p. 3.
15. Ibid., p. 1.
16. Ibid.
17. Ibid., pp. 11–12.

# 9 The Social Forms of Japanese Christianity
## Mark R. Mullins

Christianity in contemporary Japan consists of many different social and cultural forms. It includes, for example, the many churches established by Western missionaries, numerous indigenous movements (churches or sects organisationally independent of Western churches), as well as the appropriation of elements of Christianity by Japanese who are unaffiliated with any of its organisational forms. While all of these expressions of Christianity deserve serious consideration, this essay will focus primarily on the new indigenous social forms that emerged from the encounter of Western churches and missionaries with Japanese culture.

### THE PLANTING OF WESTERN CHRISTIANITY

The first encounter between Christianity and Japanese culture began with the Catholic mission to Japan from the mid-sixteenth century. Although recording remarkable numerical success for such a brief period of propagation, this first encounter had 'officially' ended by the mid-seventeenth century with government decrees prohibiting Christianity, the expulsion of European missionaries, and systematic persecution of Japanese converts. 'Unofficially', however, the encounter with Christianity continued for the next two centuries as the 'hidden Christians' (*Kakure Kirishitan*) sought to survive in the hostile environment and secretly carry on the faith they had received.[1]

The second encounter began around 1859, only six years after Commodore Perry persuaded Japan to open its doors to the West, with the arrival of the first Protestant missionaries and the return of Roman Catholics. However, it was not until after 1873, when the Japanese government removed the notices proscribing Christianity, that Christian missionary efforts began to meet with some success. Since the reopening of Japan to the West, scores of denominations and sects have made their way from Europe and North America to evangelise Japan. By the 1930s churches such as the Roman Catholic, Anglican, Presbyterian, Congregational, Methodist, Disciples of Christ, Seventh-Day Adventist, and Southern Baptist had established a significant organisational presence in Japan. In the early post-war period, numerous other evangelical churches from North America and Europe responded to General MacArthur's call for missionary reinforcements to join in building a new Japan. Thousands of post-war missionaries have established new churches, Bible schools and seminaries over the past several decades. Although on a much smaller scale, the Christian religious landscape in Japan today resembles in many ways denominational patterns in the United States. In addition to the denominations mentioned above, various Lutheran, Holiness, Baptist, and Pentecostal groups are also well established in Japan.

Considerable attention has been given to the study of these early missionary efforts and the subsequent transplantation of various mission churches.[2] In recent years several studies have also appeared that analyse the process of indigenisation in these established Japanese denominations still related to Western churches.[3] While many of these 'Western-oriented' churches have experienced significant growth periods over the past century, institutionally affiliated Christians still only amount to approximately 1 per cent of the population. When one considers the number of missionaries and the financial resources invested by both Roman Catholic and Protestant churches, it is hardly a picture of success. The NHK Survey on Japanese Religious Consciousness[4] provides a slightly more optimistic picture; it found that 2 per cent of the Japanese identify themselves as Christian and 12 per cent feel a certain empathy with Christianity.[5] Even with the more generous assessment provided by survey research, the efforts to transplant Christianity in Japan have not been too successful.

## THE NATIVISTIC REACTION

The establishment of missionary churches is hardly the whole story of Christianity in Japan. While at times the 'Westernness' of Christianity has contributed to its appeal among Japanese, for the most part it has been viewed as a problem. Many early Japanese converts to Christianity felt that their new faith was unnecessarily bound to Western organisational forms, denominational loyalties and dissensions and the missionary control. Even today, many Japanese still regard the Christian religion as 'foreign' or *batakusai* (literally, 'smelling of butter').[6]

The nativistic reaction of many Japanese Christians was expressed in rather strong terms by Nitobe Inazō as early as 1890:

> The sectarian bigots revive on a heathen land their own petty jealousies, for which their forefathers fought and burned one another.

Nothing is more ugly and repugnant to Japanese eyes than these sectarian quarrels and jealousies; worse than that, the Japanese seekers find themselves puzzled by a maze of conflicting teachings of different Christian bodies.[7]

Nitobe goes on to say that 'the divine religion of Christ, divested of all human wrappage – of sacramentalism, sacerdotalism, sectarianism – alone is welcome'. If human wrappings are necessary, Nitobe concludes, they should be 'a home-made garment'.[8] Religion without 'human wrappings', of course, is not really an option. The choice is only between imported or indigenous forms. The development of indigenous forms usually takes many years and is only achieved after difficult struggles between the initial foreign 'carriers' of the religion and the emergent native leadership. The reactions of Japanese to mission churches and their creative appropriations of Christianity have led to the development of numerous 'home-made garments', providing alternative interpretations and socio-cultural expressions of this foreign-born religion. The following list is by no means complete, but provides some indication of the variety of indigenous groups that have been organised over the past century.

| Name of organisation | Year organised |
|---|---|
| Mukyōkai (Non-church movement) | 1901 |
| Dōkai (The Way) | 1907 |
| Kirisuto Shin Shūdan (Christ Heart Church) | 1927 |
| Eikō no Fukuin Kirisuto Kyōdan (Glorious Gospel Christian Church) | 1936 |
| Ikeru Kirisuto Ichibaku Kyōkai (Living Christ One Ear of Wheat Church) | 1939 |
| Kirisutokyō Kanan Kyōdan (Christian Canaan Church) | 1940 |
| Iesu no Mitama Kyōkai (Spirit of Jesus Church) | 1941 |
| Genshi Fukuin (Original Gospel) | 1948 |
| Seisho Kenkyūkai (Bible Study Circle) | 1951 |
| Iesu no Hakobune (The Ark of Jesus) | 1960 |
| Ikeru Kami no Kyōkai (Living God Church) | 1965 |
| Ikasu Kirisuto (Life-Giving Christ) | 1966 |
| Nihon Kirisuto Shōdan (Japan Ecclesia of Christ) | 1969 |
| Sei Iesu Kyōkai (Holy Jesus Church) | 1969 |

Apart from a brief paragraph provided each year in the *Kirisutokyō Nenkan* (Christian Yearbook), we know almost nothing about most of these independent movements in Japan. The current membership of these groups varies widely, but ranges from several hundred to twenty or thirty thousand. Together, therefore, they constitute a significant segment of the Christian population in Japan.

The churches and sects established by Western missionaries and those organised by indigenous leaders can be distinguished in terms of their basic orientation and degree of indigenisation. By basic orientation I refer to the dominant reference group of the religious organisation in terms of a tendency to be either 'foreign-oriented' or 'native-oriented'. The churches established by missionaries are still 'foreign-oriented' in many ways. The Western church still functions as a primary 'reference group' for these denominations in Japan. This is readily apparent if one considers the influence of European and North American theology, church polity, and the ongoing presence of foreign missionaries. Indigenous movements, by contrast, are 'native-oriented' and do not measure their perception of religious truth by the creeds and theology of Western churches. Most of these groups produce their own literature, including monthly or quarterly magazines, editions of the Bible (sometimes specially edited versions), and collections of the founder's writings and lectures. These independent movements share the conviction that God is calling them to develop Japanese cultural expressions of the Christian faith that are at least as legitimate as the national churches and denominational forms that have emerged over centuries in Europe and North America. Some indigenous sects even claim to have *the* truth and regard Western churches and Christian traditions as apostate distortions of New Testament Christianity.

While self-government, self-support, and self-propagation are understood as the minimum requirements for an indigenous church,[9] indigenisation involves much more than mere organisational independence. It also refers to the process whereby foreign-born religions are transformed through contact with native religion and culture.[10] This transformation may involve new organisational forms, new styles of leadership, adaptations in beliefs, rituals and liturgies.

## THE CULTURAL DIVERSITY OF THE RECEIVING SOCIETY

A study of indigenous Christian movements reminds us that the Japanese population is far more heterogeneous than many popular characterisations would suggest. It is probably safe to say that the myth of the homogeneous Japanese is largely a creation of the Meiji, Taishō and Shōwa eras. Prior to the Meiji Restoration and unification of the population under the Emperor system and state Shinto, Japan lacked a strong national identity. Too often, in fact, we forget that pre-modern Japan was characterised by its diversity – various groups characterised by loyalties to different feudal lords and clans, and politicised Buddhist sects, as well as protest groups comprised of peasants and small landowners. D.C. Holtom, writing during the Second World War, explained that the unification of Japan under Shinto nationalism was extremely difficult because of this social, political, and religious diversity:

> Modern Japan has had to struggle for the unification and co-ordination of her national life in the face of strongly diversifying, not to say disintegrating, tendencies. There has been much internal heterogeneity to overcome. The particularism of a feudal regime that was split into rival clans and pocketed behind mountain barriers and secluded on separate islands has not even yet been fully transcended. *Religious diversity* has revealed itself in a tendency toward separation that seems to reflect what amounts almost to a national genius for *sect-making* and for breaking up into small esoteric groups. [emphasis mine][11]

Holtom goes on to point out that in Japan this diversity has usually been under the control of a ruling class or small elite from above. What I would like to emphasise here is that underlying the surface 'harmony' and 'order' of modern Japan is a significant degree of cultural and religious diversity. As Sugimoto and Mouer have recently stressed, there is considerable variation in behaviour and in thinking among Japanese.[12] This is a significant point when we consider the reception, understanding, and reinterpretation of Christianity by indigenous movements in Japan.

In our study of indigenisation, it is necessary to distinguish between the beliefs and practices of various social strata that constitute the native culture to which Christianity has been forced to adapt. At the very least, we must distinguish between what might be called 'elite religiosity' and 'mass religiosity', the former being associated with the educated ruling class of samurai (and their successors) and the latter with the 'ruled' majority of Japanese. The Confucian ethos has certainly been a dominant element of the elite strata, and folk religion (*minkan shinkō*) has provided the basic orientation for the masses. Without denying the important role of Confucianism and Buddhism in Japanese society, it is folk religion that scholars refer to as the comparatively stable 'substructure' of Japanese religion.[13] According to Miyake, it is within the frame of reference provided by folk religion that the organised religions have made their way into Japanese society. Only as they accommodated themselves to folk religion and its implicit norms did the institutional religions find acceptance and begin to exercise influence on people in their daily life.[14]

Early Protestant Christianity in Japan was for the most part an intellectual religion for the elite. The samurai class, the most literate and intellectual class of Japanese society, was over-represented in Christian churches. While only about 5 per cent of the Japanese population in the 1880s and 1890s were of samurai class origin, approximately 30 per cent of Protestant church membership came from this class.[15] The dispossessed samurai and their descendants found a functional equivalent to the *Bushidō* code (way of the samurai) in the strict ethics taught by the early missionaries. The intellectual character of Japanese Christianity, particularly Protestantism, can be traced to this period.[16]

## INDIGENOUS CHRISTIAN MOVEMENTS

*Mukyōkai* (non-church Christianity), founded by Uchimura Kanzō (1861–1930) and probably the most widely known and respected expression of Japanese Christianity, effectively escaped Western control but similarly represented the intellectual elite. Caldarola provided an impressive sociological study of *Mukyōkai* nearly two decades ago, showing the manner in which this Japanese social form was shaped by the cultural values of the elite social strata.[17] Rejecting Western denominationalism – its rituals (sacraments), divisive creeds, and clericalism – this movement is loosely organised into Bible study groups patterned after the Confucian teacher-disciple (*sensei-deshi*) relationship. According to Caldarola, *Mukyōkai* prides itself on being a 'manly expression of Christianity' (*otoko rashii Kirisutokyō*).[18] This is reflected not only in the dominance of male leadership, but also in the fact that over 60 per cent of the membership is male. Drawing its members primarily from the intelligentsia, this movement had approximately 35 000 members in the mid-1970s at the time Caldarola conducted his study.

*Mukyōkai* is also important for what it has given birth to throughout its history. Largely because *Mukyōkai* has no central authority or bureaucracy, it has functioned as the fountainhead of indigenous Christianity in Japan, giving rise to many other movements. One such movement, also analysed by Caldarola, is the *Genshi Fukuin* (Original Gospel) or *Makuya* (Tabernacle of Christ). Dissatisfied with the intellectualism of *Mukyōkai* Christianity, Teshima Ikurō (1910–73) founded this Pentecostal movement in 1948. Teshima was relatively open to elements of folk religion and consequently related Christianity more effectively to less educated Japanese. Like *Mukyōkai*, however, *Makuya* is also organised on the home Bible study group model and meets in the homes of leaders and in rented facilities. At the time Caldarola conducted his study, *Makuya* had 500 such groups organised around the country and a membership of approximately 60 000.

A *Makuya* leader in Tokyo informed me that there are still approximately 25 000 subscribers to their magazine *Seimei no Hikari* and 150 groups scattered across Japan that meet weekly. The decline in the number of groups, now referred to as 'ecclesia', suggests a significant decline in membership as well. This is undoubtedly related to the death of Teshima, the charismatic founder, and subsequent schisms.

## *IESU NO MITAMA KYŌKAI*: ANOTHER JAPANESE PENTECOSTALISM FORM

Although Caldarola provided a helpful analysis of indigenisation in *Mukyōkai* and *Makuya*, his study ended with the following inaccurate generalisation: 'Makuya is the *only* movement to indigenise Christianity – traditionally an upper-class religion —in the Japanese lower classes. By emphasising its pentecostal aspects, the Makuya has ingeniously succeeded in fostering the continuity of a Japanese folk-religious tradition dominated by shamanism, magic, and miracles' (emphasis mine).[19] In fact, however, there are a number of other indigenous movements that have made similar cultural adaptations and attracted members from among the less educated population. One such movement, *Iesu no Mitama Kyōkai* (Spirit of Jesus Church), provides another interesting example of the encounter between Christianity and Japanese folk religion and illustrates the process of indigenisation. The remainder of this chapter will briefly sketch the development of this movement and analyse the indigenous features that have appeared as a result of adaptations to Japanese folk religion and the ancestral cult.[20]

### Origin and historical development

The founder of the *Iesu no Mitama Kyōkai*, Murai Jun, was born in 1897, the second son of a Methodist minister. Raised in this Christian environment, he went on to study theology at the Methodist-related Aoyama Gakuin University in Tokyo. During this period Murai was deeply troubled and considered suicide. In 1918, while riding a ferry-boat in Okayama Prefecture, Murai made the decision to jump overboard and end his life. It was at this moment that he experienced the presence of the Holy Spirit in a powerful way and began speaking in tongues. This experience erased all of Murai's doubts concerning religious faith and gave him new strength and vision for Christian mission.

Murai dropped out of Aoyama Gakuin and became an evangelist, eventually becoming a pastor in the Japan Bible Church (the church that became the Japan Assemblies of God in 1949). In 1933, the pentecostal experience which had changed his life spread throughout the membership of his small congregation in Nishisugamo, Tokyo. In 1941, however, Murai separated from this church after visiting the True Jesus Church in Taiwan, a Chinese indigenous movement that had been in existence for just over 20 years.[21] Practices and beliefs Murai adopted from the True Jesus Church that led to his separation from the Japan Bible Church include sabbath worship, use of unleavened bread in the Lord's Supper, the practice of footwashing after baptism, and the 'Jesus Only' (i.e. unitarian) doctrine. The year 1941 also marks the time that his wife, Murai Suwa, received a revelation from God in which the name *Iesu no Mitama Kyōkai* (Spirit of Jesus Church) was given to them as an official church designation.[22]

Like many other Christian denominations in Japan, *Iesu no Mitama Kyōkai* did not experience significant growth until after the Second World War. In 1950 the head church in Tokyo was built and two years later a Bible school was established to train pastors. In 1953 Murai registered his church with the government and became a legal religious body (*shūkyō hōjin*). By 1958 *Iesu no Mitama Kyōkai* had grown to a membership of 28 000 and become the third largest Protestant denomination in Japan.[23] All of this was achieved without the direct assistance of foreign missionaries. This church has continued to report phenomenal growth for the past several decades.

It is necessary to point out, however, that statistics for *Iesu no Mitama Kyōkai* are less than reliable and must be viewed critically. While case-studies have revealed remarkable church growth for the Japanese context,[24] statistics for the church as a whole cannot be accepted at face value. According to church headquarters there are currently 420 000 general members (240 000 men, 180 000 women). Membership is based upon 'water' and 'spirit' baptism.[25] Anyone who has attended a meeting and received both forms of baptism (the latter being authenticated by speaking in tongues) is counted as a member. There are over 300 ministers (60 per cent women), close to 200 churches, and over 400 evangelistic house churches. The church has most recently clarified these statistics by indicating that there is an 'active membership' of 23 283; that is, individuals who regularly attend meetings and are engaged in church activities of one kind or another. Church representatives maintain, however, that the larger figure accurately reflects the number who have been 'saved' through *Iesu no Mitama Kyōkai*.

An examination of church attendance indicates that the figure for active membership is the most helpful for understanding the actual strength of this movement. One rural church in which I conducted fieldwork reports a membership of over 600 (including four house churches). Regular attendance at weekly meetings in the mother church was from three to 15 people, while close to 50 might attend the annual memorial service for the dead in August. Similarly, the Tokyo district reports a membership of over 80 000. Attendance at weekly services in the main church averages around 500. In addition, there are some 20 house meetings throughout the week with attendance ranging from 10 to 30. Attendance is greatest for the annual conference (*Daiseikai*) for pastors and laity, with approximately 1800 attending.

It might also be helpful to recognise here that Japanese religiosity and understanding of membership is quite different from Western notions. As a rule, Japanese do not commit themselves to one particular religious organisation; rather, they participate in the annual festivals and rituals of both Shinto shrines and Buddhist temples throughout the year. Regular, weekly attendance at religious meetings is the exception rather than the norm in Japan. While this church strongly discourages participation in Buddhist and Shinto rituals, their understanding of membership seems similarly undemanding. From my limited observations, there is little pressure placed upon members to attend meetings. As long as one has received 'water' and 'spirit' baptism, other obligations are viewed rather lightly.[26] Hence, the small number of regular attenders at church meetings does not seem to bother leaders. The fact that *Iesu no Mitama Kyōkai* is no longer experiencing significant growth is undoubtedly related to this more relaxed attitude toward membership and recruitment.

## Leadership and organisational structure

The observations above regarding membership are clearly related to the organisational structure and definition of clergy and laity responsibilities. Although *Iesu no Mitama Kyōkai* has a bishop, the role is largely a symbolic one. The current bishop, Murai Suwa, the wife of the deceased founder, is highly respected by pastors and members alike. Nevertheless, the role of bishop carries no official political power. There are no church councils or meetings over which to preside. As bishop, the Revd Murai symbolically represents the authority of the church and officiates at the communion service each year at the annual conference.

The actual control of the church is in the hands of each local pastor. A phrase one commonly hears in the church to express this socio-political reality is *bokushi ichinin shugi*, which in essence means that each pastor is entrusted with the responsibility of a local church. No outside interference is permitted. The laity in each local church are under the authority of the pastor and have no official role in church government. There are no congregational meetings and no lay leaders (elders or deacons). Neither is there a treasurer.[27] The pastor is in charge of the finances of the local church. Members, of course, are urged to tithe; but the use of church funds is determined by each pastor. In sum, *Iesu no Mitama Kyōkai* is a streamlined religious organisation with no committees or bureaucracy.

The responsibilities of the laity are summed up with the often-heard expression: *hitsuji ga hitsuji o umi, soshite bokushi ga yashinau*. Roughly translated, sheep are expected to give birth to more sheep and the pastor is expected to shepherd the flock. The choice of image here is important. As 'sheep' laity have only a passive role to play. One leader suggested that pastors viewed themselves as a family of priests, much like Aaron and the Levitical priests in the Old Testament.[28] They have been set apart from ordinary believers for their priestly activities. In order to train pastors for this 'high' calling, a two-year Bible School programme is maintained in the church headquarters in Tokyo. Each year there are 10–20 students attending the training programme. The Bible and the writings of founder Murai Jun form the content of the curriculum. After completing the two-year course, graduates assist in the work of the head church or engage in new church development.

It should be noted here that the relatively high status and power of pastors in this church probably contributed to the earlier growth of this movement. Religious diffusion via kinship ties is particularly evident at the leadership level. Anzai's study of the growth of *Iesu no Mitama Kyōkai* in Okinawa revealed that the founder of the church in that area effectively passed on the faith to his family.[29] Following his death, his wife continued to work in the church, one daughter and one son became pastors, and two daughters became wives of pastors in this movement. In my study of a church in Shikoku, I discovered a similar pattern. The pastor's father had converted to the Spirit of Jesus Church from an Assemblies of God congregation and become a pastor in the movement. Two of her brothers and one sister also became pastors. At the present time, two nieces and a nephew are serving as pastors, and two other nieces are in the Bible School preparing for pastoral work. If this pattern is the norm, one can understand why this movement has experienced significant growth.

## Dispensational and pentecostal connections

Although the historical link has not been established, the influence of dispensationalism upon the theology of the founder is unmistakable. An examination of Murai's *Seisho Shingaku* (Biblical Theology) and

*Kirisutokyō Annai* (A Guide to Christianity, No. 1) reveals that Scofield's notes must have been a handy reference in Murai's study of the Bible. With the dispensational eschatalogy imported from the West, Murai combined the features of pentecostal Christianity. Like other pentecostal groups, *Iesu no Mitama Kyōkai* rejects intellectualism and emphasises the importance of religious experience. Speaking in tongues, anointing with oil, dancing in the spirit, miracles of healing, and revelations from God are all basic components of everyday religious life. The symbolic world of the 'believer' is filled with spirits, signs, miracles, and wonders. Miracles of healing and religious experience, rather than intellectual or theological sophistication, are key characteristics of this church. Church services usually include scripture reading, singing, glossolalia and anointing with oil for healing and blessing.

Anyone familiar with dispensationalism and pentecostalism in North America will not be surprised at this synthesis of beliefs. Murai and his followers, however, have adapted this theology to various features of Japanese folk religion, creating a new indigenous expression of Christianity. It is this aspect of *Iesu no Mitama Kyōkai* that I would like to focus on in the remainder of this study.

### Cultural adaptations in *Iesu no Mitama Kyōkai*

It has long been recognised that the ancestral cult is a central feature of Japanese folk religion. In its classical or traditional form, the ancestral cult refers to the 'belief in the superhuman power of the dead who are recognised as ancestors, and the rituals based on this belief'.[30] Ancestors were originally understood as the founder of a household – and successive household heads. Thus, ancestor veneration was essentially a patrilineal phenomenon. Studies have indicated that modernisation and urbanisation have modified both the family structure and conception of ancestors in significant ways. Nevertheless, the concern with ancestors and appropriate care for the deceased is still a dominant feature of contemporary Japanese religion and culture.[31]

One unique feature of *Iesu no Mitama Kyōkai* that appears to provide an effective point of contact with traditional Japanese religiosity is its practice of baptism for the dead. While this church dissociates itself from Buddhist-related ancestor veneration, it seems to have found a functionally equivalent ritual that meets the needs and concerns of Japanese for their ancestors. According to church representatives, the traditional Buddhist ancestral cult is nothing other than 'idol worship' and violates the second commandment (Exodus 20). The rejection of Buddhist-related practices, in some cases, is 'symbolised in its burning of ancestor tables'.[32] In spite of this negative evaluation of traditional practices, *Iesu no Mitama Kyōkai* by no means neglects the ancestors. Their understanding of 'household salvation' (Acts 16:13-32) is interpreted from a Japanese cultural perspective and linked to baptism for the dead (1 Corinthians 15).

The Japanese household includes both present and past members (ancestors). Through the ritual of baptism for dead ancestors (*senzo no migawari senrei*) the blessings of salvation can extend not just to future generations but to past generations as well. In *Seisho Shingaku* (Biblical Theology) considerable emphasis is placed upon this teaching.[33] According to Murai, the Biblical teaching of the salvation of the dead had been hidden from the church since the second century, when the church abandoned water and spirit baptism. 'It is in these last days,' Murai writes, 'that this great mystery has been revealed to *Iesu no Mitama Kyōkai*'.

The salvation of ancestors is explained as follows: the spirits of all those who died without salvation and without receiving water and spirit baptism are presently in Hades. Although their bodies decay in the grave, their spirits can be saved through the forgiveness of sins. The authority to forgive sins, Murai maintains, has been forgotten by the modern church along with all the signs, miracles and wonders that characterised the early church. Through the ritual of vicarious baptism, the good news of the forgiveness of sins is communicated to the dead and their spirits are transported from Hades to Heaven. Believers are assured that all their doubts and misgivings regarding the state of their ancestors can be resolved through this ritual of baptism. This ministry to the dead is simply carrying on the work begun by Jesus Christ when he descended into Hades and preached to the imprisoned spirits (see 1 Peter 3:18-22).

How does this work out in practice? Members can request baptism for ancestors at the time of their own baptism or later when they become concerned about the salvation of those who have gone before. One simply states the name and one's relationship to the ancestor and then receives baptism by immersion on their behalf.[34] This understanding of vicarious baptism is expressed clearly in a hymn by that title in the church's *Rei Sanka* (Spirit Hymns).[35]

Vicarious Baptism

The spirits of our long-sleeping ancestors
still now are weeping in sorrow
Spring passes, summer comes, autumn goes and winter comes
But Hades is eternally winter's dead of night.

> Like the never ending shadowy darkness of Hades
> tears are flowing
> Crossing over the river of death, the anguish of that day
> Even now they are in the bitter harbour.[36]

> The ship which goes out knows no bottom
> Sinking deeper and deeper in the depths
> Still now the salvation of our ancestors is closed
> Eternal spirits anguishing ceaselessly.

> Evil spirits come like a whirlpool
> Frantically seeking salvation
> Faintly hearing the splash of water
> The mysterious work of atonement in songs from heaven.

> By and by the gates of Hades are opened
> Through the name of Jesus
> The substitutionary baptism of descendants in the world
> Oh what immeasurable grace.

> Oh, the cries of joy reverberate
> Our ancestors have been saved
> The light of grace shines all around
> The songs of the angels thunder throughout heaven and earth.

According to the church, through vicarious baptism the spirit of a dead person is released from Hades and is transported to Heaven where he or she prays for family members remaining upon earth. Just as a dead person is transformed into a benevolent ancestor through Buddhist memorial services, *Iesu no Mitama Kyōkai* transforms their dead through baptism into benevolent ancestors who perform intermediary prayers (*torinashi no inori*) on their behalf.

Concern for the dead does not end with the ritual of baptism. The *gōdō irei sai* (festival for comforting the spirits) is also an important service in all churches. According to one church representative, the significance of this service is that it is an occasion when the spirits of the dead join with those believers remaining on earth in common prayer to Jesus Christ. This emphasis certainly resembles the role of the Buddhist Bon festival held annually throughout Japan. The idea of reunion and fellowship with the dead is a central motif of this celebration. There is some variation in the observance of this service from church to church. In one church on the island of Shikoku, for example, this service is held each August. Members bring a list of deceased family members to be remembered in prayer.[37]

This timing is not without significance. The Bon festival is also held throughout Japan in either July or August. In the Tokyo Church, memorial services are performed numerous times throughout the year according to the requests of members. This follows the Buddhist custom of performing memorial services (*hōji*) for the dead after a set number of days, months or years. This *gōdō irei sai* is clearly the functional equivalent of the Buddhist memorial service that Japanese view as important for showing proper respect to ancestors and for assuring their eternal peace.[38]

## CONCLUSION: THE WAYS OF JAPANESE CHRISTIANITY

*Iesu no Mitama Kyōkai* shows us another way in which Japanese have reinterpreted Christianity in light of native traditions and concerns. This movement serves a clientele largely unreached by other Protestant churches and indigenous movements like *Mukyōkai*. While Caldarola regarded *Mukyōkai* as 'Christianity the Japanese Way', we must add that it is the 'way' for a small group of highly educated elites. These two movements differ not only in clientele, but also in the nature of leadership and worship. In contrast to the dominance of male teachers in *Mukyōkai*, for example, 60 per cent of the ministers in *Iesu no Mitama* are women, perhaps reflecting their central role in traditional folk religion and shamanism. While emotional preaching and healing services are central to *Iesu no Mitama Kyōkai*, Bible study, teaching and publications form the core of *Mukyōkai* religious practice. There are clearly many different 'ways' to be Christian and Japanese.

Just as Europeans or North Americans require diverse cultural expressions of Christianity, the Japanese also have different tastes and dispositions. For that reason Japanese belong to a variety of denominations and sects originally from Western countries as well as to a variety of indigenous Christian groups – high church, low church, evangelical, pentecostal, shamanistic, and so on. With all due respect to Nitobe, we must add that Western churches are not fully responsible for the denominationalism and conflicting interpretations of Christianity in Japan. As Holtom pointed out, Japanese religious history reveals a tendency toward sect-making, a pattern that has been repeated in the history of indigenous Christian movements since the turn of the century.

Without denying the widespread influence of *Mukyōkai* and other indigenous movements in Japanese society, it remains to be said that none of these groups appears to be recording significant growth today. It seems that most hold little more attraction for the average Japanese than other

Protestant churches. The fact that these indigenous movements are currently declining in membership suggests that they are no longer viewed as culturally relevant. 'What will give one generation a sense of unifying tradition,' Yinger[39] correctly notes, 'may alienate parts of another generation who have been subjected to different social and cultural influences.' Commitment to an indigenous form that may have been meaningful a half-century ago undoubtedly discourages the creation of new forms relevant to different cultural situations or settings.[40]

## NOTES

1. The Japanese literature on this indigenous form is vast; for a helpful English analysis see the articles by Turnbull and Whelan in this volume and Ann M. Harrington's 'The Kakure Kirishitan and Their Place in Japan's Religious Traditions', *Japanese Journal of Religious Studies* 7:4 (1980).
2. See, for example, Iglehart, *A Century of Protestant Christianity in Japan*; Morioka, *Nihon no Kindai Shakai to Kirisutokyō*; and Yamamori, *Church Growth in Japan*. Of these, by far the most authoritative study of this early period of Protestant missions in Japan is undoubtedly Morioka's work which provides a social history along with an analysis of mission work and church formation from 1859 to 1912. Yamamori's work is also useful in that it provides a comparative analysis of growth patterns in the Anglican, Presbyterian, American Baptist, Congregational, Methodist, Disciples of Christ, Southern Baptist and Seventh-Day Adventist churches during five historical periods. Yamamori gives attention to both the socio-cultural setting (contextual factors) and institutional factors that influenced growth patterns in each period.
3. See, for example, Reid, *New Wine*, Nishiyama, 'Indigenization and Transformation of Christianity'; and Doerner, 'Comparative Analysis of Life After Death'.
4. The NHK study (published by Aono in 1984) was conducted in November 1981. It was based upon 3600 interviews with individuals 16 years of age or older at 300 different locations throughout Japan. Of that number 2692 (74.8 per cent) were usable.
5. The higher percentage indicated by survey research is probably related to the influence of the numerous Christian educational institutions throughout Japan. The close to two thousand Protestant and Catholic institutions – from kindergartens to universities and graduate schools – have combined enrolment of over 600 000 students. Many of these schools provide chapel services and religious education. Although only a few students actually make church commitments, it seems that a number of others identify themselves as Christians as a result of this educational experience.
6. In a recent interview, the pastor of an indigenous Christian church in Tokyo used the expression *batakusai* to refer to aspects of Christianity planted by Western churches in Japan.
7. Nitobe Inazō, *The Intercourse between the United States and Japan*, p. 468.

8. Ibid., p. 470. Sociologist Anzai Shin similarly suggests, 'the Church has forgotten to distinguish, even in its own western terms, the essential from the non-essential. It took many centuries for western Christianity to fashion a beautiful square peg, and she has been trying to drive it into a round hole in Japan; the peg will not fit ...' (quoted in Caldarola, *Christianity the Japanese Way*, p. 13).
9. Smalley 'Cultural Implications of an Indigenous Church', pp. 147–51.
10. This is the definition provided by Morioka in 'Gairai shūkyō no dochakuka' (p. 52) in a passage where he distinguishes between 'acculturation' and 'indigenisation'. According to Morioka, in studies of acculturation the central focus or concern is to what extent the native culture has changed under the influence of a foreign religion. Studies of indigenisation, on the other hand, are primarily concerned with the nature and degree of change in the foreign-born religion through contact with native religion and culture.
11. Holtom, *Modern Japan and Shinto Nationalism* (rev. edn), p. 67.
12. Sugimoto and Mouer, *Constructs for Understanding Japan*, p. 160.
13. Hori, *Folk Religion in Japan*, p. 18.
14. Miyake, 'Folk Religion', p. 122. Hori similarly writes that 'the temptation to accommodate folk religion has really been the weak point of institutionalized religion in the history of Japanese religion from ancient times to the present'.
15. Yamamori, *Church Growth in Japan*, p. 53.
16. Ariga Tetsutarō suggests that the failure of Christianity to penetrate all of Japanese society is related to this early 'elitism', writing that many of the 'Christian leaders of the Meiji Period, being of samurai origin, had shared the samurai prejudice against Buddhism and Shinto. For precisely because these were the religions of the lower classes upon which the samurai looked down, they were bound to be more important factors of the society where all the former classes were mixed. This point they seemed to have missed. And here perhaps should be sought the chief reason why Japanese Protestantism has neither been able to extend its influence widely beyond the educated middle classes nor to answer successfully the challenges made by Buddhism, Shinto, and more recent popular sects.' (Ariga, 'From Confucius to Christ', p. 11).
17. See Caldarola, *Uchimura Kanzō to Mukyōkai* and *Christianity the Japanese Way*.
18. Caldarola, *Uchimura Kanzō to Mukyōkai*, p. 178.
19. Caldarola, *Christianity the Japanese Way*, p. 208.
20. This section draws from my earlier case study, 'Japanese Pentecostalism and the World of the Dead'.
21. Yoshiyama, 'Mitama ni Michibikarete', p. 23.
22. I was informed that only the Japanese 'Iesu no Mitama Kyōkai' is acceptable to the church. Since the name was given in a revelation from God, the English rendering 'Spirit of Jesus Church' is not permitted. In all foreign missionary contexts, the Japanese designation 'Iesu no Mitama Kyōkai' is used.
23. Iglehart, *A Century of Protestant Christianity in Japan*, p. 339. Actually, Protestant is a designation which *Iesu no Mitama Kyōkai* members reject. They maintain that they are neither Catholic nor Protestant, but a recovery of the authentic 'primitive' church. In any case, outsiders tend to classify

154        *Japan and Christianity*

      this church as 'Protestant', though often adding that it is 'heretical' in its
      rejection of the Trinity and in its practice of baptism for the dead.
24.   Anzai, 'Iesu no Mitama Kyōkai – Okinawa Dendō'.
25.   On more than one occasion I have inquired whether the membership statistics included 'baptisms for the dead' (see subsequent discussion). Church leaders indicated that such baptisms were recorded in a separate category and had nothing to do with their membership statistics.
26.   Comparison with membership in another new religious movement might be helpful here. In his study of *Sūkyō Mahikari*, for example, Davis writes: 'I would estimate that although as many as one million amulets have probably been distributed to new members, the *de facto* membership probably numbers about 100 000 to 200 000 or even less'. (Davis, *Dojo: Magic and Exorcism in Contemporary Japan*, p. 7).
27.   One pastor reminded me in an interview that it was Judas, the 'treasurer', who caused Jesus so much trouble. In other words, it is best not to entrust laity with heavy responsibility in financial matters.
28.   The strong influence of the Old Testament is also apparent in other areas of *Iesu no Mitama Kyōkai*. For example, this church observes the Sabbath as the primary day of worship (although they still hold meetings on Sunday). Also, 'unleavened bread' must be prepared for communion.
29.   Anzai, 'Iesu no Mitama Kyōkai – Okinawa Dendō', p. 42.
30.   Morioka, 'Ancestor Worship in Contemporary Japan', p. 201.
31.   Regarding change and continuity in the ancestral cult, see, for example, Smith, *Ancestor Worship in Contemporary Japan*, pp. 220–6; Morioka, 'Ancestor Worship in Contemporary Japan', p. 206; Hardacre, *Lay Buddhism in Contemporary Japan*, pp. 101–3; and Komoto, 'Gendai Toshi no Minzoku Shinkō', p. 49 and pp. 71–4.
32.   Anzai, 'Newly-adopted Religions and Social Change', p. 69.
33.   Murai, *Seisho Shingaku*, pp. 32–3.
34.   It is significant to note here that the church also performs baptism for *mizuko* (literally 'water-child'), or aborted and stillborn children. In this way, the *Iesu no Mitama Kyōkai* is responding to the felt needs of Japanese women to deal with the sense of guilt and the curse associated with the spirit of a *mizuko*. See Hoshino and Takeda, 'Indebtedness and Comfort' and Young, 'Abortion, Grief and Consolation' for helpful discussion of the growing trend of *mizuko kuyō* (memorial services for aborted or stillborn children) in contemporary Japanese religion.
35.   This is a collection of 166 hymns all said to have been received from heaven by Tsuruhara Tama, a woman who was active in the early years of this church. Since the hymns were given in a revelation directly from God, no changes are permitted. One sociologist has commented on the 'indigenous' character of this hymn book and suggested that these songs do not have the melodies and rhythms of Western hymns, but are more like Japanese folk songs. (Anzai, 'Iesu no Mitama Kyōkai', pp. 277–8). A young Japanese woman to whom I showed these songs was similarly impressed. She was immediately struck by the Buddhist influence evident in the lyrics and the Japanese-sounding melody.
36.   The imagery of these last two lines, the 'river of death' and the 'bitter harbour', reflects the Japanese Buddhist expression for dying, *Sanzu no*

*kawa o wataru*. In expressing the sorrow in the world of the dead, the author of this hymn is clearly drawing upon this cultural heritage. In the last line of the second verse, my translation of the term bitter is from the Japanese word *urami*. It is interesting to note that in Japanese folk religion often wandering spirits 'are said to be suffering from the emotional state of *urami* – bitterness, ill will, enmity, spite or malice' (Smith, *Ancestor Worship in Contemporary Japan*, p. 44). Individuals suffering misfortune in this life often see the cause in the *urami* of some unpacified spirit. In order to pacify such spirits, individuals follow the instructions of shamans to perform memorial services or make special food offerings.

37. This, along with records of those 'baptised vicariously', resembles the practice of *Reiyukai* members in keeping a death register or Book of the Past (*kakochō*). See Hardacre, *Lay Buddhism in Contemporary Japan*, pp. 65–6.

38. The concern for the dead is also manifested in the annual *daiseikai*, a several-day meeting held annually in each district or region. In the Kantō district, for example, a memorial service is observed during the *daiseikai* each May for the founder and for pastors who have died. In addition to the general memorial services for the dead, the Tokyo church (headquarters) also observes annually in March a special memorial service for the founder and first bishop of the *Iesu no Mitama Kyōkai*. Reid has observed a similar pattern of 'ritual respect' accorded founders of other Christian institutions in Japan. (Reid, *New Wine*, p. 28).

39. Yinger, *The Scientific Study of Religion*, p. 112.

40. John H. Connor considers this problem from a missiological and theological perspective in his article, 'When Culture Leaves Contextualised Christianity Behind', *Missiology: An International Review* 19:1 (1991).

# 10 From Out of the Depths: The Japanese Literary Response to Christianity
## Mark Williams

> *The Christian must distance himself from Evil. He is forbidden from approaching Evil. But the author is not permitted to avert his gaze from any aspect of the human soul – which includes not only the beautiful and good aspects, but also the objectionable and evil realm. He must confront every aspect of the human heart. Thus, anyone confronted with the duty of the believer on the one hand and the obligations of the author on the other cannot help but experience the pain of this contradiction.*[1]

In thus highlighting the apparent irreconcilability of literature and religion, Endō Shūsaku, one of the most prominent authors in contemporary Japan, is here touching upon an issue that has long been a topic for debate in both literary and religious circles. Whilst clearly not unique to Japan, the concept would appear to have exerted an undue influence on the development of the literature of a nation which at no stage this century has boasted more than 1.5 per cent of its total population as adherents to Christianity. It is the aim of this essay to assess the extent to which Japanese literature has been influenced by Christianity over the past century and, in so doing, to explore several possible explanations for this apparently disproportionate influence. In this, the intent is clearly not to posit a new genre of 'Christian literature': to do so would be not only to ignore the differing awareness of problems which form the basis of each author's art, but also to overlook the extent to which each has been integrated – or rather, has succeeded in integrating himself – into the mainstream of contemporary Japanese literature.[2] Nevertheless, in focusing on these authors struggling against the contradictions and irrationality of the age, certain similarities of approach do emerge, and it is these which this essay will seek to address. Before this is possible, however, consideration must be made of the often uneasy coexistence between the Christian faith on the one hand and the world of fiction on the other.

# CHRISTIAN LITERATURE AS OXYMORON?

It was the French novelist François Mauriac who highlighted the issue by remarking, 'I am a novelist. I am a Catholic. Therein lies the challenge.'[3] And it was the same perception of the problems confronting the 'Christian artist' that led Uchimura Kanzō, the foremost Japanese Protestant theologian of the modern era, to conclude:

> Literature is the worst possible path that the person seeking to interpret Christianity can choose .... As a Christian, one may be a critic, a dramatist – even, in certain circumstances, a poet. The man of letters, however, tends to be too feeble, too delicate and too cowardly to be a cross-bearing follower of Christ.[4]

Whether such comments were intended by way of genuine conviction, or as a challenge to the literary intellectual is impossible to determine. Through their hyperbole, however, such comments do suggest perception of a strict line of demarcation between religion, seen by Uchimura as seeking to bring man into harmony with some transcendent absolute, and literature, which he portrayed as focusing on an artistic and fictitious world through mediation and close observation. For such authors, the challenge seems clear: they are obliged to seek the potential for reconciliation between the necessity, accruing to themselves as authors, to remain honest to their observations of human nature, and their duty, as Christians, to seek within man the potential for salvation.

Plagued by these doubts, such authors inevitably come to question the very nature of their art, and many are driven to concentrate on an 'apologetic' form of literature in which the main focus is proselytisation rather than a concerted attempt to reveal the reality of the life of the individual and to plumb the depth of human experience. Others, however, intent on a successful resolution of the dichotomy with which they find themselves confronted, come to view as paramount the need to judge the artistic merits of the novel on the basis of a poetics of literature as opposed to theological criteria, and to concur with the conclusion offered by another author struggling with the same dichotomy, Graham Greene, who confessed: 'I am not a Christian author. It is just that Catholic padres happen to populate the pages of my works.'[5]

To Endō, Greene and others, the danger for the author of Christian persuasion is that the literary text will be relegated to secondary importance by the author's determination to seek within his work the possibility of salvation, not only for his creations, but also for himself. And, as Endō recognised at the outset of his career:

> If, for the sake of creating a truly 'Catholic literature', or for the purpose of preserving and propagating the Catholic doctrine, the personalities of the characters in a novel are subjected to artifice and distortion, then the work ceases to be literature in the true sense of the word.[6]

In thus emphasising the need for the artist to focus on his inner thoughts, Endō made no attempt to deny his debt to Western literature, and continued:

> The psychoanalytical self-examination of Freud and Bergson, the novelistic technique and psychology of contradiction that permeates the works of Dostoevsky, the question of self-integrity in Gide and the techniques of Proust ... are problems that the Catholic authors after Bourget and Bourdeaux could not deny, issues with which they had to grapple and which had to be overcome. Even if this conflicted with the goal of proselytisation, they adopted such techniques in that they contributed to the science of human observation. At that time, these new Catholic writers sensed an urgent need to remove themselves from the lofty heights of 'apologetic literature' and to examine 'godless man' as human beings.[7]

Viewed in this light, the 'Christian author' is the novelist who seeks to create his artistic world through consideration of the dramatic tension that ensues when religion and literature are placed in opposition. Equally, it is only with recognition of the existence of art created by examination of the violent internal struggles within man that one can see the integral relationship that exists between the two. In this, the danger is inevitably inherent that the author will be prevented, through a sentimental attitude towards religious motifs, from a deeper probing of human nature. But, provided that the author persists with the examination of the fundamental essence of his characters, rather than seeking to force them into a closer proximity with a symbol of divinity, then the potential for a literature born of this duality remains. The point is that stressed by Gibson in his study of the religious nature of the art of another to have confronted this dichotomy, Dostoevsky:

> The Christian [novelist] does not write novels about God; he writes them about people in their perplexities about God. He may, indeed he cannot but, reveal his personal convictions, but it will be dissolved in the structure of the novel; it is the people, with their unfulfilments, their stresses, their defiances and also their complacencies and compromises, and their exposure to the light which they may accept or decline, who absorb his attention.[8]

The result, in the works of Dostoevsky and the other novelists mentioned above, is a body of works in which consideration of the various dualities inherent within Christianity (for example, God vs. Devil, Spirit vs. Flesh, Good vs. Evil) is afforded a literary treatment, with the 'success' of such works traditionally determined by the extent to which the author is able, in this way, to progress beyond an intellectual understanding of man to a fuller understanding of human nature *per se*.

THE JAPANESE DIMENSION

In the case of the 'Christian author' in Japan, however, the dichotomy addressed by Dostoevsky can be viewed as further exacerbated. Forced to operate within a cultural and spiritual framework in which a metaphysical sensibility has traditionally been superseded by a powerful realistic and empirical tendency, these authors have consequently received less encouragement for the development of literary themes dealing with the spiritual drama of the relationship between God and man. In brief, the challenge has been to present the dichotomy, as outlined above, to a Japanese readership imbued with very different expectations concerning the proper domain of literature – and to counter the conviction, epitomised by the literary critic, Kamei Katsuichirō, who on the occasion of the baptism into the Protestant church of the prominent *sengoha* (post-war) author, Shiina Rinzō, remarked, 'Shina-san, you're going to have to make a choice between religion and literature'.[9] In this belief, Kamei was by no means alone. Another to express similar sentiments regarding this perceived incompatibility was the critic Matsubara Shin'ichi who advised another post-war novelist to seek baptism, Shimao Toshio, that, since the true Christian will be led to seek resolution to all conflicts in the world of religion, he should have no need for literature as an alternative source of salvation.[10]

It is difficult to gauge the extent to which the decisions reached by these and the other Japanese Christians who determined to persist with their literary ambitions in the face of such cynicism were deliberate attempts to prove a point, but there is evidence, especially in their immediate reactions to such comments, that these were taken seriously, if not necessarily ultimately heeded. Shimao's response to Matsubara for example, betrays a profound sense of unease and betrayal:

> We Japanese have been influenced by Catholicism for quite some time now, some four hundred years, and yet there is something about the spiritual climate, a sense of attachment (if that is the correct word) which we Japanese experience and which is totally unrelated to Christianity. That something is very deep-rooted within us, so that, when one enters the

Catholic church, one cannot escape a sense of having somehow betrayed something, however illogical that sentiment may be.[11]

And Endō was to express similar concerns when he confessed:

> As a Christian, a Japanese and an author, I am constantly concerned with the relationship and conflict created by these three tensions. Unfortunately, I have yet to reconcile and create a certain unity between these three conditions in my mind and, for the most part, they continue to appear as contradictory.[12]

The challenge for all these writers was to 'find God on the streets of Shinjuku or Shibuya, districts which seem so far removed from Him',[13] and in responding to these challenges, Japanese authors over the past century have reacted in differing ways. It is, however, possible to discern four distinct stages to the process that culminated in the intense scrutiny of the 'religion vs. literature' duality by a group of postwar Japanese novelists, and a brief examination of these now follows.

## FOUR STAGES OF DEVELOPMENT

The first phase, corresponding roughly to the first 25 years of the Meiji era (until c. 1890), saw the emergence of a series of translations, not only of the Bible itself, but also of an extensive corpus of theological tracts and novels premised upon Christian themes. At the same time, the period saw the emergence of a number of orthodox Christians into Japanese public life, with the likes of Yuasa Hangetsu and Iwamoto Yoshiharu assuming positions of considerable prominence in society. Mostly born of samurai stock, the majority of these early Meiji Christians had been raised in an ethical void – and sought in Christianity new values and morals. In this, however, they were inevitably strongly influenced by the Puritan morality of the early American missionaries. Writing, moreover, before the period of self-awakening, their works tend to lack the humanism and individualism of the subsequent era, and the majority of these authors, influenced by *fin de siècle* European literature, ultimately renounced their adopted faith.

In the search for more concerted attempts to define modern individualism using a predominantly Christian vocabulary, therefore, it is to the second era, from 1890 to the end of the Taishō era in 1926, that one must turn. The literature of the time betrays the stirrings of a variety of emotions, interesting as part of the larger process of the spiritual revolution of the Meiji and Taishō eras and, confronted by the apparent opposition between religion and literature, most felt obliged to succumb to the choice between their careers and their faith. Some, like Uchimura Kanzō and Uemura Masahisa, began their careers by positing the existence of a 'pure' literature which the former defined as a 'fight against ugliness, against injustice, coldheartedness, flattery and deceit', with all literature that fails to wage war on the various wrongs within society being dismissed as 'the work of the Devil'.[14] As their careers progressed, however, such critics came to despair of the possibility of a 'Christian literature', and ended up denying the way of literature in order to become Christian leaders.

Others, however, chose the opposite path. Initially attracted through youthful zeal to the essential message of hope of the Christian gospel, many were personally baptised by Uchimura and Uemura. Nevertheless, troubled by the perceived demands for justice delivered by an Absolute God, the majority subsequently proved unable to convert their initial sense of optimism into a consciousness of social issues, their writings betraying rather concern with the interacting of confession, sin consciousness and sexual desires. The trend amongst this generation towards an increasing distance from Christianity in favour of a more realistic humanism is marked, leading subsequent critics like Endō to question the depth of their initial affiliation to the faith:

> They received baptism as young men oblivious to the anti-Christian sentiment that lurked within them as members of the Japanese race – with the result that their faith never became an integral part of their lives.[15]

Overwhelming amongst the concerns of this generation were the emergence and development of the modern self, the first to stress the connection between this concept and Christianity being Kitamura Tōkoku. To Kitamura, the emerging self came to be viewed as the 'inner life' (*naibu seimei*), of which he wrote:

> In the intellectual world of Meiji Japan, in investigating the legacy of our Christian forebears who were pioneering new ground, they were doing nothing if not planting the so-called 'tree of life' in the heart of man (to coin the religious terminology).[16]

To Kitamura and a number of his pupils who sought to continue his legacy following his suicide in 1894, the life of which he was here speaking was far divorced from the natural life, but stemmed rather from God as a supernatural form of existence in which direct communication between God and His creation was emphasised, the intercessory role of Jesus Christ reduced in importance.

Kitamura was baptised in 1888, believing the major achievement of Christianity in Japan to have been the gift to the Japanese of a philosophy of inner life based predominantly on personal experience. The consequent Puritanism of his view of love (*ren'ai*) and his respect for the metaphysical world thus appear closely linked to his adopted faith. But as this came increasingly into conflict with his deep longing for traditional Japanese views of Nature, he was driven ever more to oppose the often indiscriminate cultural integration upon which his nation was embarked – and to view as the true function of literature an assault on the false reality and emptiness with which he sensed himself surrounded. The result was a man driven increasingly to despair, his suicide at the age of 26 serving as a poignant symbol of the religion/literature dichotomy with which he was ultimately unable to find reconciliation.

Following Kitamura's death, there were several other authors who were initially attracted to the message of hope they discerned in the Christian gospel but who were ultimately unable to reconcile this with their chosen careers as artists and who ended up travelling the path towards Marxism and aesthetic hedonism. Of these, probably the most influential was Masamune Hakuchō, whose vision of God as the terrifying, paternal figure of the Old Testament standing in judgment over His forlorn creation was to prove so influential to future generations of authors. It was this image, in which Christianity was viewed not as a religion of love and harmony but as an oppressive trend, that remained so prevalent in literary circles in Japan throughout the first half of the twentieth century and that remained a persistent catalyst for the attempts at depictions of a more maternal figure even in the post-war period. Masamune's image of God is encapsulated in the following assessment.

> I came to see Christianity as a severe religion. I saw it as forcing man towards martyrdom. All those worthy of the name believer are martyrs to the faith. They must renounce all pleasures. They must live their whole lives as though in a Mediaeval monastery. All attempts to enjoy the beauties of Nature are deviations from the mysteries of Christianity.[17]

Given the overwhelmingly negative tenor of Masamune's assessment, his decision to repudiate his earlier baptismal vows comes as little surprise – although it is interesting to note that, later in life, he came to temper that with a recognition of the less harsh qualities of the New Testament figure:

> To me, I treat Christ in a special way. It doesn't matter if my thoughts are bad. Whatever I do, Christ will help me and preserve me. In *The Book of Revelation*, God appears and, recognising that He has caused

pain and anguish to His people over the years, explains that that is now finished and that He will now accept them as they are. Moral values now count for nothing. Whatever man does, God will finally come to his rescue, take pity on man for having caused him so much pain and summon man to Himself. This is the message at the end of the Book.

I find this a most gratifying teaching ... There will probably be various theories on this, but the ultimate message is that Christ will be our salvation. It makes no difference how one has spent one's life. In the final analysis, Christ will welcome us into His heart just as a hen protects her chicks.[18]

The impact of Masamune's vision can be discerned in the writings of several of the leading figures in the literary world of this period, most notably Akutagawa Ryūnosuke, Natsume Sōseki, Shimazaki Tōson, Arishima Takeo and Kunikida Doppo.

Of this group, the author to have grappled most persistently with the conflicting pulls of Christianity and his chosen profession was Akutagawa, whose interest in Christianity, as with his adulation of the West, was based on his fascination with exoticism, but who struggled continuously with a profound sense of rejection by a 'Western' God and who related this as though representing a major defeat.[19] By his own admission, Akutagawa's contact with Christianity brooked three distinct stages for, as he writes in the introduction to his penultimate work:

About ten years ago, I loved Christianity – and in particular Catholicism – in an artistic sense. The temple of the Holy Mother in Nagasaki is still engraved on my memory. I am but a crow who picked up the seeds sown by Kitahara and Kinoshita. Then, a few years ago, I came to experience an interest in the Christian martyrs. The psyche of the martyr, like that of the fanatic, provided a morbid fascination to me. Finally, just recently, I have come to love the Christ portrayed to us by the four gospel writers. I no longer look at Christ as a passing stranger.[20]

Throughout his career, however, there is evidence of an author intent upon an examination of the claims of the Bible in his literature – as evidenced, for example, in 'Hōkyōnin no Shi' (The Death of a Martyr, 1918) and 'Kirishitohoro-jō Hitoden' (A Life of St Christopher, 1919), works that expound upon the author's candid feelings concerning the lives of two saints. Such works were clearly inspired by more than mere intellectual curiosity: Akutagawa's strong sense of affinity with their struggles suggests a very human and universal type of suffering. But the image of Christ with which the author ultimately found himself confronted remained couched in abstract terminology – and, within days of producing the following testimony, Akutagawa found himself drawn to take his own life:

> [Christ] was both a journalist and a character within journalism; alternatively, he was both a writer of short stories (in allegorical form) and the hero of a fictional biography called *The Complete Works of the New Testament*.[21]

In the case of Natsume Sōseki, interest in the faith failed to arouse in the author a desire to seek formal affiliation into the Christian church through baptism. He was, however, probably the first author in Japan to base his writing on an awareness of the fact that, in both religion and literature, every man is viewed as an individual – and it was the introduction of the notion that every man stands before God individually that afforded his work a fresh perspective. The motif recurs throughout Sōseki's oeuvre, but it is in *Kokoro* (Kokoro, 1914), as the protagonist reflects on the sin he has committed, that the author expounds upon his view of sin – especially, as in this case, sin at the level of the individual – as possessing the capacity to destroy human nature. For Sōseki, the sole means of escape from the darkness of his world was through literature, his frequent resort to the literary technique that subsequently came to epitomise his style, *sokuten kyoshi* (Follow Heaven and forsake the self), suggesting no mere literary ornamentation, but a heartfelt desire to live. The result is a literary corpus replete with biblical themes and several titles to his novels with overt biblical allusion.[22]

In the case of Shimazaki, who had been drawn to both Christianity and the world of literature by his mentor, Kitamura, his initial interest in Christianity is best depicted in the respect for life evidenced by early protagonists. But, following the success of his first major work of fiction, *Hakai* (The Broken Commandment, 1905), there is increasing evidence of an author whose respect for life has been reduced to a respect for the self that is often indistinguishable from egoism. The more immersed he became in his own immediate world, the more he came to view his writing as 'but confessions of a gnawing anguish',[23] this being reflected in his literature in a shift from sensitivities nurtured by Christian ethics to the charms of Greek humanism. Shimazaki's subsequent distancing from the church comes therefore as little surprise, his attitude appearing to reflect that of Sutekichi, the protagonist of one of his later novels, *Sakura no Mi no Jukusuru Toki* (When the Cherries Ripen, 1919), who remarks on one occasion:

> When asked by someone, 'Are you Christian?', I could not reply that I was the person who had earlier been baptised at Asami-*sensei*'s church

... 'Well, do you believe in God?' When asked that, I wanted to reply that, though still young, I was seeking God. I wanted to reply that I had been baptised by mistake ... that, if I were to be truly baptised, that still remained in the future.[24]

For the writers of the era attracted at the outset of their careers to the Christian gospel but subsequently driven to reject their faith as a perceived prerequisite for a literary career, however, the fundamental catalyst for their volte-face was the tension they discerned between the prevailing trend towards a Naturalist literature on the one hand and their creed on the other. Torn between the Naturalist emphasis on objective description of the contemporary world of human physicality and desires and the obligation, imposed upon them by their faith, for a certain subjective involvement, most found themselves unable, or unwilling, to pursue themes related to the salvation of the individual to any great depth in their literature. In seeking to emphasise, instead, the objective salvation of the entire society, these authors chose rather to divorce expression of the pain stemming from the contradictions and tensions that would have accompanied the process of baptism and subsequent apostasy from their writings, and have consequently been dismissed by many as lacking the powers to confront the great intellectual issues of the day.[25] For all their rejection of their baptismal vows, however, such authors remained under the sway of Uchimura and other theological leaders of their generation, who continued to exert a considerable, if indirect, influence on their subsequent writings. The result was an unprecedented moral, humanistic and social consciousness betrayed by their literary successors.

The third period that can be posited extends from the beginning of the Shōwa era in 1926 through the Pacific War, an era that saw the erosion of earlier idealism replaced amongst several of the literati by a renewed interest in Christianity. The result was a succession of authors who evidenced considerable interest in the Bible and deep insights into the faith, but who, as with their predecessors, ultimately failed to discern in Christianity the potential for salvation for the destroyed individual. Included in this number are the likes of Shiga Naoya, Mushanokōji Saneatsu and Dazai Osamu, all of whom were initially attracted to Christianity as a result of consideration of various issues concerned with the freedom of the individual but who, in coming to perceive the self as the window to all truth, ultimately spurned Christianity in the belief that they could obtain thereby an even greater freedom. The focus of the works of these authors thus became increasingly confessional, confined to narrow psychological concerns, as reflected in the works of, initially, the

*Shirakaba-ha* (literally, 'White birch society') and thereafter, the writers of the *shishōsetsu* genre.

The main exception to this trend was Dazai who has been seen by several critics as paramount in securing the transition to the fourth category of post-war writers for whom the 'literature vs. religion' duality represented the catalyst for their literature.[26] Biblical allusions are so numerous in Dazai's works as to warrant Sako's monograph, *Dazai's Osamu to Seisho* (Dazai Osamu and the Bible, 1983), devoted entirely to an analysis of these references, leading the critic Kamei to remark, 'One cannot understand Dazai without considering his relationship with the Bible.'[27]

To be sure, as Donald Keene suggest, '[Dazai's constant Biblical references] do not imply that he was a believer, nor even that he sought to believe – merely that they attracted his curiosity. He found in the Bible phrases that perfectly expressed his own feelings and mood.'[28] To dismiss entirely the importance of biblical motifs in Dazai's oeuvre is, however, to belittle the continuous soul-searching evidenced in his literature – as suggested by the following comment in his essay 'HUMAN LOST': 'By one book, the Bible, the history of Japanese literature was clearly divided into two parts, with such a distinction as was impossible in the past.'[29]

As with Masamune, the God whom Dazai discovered in the Bible was the overpowering figure of the Old Testament, not a saving God. Significantly, therefore, in searching for an antonym for the word 'sin', Yōzō, the protagonist of *Ningen Shikkaku* (No Longer Human, 1948) alights on various possibilities (including law, God, salvation, punishment, confession, repentance), but fails to arrive at the 'orthodox' answer: forgiveness. On his own admission, Dazai did not possess faith in the forgiving God of the New Testament, and *Ningen Shikkaku* and other Dazai novels consequently read as the tragedies of the man who perceives God, but remains unable to place absolute trust in Him.

Despite the tendency to remain obsessed with problems in their past and the consequent trend towards a single-level perspective, therefore, the fact that several writers from this group secured for themselves a place at the heart of the contemporary literary world in Japan suggests that their struggles to come to terms with the conflicting demands of religion and literature were by no means totally unsuccessful. In their attempts to secure a literature derived immediately from the dichotomy with which they found themselves confronted, however, their contribution remains limited, and in the search for a group of authors who drew their literary lifeblood more directly from this opposition, one must turn to the fourth generation of authors, those who reached literary maturity following the cessation of Pacific War hostilities in 1945.

Particularly in view of the fact that, on 15 August 1945, there was no single author of national acclaim engaged in active consideration of the dichotomy between religion and literature, the emergence of a mature 'Christian literature' in the ensuing decades appears the more remarkable. Authors such as Endō Shūsaku, Shimao Toshio, Takahashi Takako, Shiina Rinzō, Miura Shumon, Sono Ayako, Miura Ayako, Ariyoshi Sawako, Inoue Hisashi, Ogawa Kunio and recent convert Yasuoka Shōtarō, in addition to the playwrights Yashiro Seiichi and Takado Kaname, have all contributed to the process from a literary perspective, with Kagawa Toyohiko and Tanaka Kōtarō following on the tradition of Christian intellectual leadership in society initiated by Uchimura Kanzō and Uemura Masahisa.

Viewed as a literary group, distinctions between these post-war 'Christian authors' and their literary forebears, even those active in the immediate pre-war period, are marked and, in this regard, the influence of their wartime experiences cannot be overemphasised. Some, including Endō and Takahashi, may not have seen active service at the front, but, confronted with the ruins of a defeated nation in 1945, all looked to Christianity as a means to rebuild destroyed man. Unlike their predecessors, whose beliefs tended to stem from an intellectual search, the faith of this post-war generation grew out of very real struggles and doubts occasioned by the war, with the result that many found themselves in a position to smile with an inner knowledge on situations which threatened to overcome them in a way not achieved by the pre-war writers. Thus, whereas Dazai and his contemporaries sought, through literature, to escape life, the post-war generation tended to follow the lead established by Shiina in setting himself to 'endure' – and ultimately to secure individual freedom.[30]

The above contrast is indicative, however, of a more fundamental difference in approach between the pre- and post-war generations of 'Christian writers' in Japan – as it suggests a growing recognition of the need to focus on a deeper level of the individual being, the realm of the unconscious, in order to reconcile the various dualities with which their faith had confronted them. Again, it was Endō who highlighted the integral relationship between Christian literature and examination of the unconscious with the following assessment:

> The Catholic author views this world as a shadow of the supernatural world and, even whilst observing human psychology, he will detect, behind the 'second dimension' psychology of Freud, Bergson and Proust, the 'third dimension' of which Jacques Rivière happened to make

mention. As a result, the Catholic writer can conceive as reality the introduction of the supernatural world into the world of man, even if the non-Catholic reader is apt to misinterpret this as a distortion of reality.[31]

One would be hard pressed to discover such explicit recognition of the relationship between Christianity and the 'third dimension' in the pre-war literature considered above and, in a subsequent essay devoted more specifically to the distinction between the various levels of consciousness, Endō sheds further light on the implications that his holds for the author intent on an honest portrayal of human nature:

> The mind is the first dimension, the unconscious behind the mind is the second dimension. And to describe man's inner self, we must probe further to the third dimension ... the territory of demons. One cannot describe man's inner being completely unless one closes in on this demonic part.[32]

By this stage, the author's awareness of the relationship between a literature born of the religion/ literature duality and examination of the inner being is readily apparent. The more he came to focus on this connection, moreover, the more he has come to acknowledge this as the realm of the unconscious, leading to the conclusion that has influenced several of the other writers in this post-war category:

> Nowadays, it may be possible to discuss ideology without resort to the question of the unconscious; but it is not possible to consider literature and religion in that way ... Religion is more than the product of the intellect; it is a product of the subconscious transcending all intellectualisation and consciousness.[33]

Again, the debt to Western precedent is apparent, and it was not long before a closer examination of this relationship by Endō and several of the other members of this post-war group was to lead to a move away from a Freudian view of the unconscious. Modifying their vision of this realm as a 'swamp that houses those desires and urges which, though present in our subconscious, must remain suppressed and unexpressed',[34] they renewed their efforts to secure an interpretation that could be reconciled with their obligation, as Christians, to seek within man the potential for salvation. The result was recognition of a spiritual element to the unconscious (a quality which Endō has chosen to describe as the 'X within man') and the emergence of an image of the dual nature of the unconscious – as both the fount of Evil and the potential source of the redemption of the individual – that is unashamedly Jungian in emphasis.

The literary technique to emerge from this recognition has been described by one Japanese critic as that of 'paradoxical inversion',[35] for in seeking to probe a realm in which 'the desire for Good conflicts with our penchant for Evil ... where our appreciation of Beauty conflicts with our attachment to the Ugly',[36] the onus is on the author to suggest a fusion of qualities that, at first glance, appear irreconcilable.

Seen in this light, the stance adopted by these authors can be seen as heavily indebted to Gide, another to have addressed the 'religion vs. literature' dichotomy, who upheld the 'cooperation of the Devil' as the *sine qua non* for all literary activity and who was instrumental in the vision of God as at work, 'not merely in the beautiful parts of our being, but also over sullied parts, our sins'.[37] The result is a plethora of works from this post-war group that depict characters pulled by two opposing forces, Good and Evil – works that bear out Mauriac's conclusion that:

> If there is a reason for the existence of the novelist on earth, it is to show the element which holds out against God in the highest and noblest characters – the innermost evils and dissimulations – and also to illumine the secret source of purity in creatures who seem irreparably fallen.[38]

The tendency to focus on the ugly, the frightening and the grotesque is reminiscent of Dante's ability to portray Hell: just as such a depiction required a Christian perspective, so it remained for the 'Christian novelists' here under discussion to create realistic portrayals of the secular and chaotic world. In the light of the pioneering works in this sphere, the conviction grew of the impossibility of portraying the holy without an understanding of its antithesis, and several authors attributed their successes with this technique to a confidence in the existence of a transcendental figure. Not only could such a being be seen as lending a certain meaning to the chaos of life, the existence of such a figure also enabled these authors to portray those aspects of human nature they found themselves unable to probe alone. The consequent literature is founded upon a scrutiny of the darker elements of human nature – frequently portrayed in terms of a plumbing of the soul – in an attempt to discern thereby the inverse qualities within man; like Dostoevsky, these authors chose to 'select the dark corners of the world – if only to show that the light which could not penetrate them would not be worthy of worship'.[39]

In keeping with Western precedent, therefore, to Endō and the other post-war Japanese who sought to address the religion / literature dichotomy in their literary works, the realisation that the way to detect the holy was to portray it shining forth from the darkest recesses of the soul encouraged them to focus, as literary creators, on the 'living chaos within man'[40] as the formula for the creation of 'living human beings'.[41] Only thus, by penetrating to the core of the human unconscious and probing both the mystery and misery of the human drama, could these authors hope to 'understand, not only their characters' psyche and personality, but also their true flavour, their pain and struggles, everything about them'.[42] And only thus could they do justice to their vision of the individual as an amalgam of forces which, although seemingly in direct opposition, contained within themselves the potential for reconciliation at the level of the unconscious.

Another such duality which these authors frequently address and which consequently comes to be viewed less as the diametric opposition it traditionally represents, more as a combination of two mutually interdependent qualities, is that between faith and doubt. The result is a body of texts in which the most profound faith appears only to be expressible through the language of doubt and scepticism – a technique well known to readers of Dostoevsky's classic work *The Brothers Karamazov*, in which depiction of the dark sceptical soul of Ivan is countered by portrayal of the pure soul of Alyosha. The consequent text, indicative of a coexistence of faith and doubt within the author's own being, suggests a chaos in which the one supports the other and stands as a vivid reminder of the ability of literature to encapsulate faith, not through lucid confessions, but through the metaphor of doubt. The ability stems from the poetics of literature, whereby man should be portrayed without embellishment. The consequence, however, is that, in seeking to capture the hearts of his characters at the moment of greatest internal drama – as their inner beings are racked by fundamental doubts concerning the underpinnings of their lives – the author succeeds, paradoxically, in highlighting the potential for fusion between forces initially perceived as in opposition.

As Christians, however, all such dualities remained premised upon one fundamental relationship, that between man and God, and each of the oppositions established textually by these authors can consequently be traced back to this basic duality. But once more awareness of the need for literature to refrain from the incorporation of a specifically theological lexicon – to seek a portrayal, not of God, but of man in his relationship with God – remained paramount, and these authors found themselves resorting once more to Western precedent – in the deployment of the image most widely used in this literature to signify the creator / creation paradigm: that of the lover. In this, the author was concerned, not so much with similarities between the mentality of the lover and that of the believer *per se*, rather with the potential with which this, as symbol of mundane experience, invested him to reveal God working, not merely in the pure and transparent, but also in the inauspicious.[43]

There remains, however, one further corollary to the tendency for this generation of authors to focus on the inner being and to discern there a succession of seemingly conflicting qualities. For having come to view man's inner world as a battleground, especially for forces of a psychic nature, these authors came increasingly to a vision of man as irrational, driven by subtle, unknown and unknowable psychic motives. The result is a preponderance of characters depicted as confronted by 'another self' – a *dopplegänger* – which reflects not only Western precedent,[44] but also the above-mentioned interest in the Jungian image of man. As recognised by Takahashi Takako, for years an active member of this group of post-war writers who sought to address this 'religion vs. literature' duality, the issue cannot be divorced from the 'Christian concept of the dualism of man'.[45] Significantly, however, in contrast to the Western model, in which such duality of thought tends to be traced back to two clearly differentiated sources that can be attributed to the tension of a binary opposition, these Japanese depictions of an 'alter ego' behind a literary creation tended to be viewed as the product of a literary heritage in which the tension of such internal oppositions had traditionally been overlooked and, as such, were less readily accepted.[46]

In thus seeking to depict how some form of contact with Christianity can be seen as impacting upon the actions of the individual and being led thereby to concentrate on the inner being, these authors have betrayed an intellectual element, lacking in so much pre-war 'Christian literature'. On occasions, to be sure, these authors have become so embroiled in the intellectual and metaphysical implications of this search that they have ignored the fundamental changes that this search can induce in the behaviour and attitudes of their creations – with the result that some protagonists appear to have been reduced to the level of mere mouthpieces of authorial philosophy. However, in discerning within the unconscious the potential for reconciliation of positive and negative forces, these authors were in a position to address another issue which, as indicated earlier, was to prove the ultimate impediment for several of the pre-war authors – the image of God, as purveyed by Masamune, as the punishing and paternal figure of the Old Testament.

At the outset of their careers, many of this generation would have concurred with Endō in his attribution of this fundamentally negative perception of Christianity to a 'lack of sensitivity towards God, towards sin and towards death.'[47] As their consideration of human nature progressed, however, and as they came increasingly to view the individual as a composite of opposing forces, so they were able to isolate a more positive vision and to present this in a language with which their Japanese readership could more readily identify.

172  *Japan and Christianity*

Given Japan's somewhat tenuous links to the Christian church, the progression outlined above is indeed remarkable. In the space of little more than one century, Japanese authors addressing the 'religion vs. literature' dichotomy have developed from the first tentative steps to imitate Western models to the literary depictions by the post-war group of faith within, and through, doubt. In so doing – and in generally avoiding the stigma that accrues to all works of literature which encroach too overtly into the realm of theology – these authors have come to an increasingly optimistic vision of the possibility for effective communication across various national, religious and cultural divides. They have also succeeded in acquiring the type of confidence betrayed by Shiina in his eventual rejection of Kamei's pessimistic assessment of the prospects for a literary career for one on the threshold of baptism:

> I still write novels and remain a Christian. According to Kamei's logic, as long as I keep writing literary works, I cannot be a true Christian – but remain a fake. Equally, as long as I remain a Christian, I cannot, by definition, be a man of letters. Here, too, I remain a mere fake. In other words, whichever option I adopt, I am no more than an impostor.
>
> It is an indisputable fact that religion and literature are two distinct entities. At the same time, however, it is clear that it is possible to be both Christian and author. Needless to say, any religion, be it Buddhism, Christianity or any other belief, is premised on the concept of salvation. But salvation equals freedom ... As such, to have a religious faith is to live in the freedom that each religion furnishes and that freedom will cast a light upon life and the world very different from that provided by any other sense of freedom, causing them to be perceived in a different light. And that freedom has its own unique logic of denial. This is the religious reality of Buddhism, of Islam, of Christianity. There is no inconsistency in being a Christian believer who writes novels.[48]

## NOTES

The author acknowledges with gratitude a generous grant received from the Daiwa Anglo-Japanese Foundation. He also wishes to thank a series of audiences at lectures presented at the University of Leeds, at the annual Conference of the British Association for Japanese Studies (Bath, 1992) and at the International Christian University (Tokyo, 1993) for several questions that helped stimulate the ideas developed in this essay. An earlier version appeared in the I.C.U. *Journal for the Institute of Asian Cultural Studies* 20 (March 1994).

1. Endō, *Watashi no Aishita Shōsetsu*, p. 176.
2. As shown in the subsequent discussion, the issue is by no means limited to male authors. For the sake of convenience, however, the male pronoun will be used throughout.
3. Cited in Endō, 'Katorikku Sakka no Mondai', p. 29.
4. 'The Faith of a Literary Man', 1919. Cited in Takadō, 'Kirisutosha no Bungaku no Kanōsei', p. 45.
5. Cited in Endō, *Ningen no Naka* no. X, p. 137.
6. Endō, 'Katorikku Sakka no Mondai', pp. 20–1.
7. Ibid., pp. 21, 23.
8. Gibson, *The Religion of Dostoevsky*, p. 54.
9. Cited in Takadō, 'The Challenge of Christian Literature', p. 85.
10. Matsubara makes this claim in a discussion with Shimao and Morikawa Tatsuya in *Bungaku Sōzō no Himitsu*, pp. 130–6.
11. Ibid., p. 131.
12. Endō 'Nihonteki Kanjō no Soko ni aru Mono', p. 146.
13. Endō, 'Watashi no Bungaku', p. 370.
14. Cited in *Kokubungaku: Kaishaku to Kanshō* (1974:7), p. 68.
15. Endō, 'Watashi to Kirisutokyō', p. 357.
16. Kitamura, 'Naibu Seimei-ron', p. 240.
17. Cited in Endō, 'Chichi no Shūkyō: Haha no Shūkyō', p. 181.
18. 'Bungaku Hachijū-nen'. Cited in Takeda Tomoju, *'Chinmoku' igo*, pp. 121–2.
19. Cf., for example, his story 'Haguruma' (Cogwheels), 1927.
20. Akutagawa, *Seihō no Hito*, p. 112.
21. Ibid., p. 148.
22. eg. *Mon* (The Gate), *Kusamakura* (lit. Pillow of Grass) and *Kokoro*.
23. Cited by Kuyama Yasushi in Kuyama et al., 'Christian Influences', p. 206.
24. Cited in *Kokubungaku: Kaishaku to Kanshō* (1974:7), p. 78.
25. Cf., the opinion expressed by Kamei Katsuichirō in Kuyama et al., 'Christian Influences', p. 204.
26. Critics to have expressed this view include Sako Jun'ichirō in Sako, ed. *Dazai Osamu to Seisho* and Shimizu Hiromu in a lecture at Dōshisha on 24 June 1982.
27. Cited in *Kokubungaku: Kaishaku to Kanshō* (1974:7), p. 92.
28. Ibid.
29. 'HUMAN LOST', p. 106.
30. The theme of 'endurance' is integral to Shiina's maiden novella, 'Shin'ya no Shuen' (The Midnight Banquet, 1947) and remains a prominent motif in the author's subsequent writings.
31. Endō, 'Katorikku Sakka no Mondai', p. 27.
32. Endō, 'The Anguish of an Alien', p. 184.
33. Endō, *Watashi no Aishita Shōsetsu*, pp. 21, 30.
34. The depiction is Endō's in *Watashi no Aishita Shōsetsu*, p. 20.
35. Yamagata, '*Eien naru* Joshō-ron', p. 69.
36. Endō, *Watashi no Aishita Shōsetsu*, p. 13.
37. Ibid., p. 73.
38. Mauriac, 'Dieu et Mammon', p. 315.
39. Gibson, *The Religion of Dostoevsky*, p. 75.
40. Endō, *Watashi no Aishita Shōsetsu*, p. 13.

41. Endō, 'Shūkyō to Bungaku', p. 117.
42. Ibid., p. 119.
43. The process is that described by Endō as 'transposition', whereby the author seeks a gradual and imperceptible replacement of one object by another – to transform the presence of a lover within a character's heart into the presence of God. cf. *Watashi no Aishita Shōsetsu*, p. 70ff.
44. Cf., Graham Greene's, *The Man Within*, and Dostoevsky's *The Double*.
45. Takahashi, 'Dopperugengeru-kō', p. 15.
46. This claim is borne out by the relatively muted reception accorded to Endō's most complete treatment of the *doppelgänger* theme to date, his recent novel, *Sukyandaru* (Scandal, 1986).
47. Endō, 'Watashi to Kirisutokyō', p. 355.
48. Shiina, 'Shūkyō to Bungaku', p. 87.

# Select Bibliography

*All works are published in Tokyo unless otherwise stated.*

Abe Iso, *Shakaishugisha to naru made*. Kaizōsha, 1932.
Adams, A.O., *A History of Japan* (2 vols). London. 1875.
Akutagawa Ryūnosuke, *Seihō no Hito: Zoku-Seihō no Hito*. Shinchōsha Bunko. 1988.
Anzai Shin, 'Newly-adopted Religions and Social Change on the Ryukyu Island (Japan)', *Social Compass* 23:1 (1976).
—— 'Iesu no Mitama Kyōkai – Okinawa Dendō no Shosō', in Wakimoto Tsuneya, ed., *Shūkyō to Rekishi*. Yamamoto Shoten, 1977.
—— 'Iesu no Mitama Kyōkai', in Sakurai Tokutarō, ed., *Minzoku Shūkyō to Shakai*. Kobunsha, 1980.
Aoikawa Nobuchika, *Hokkyōdan*. Tokyo, 1874.
Aono Masaya, ed., *Nihonjin no Shūkyō Ishiki*. NHK, 1984.
Arai Hakuseki, *Arai Hakuseki Zenshū, 4: Seiyō Kibun*. 1906.
Ariga Tetsutarō, 'From Confucius to Christ: A Feature of Early Protestantism in Japan', *Japanese Religions* 2: 2–3 (1961).
Asao Naohiro, *Nihon no Rekishi, 17: Sakoku*. Shōgakkan, 1975.
Ballhatchet, Helen, 'Confucianism and Christianity in Meiji Japan: The Case of Kozaki Hiromichi', *Journal of the Royal Asiatic Society* 2 (1988).
Banno Junji and Miyachi Masato, eds, *Nihon Kindaishi ni okeru Tenkanki no Kenkyū*. Yamagawa Shuppan, 1985.
Bohner, A., 'Tenchi Hajimari no Koto: Wie Himmel und Erde Enstanden', *Monumenta Nipponica* 1:2 (1938).
Boxer, C.R., *The Christian Century in Japan, 1549–1650*. Rev. edn. Manchester: Carcanet Press, 1993.
Breen, John, 'Heretics in Nagasaki: 1790–1796', in Ian Nish, ed., *Contemporary European Writing on Japan*.
—— 'Emperor State and Religion in Restoration Japan'. (Unpublished PhD dissertation, Cambridge University, 1992).
—— 'Accommodating the Alien: Ōkuni Takamasa and the Religion of the Lord of Heaven', in P. Kornicki and I.J. McMullen, eds, *Arrows from Heaven*. Cambridge: Cambridge University Press (forthcoming).
Buraku Kaihō Kenkyūjo, ed., *Buraku Mondai Gaisetsu*. Osaka: Kaihō, 1987.
Burnstein, Ira, J., *The American Movement to Develop Protestant Colleges for Men in Japan, 1868–1912*. Ann Arbor: University of Michigan, 1967.
Caldarola, Carlo, *Uchimura Kanzō to Mukyōkai: Shūkyō Shakaigakuteki Kenkyū*. Shinkyō Shuppansha, 1978.
—— *Christianity the Japanese Way*. Leiden: E.J. Brill, 1979.
Cary, Otis, *A History of Christianity in Japan: Roman Catholic, Greek Orthodox and Protestant Missions*. Rutland Vt.: Tuttle, 1976.
Chō Takeda Kiyoko, 'Shinkaron no Juyō Hōhō to Kirisutokyō', *Bungaku* 47 (April 1979).

Cieslik, Hubert, 'Shūkyō Shisōshi kara mita Bareto Shahon', *Kirishitan Kenkyū* (1962).
—— 'Kirishitansho to sono Shisō', in Ebisawa Arimichi et al., eds, *Nihon Shisō Taikei, 25: Kirishitansho, Haiyasho*.
Cooper, Michael, ed., *The Southern Barbarians*. Kodansha International, 1971.
—— *Rodrigues the Interpreter*. Weatherhill, 1974.
—— 'Teatro Jesuitico no Japao', *Anais* (1976).
Cortazzi, Hugh, ed., *Mitford's Japan: the Memoirs and Recollections (1866–1906) of Algernon Bertram Mitford, the First Lord Redesdale*. London: Athlone Press, 1985.
*Date Munenari Shuki*. Tōkyō Daigaku Shiryō Hensanjo.
Davis, J.D., 'A Mission Problem in Japan', *Missionary Herald* (May 1875).
Davis, Winston, *Dojo: Magic and Exorcism in Contemporary Japan*. Stanford: Stanford University Press, 1980.
Dazai Osamu, 'HUMAN LOST', in *Dazai Osamu Zenshū*, 1. Chikuma Shobō, 1955.
de Forest, Charlotte B., *The Evolution of a Missionary: A Biography of John Hyde de Forest*. New York: Fleming H. Revell, 1914.
de Sande, Eduardus, *De Missione Legatorum Iaponensium ad Romanam curiam*. Macao, 1590 (facsimile edition, Tōyō Bunko, 1935).
de Visser, M.W., 'The Tengu', *Transactions of the Asiatic Society of Japan* 26:2 (1908).
de Vos, G. and Wagatsuma, H., *Japan's Invisible Race: Caste in Culture & Personality*. Berkeley: University of California Press, 1966.
Doerner, David L., 'Comparative Analysis of Life After Death in Folk Shinto and Christianity', *Japanese Journal of Religious Studies* 4: 2–3 (1977).
Doi Akio, *Nihon Purotesutanto Kirisutokyōshi*. Shinkyō Shuppansha, 1980.
Ebina Danjō, 'Seisho Shinkasetsu', *Rikugō Zasshi* 78 (June 1887).
Ebisawa Arimichi, *Nanban Gakutō no Kenkyū*. Sōbunsha, 1958.
—— *Nihon Kirishitanshi*. Hanawa Shobō, 1966.
—— *Amakusa Shirō*. Jinbutsu Ōraisha, 1967.
—— et al., eds, *Nihon Shisō Taikei, 25: Kirishitansho, Haiyasho*. Iwanami Shoten, 1970.
—— *Nihon no Seisho: Seisho Wayaku no Rekishi*. Nihon Kirisutokyō Shuppankyoku, 1981.
Elison, George, *Deus Destroyed: The Image of Christianity in Early Modern Japan*. Cambridge, Mass.: Harvard University Press, 1988.
Endō Shūsaku, 'The Anguish of an Alien', *Japan Christian Quarterly* 40:4 (Fall 1974).
—— 'Shūkyō to Bungaku', *Endō Shūsaku Bungaku Zenshū, 10*. Shinchōsha, 1975.
—— 'Katorikku Sakka no Mondai', in ibid.
—— 'Nihonteki Kanjō no Soko ni aru Mono: Metafijikku Hihyō to Dentōbi', in ibid.
—— 'Watashi no Bungaku', in ibid.
—— 'Watashi to Kirisutokyō', in ibid.
—— 'Chichi no Shūkyō: Haha no Shūkyō', in ibid.
—— *Ningen no Naka no X*. Chūō Kōronsha, 1978.

―― 'Nihon no Numa no Naka de: Kakure Kirishitankō', in idem, *Kakure Kirishitan*. Kadokawa Shoten, 1980.
―― *Watashi no Aishita Shōsetsu*. Shinchōsha, 1985.
Farmer, D.H., *The Oxford Dictionary of Saints* (2nd Ed). Oxford: Oxford University Press, 1987.
Faulds, Henry, *Hensenron*. Kobe: Beikoku Idenkyōshi Jimukyoku, 1881.
Frois, Luis, *La Première Ambassade du Japon en Europe, 1582–1592*, J.A. Abranches Pinto et al., eds, Monumenta Nipponica Monographs 6, Sophia University Press, 1941.
Frois, Luis, *Historia de Japam*. Lisbon: Biblioteca Nacional, 1976–1984.
Fujii Sadafumi, 'Senkyōshi no Nagasaki Kaikō', *Kokushigaku* 44.
―― 'Senkyōshi no Kenkyū', *Kokugakuin Zasshi* 49: 5, 6.
Fujiki Hisashi, *Nihon no Rekishi, 15: Oda Toyotomi Seiken*. Shōgakkan, 1977.
Fukaya Katsumi, 'Shimabara no Ran', in Sasaki Junnosuke, ed., *Nihon Minshū no Rekishi, 3: Tenka Tōitsu to Minshū*. Sanseidō, 1974.
―― *Zōho Keiteiban Hyakushō Ikki no Rekishiteki Kōzō*. Kōsō Shobō, 1986.
Fukushima Kunimichi, *Santos no Gosangyō: Honji Kenkyūhen*. Benseisha, 1978.
Funayama Shin'ichi, *Zōho Meiji Tetsugakushi Kenkyū*. Minerva Shobō, 1965.
Furuno Kiyoto, *Kakure Kirishitan*. Shibundō, 1984.
Gaimushō, ed., *Nihon Gaikō Monjo* (5 vols). Nihon Kokusai Kyōkai, 1937.
Gibson, A. Boyce, *The Religion of Dostoevsky*. London: SCM Press, 1973.
Greene, Daniel C., 'The Influence of Modern Anti-Christian Literature upon the Missionary Work in Japan', in *Proceedings of the General Conference of the Protestant Missionaries of Japan, held at Osaka, Japan, April 1883*. Yokohama: R. Meiklejohn, 1883.
Greene, Evarts B., *A New Englander in Japan: Daniel Crosby Greene*. Boston: Houghton Mifflin, 1927.
Griffis, William Elliot, *Verbeck of Japan: A Citizen of No Country*. New York: Flemming H. Revell, 1900.
Gutierrez, Fernando G., 'A Survey of Nanban Art', in Michael Cooper, ed. *The Southern Barbarians*.
Haga Shōji, 'Meiji Jingikansei no Kakuritsu to Kokkasaishi no Saihen', *Jinbun Kagaku Kenkyūjo Kiyō* 49, 51.
―― 'Shintō Kokkyōsei no Keisei – Senkyōshi to Tennō Kyōken', *Nihonshi Kenkyū* 264.
Hall, J., *Dictionary of Subjects and Symbols in Art*. London: John Murray, 1974.
Hardacre, Helen, *Lay Buddhism in Contemporary Japan: Reiyūkai Kyōdan*. Princeton, NJ: Princeton University Press, 1984.
―― *Shinto and the State 1868–1988*. Princeton: Princeton University Press, 1989.
Hashimoto Shinkichi, *Hashimoto Shinkichi Chosakushū, 11: Kirishitan Kyōgi no Kenkyū*. Iwanami Shoten, 1961.
Haugen, Einar, 'The Analysis of Linguistic Borrowing', *Language* 26 (1950).
Hayashi C., *Nihonjin no Shūkyōteki Taido*. NHK Publications, 1982.
Hayashi Tetsuyoshi, ed., *Shimabara Hantōshi* (vol. 2). Shimabara: Nagasakiken Minami Takakigunshi Kyōikukai, 1954.
Hennecke, E., *New Testament Apocrypha, 1: Gospels and Related Writings*. London: Lutterworth Press, 1963.
*Higohan Kokuji Shiryō (Kaitei)*. (10 vols). Kumamoto: Kōshaku Hosogawake Hensanjo, 1932.

Hirai Seiji, '"Goshuin Shishoku Kokaku" to Yamada Mikata – Toyotomi Hideyoshi no Kirishitan Kinrei o megutte', *Komonjo Kenkyū* 25 (1986).

Hirota Ichijō, *Kirisutokyō to Bukkyō: Fukyō Shinjitsu*, 2. Kyōto: Hozōkan, 1899.

Holtom, D.C., *Modern Japan and Shinto Nationalism: A Study of Present-Day Trends in Japanese Religions*. New York: Paragon Book Reprint 1963.

Hori Ichirō, *Folk Religion in Japan: Continuity and Change*. Chicago: University of Chicago Press, 1983.

Hoshino Eiki & Takeda Dosho, 'Indebtedness and Comfort: The Undercurrents of *Mizuko Kuyō* in Contemporary Japan', *Japanese Journal of Religious Studies* 14:4 (1987).

Howes, John F., 'Japan's Enigma: The Young Uchimura Kanzō'. (Unpublished PhD dissertation, Columbia University, 1965).

Iglehart, Charles W., *A Century of Protestant Christianity in Japan*. Charles E. Tuttle, 1959.

Ikeda Tetsurō, 'Eigo Kyōkasho', in Nihon no Eigaku Hyakunen Henshūbu, ed., *Nihon no Eigaku Hyakunen*. Kenkyūsha, 1968.

Imanaka Kanshi, '*Rikugō Zasshi* ni okeru Kozaki Hiromichi', in Dōshisha Daigaku Jinbunkagaku Kenkyūjo Kirisutokyō Shakai Mondai Kenkyūkai, ed., *Rikugō Zasshi no Kenkyū*. Kyōbunkan, 1984.

Inagaki Hisao, *A Dictionary of Japanese Buddhist Terms*. Kyoto: Nagata Bunshodō, 1984.

Inoue Enryō, *Shinri Kinshin, 1: Yasokyō o haisuru wa Riron ni aru ka*, in Yoshino Sakuzō, ed., *Meiji Bunka Zenshū, 11*. Nihon Hyōronsha, 1928.

Inoue Nobutaka and Sakamoto Koremaru, eds, *Nihongata Seikyō Kankei no Tanjō*. Daiichi Shobō, 1987.

Ishii Ryōsuke, ed., *Kinsei Hōsei Shiryō Sōsho* (vol. 2).Sōbunsha, 1959.

—— *Tokugawa Kinreikō*. Sōbunsha, 1959.

Ishikawa Chiyomatsu, 'Mōsu-sensei to Shinkaron', in Dai Nihon Bunmei Kyōkai, ed., *Meiji Bunka Hasshō Kinenshi*. Dai Nihon Bunmei Kyōkai, 1925.

—— *Ningen Fumetsu*. Manrikaku Shobō, 1929.

Itō Tasaburō, 'Kinsho no Kenkyū (jō, ge)', *Rekishi Chiri* 68: 4 and 5.

Iwamoto Yutaka, *Nihon Bukkyōgo Daijiten*. Heibonsha, 1988.

Iwazawa Harahiko, 'Toyotomi Hideyoshi no Bateren Seihai Shuinjō ni tsuite', *Kokugakuin Zasshi* 80: 11 (1979).

James, M.R., *The Apocryphal New Testament*, Oxford: Clarendon Press, 1924.

*Japanese English Buddhist Dictionary*. Daitō Shuppansha, 1965. And revised edn. Daitō Shuppansha, 1991.

Kamei Takashi et al., *Nihon Iezusukaihan Kirishitan Yōri: Sono Honan oyobi Hon'yaku no Jittai*. Iwanami Shoten, 1983.

Kashiwabara Yūsen and Fujii Manabu, eds, *Nihon Shisō Taikei, 57: Kinsei Bukkyō no Shisō*. Iwanami Shoten, 1973.

Kataoka Yukichi, *Urakami Yonban Kuzure*. Chikuma Shobō, 1963.

—— *Kakure Kirishitan*. NHK Books, 1967.

—— *Nihon Kirishitan Junkyōshi*. Jiji Tsūshinsha, 1979.

Katsu Yasuyoshi, *Kaishū Zadan*. Iwanami Shoten, 1928.

Kawaguchi Z., *Kakure Kirishitan Orashio no Shiori*. Nagasaki: Kirishitan Kenkyūkai, 1954.

Kawakita Airo, 'Uchimura Kanzō no "Tennen"-kan', *Uchimura Kanzō Kenkyū* 2 (June 1974).

Kido Takayoshi, *The Diary of Kido Takayoshi* (3 vols). Sidney Devere Brown, Akiko Hiroko, trans. University of Tokyo Press, 1985.
Kitamura Tōkoku,'Naibu Seimei-ron', in Katsumoto Seiichirō, ed., *Kitamura Tōkoku Zenshū*, 2. Iwanami Shoten, 1950–60.
Komoto Mitsugu, 'Gendai Toshi no Minzoku Shinkō', in Ōmura Eisho, Nishiyama Shigeru, eds, *Gendaijin no Shūkyō*. Yuhikaku, 1988.
Kozaki Hiromichi, 'Kirisutokyō to Shinpo', *Rikugō Zasshi* 96 (December 1888).
—— *Reminiscences of Seventy Years: The Autobiography of a Japanese Pastor*, Kozaki Nariaki, trans. Kyōbunkan, 1934.
—— *Nihon Kirisutokyōshi*, in *Kozaki Zenshū*, 2. Kozaki Zenshū Kankōkai, 1935.
*Kumamotoken Shiryō: Chūsei* (vol. 4). Kumamoto, 1967.
Kunaichō, ed., *Meiji Tennōki*. (5 vols) Yoshikawa Kōbunkan, 1969.
Kuyama Yasushi et al., 'Christian Influences on Meiji Literature: A Roundtable Discussion', Swain, D., trans., *Japan Christian Quarterly* 46:4 (Fall 1980).
Laures, Johannes, ed., *Kirishitan Bunko: A Manual of Books and Documents on the Early Christian Mission in Japan*. Monumenta Nipponica Monographs 5, Sophia University Press, 1957.
Levy, Marion, *Modernization and the Structure of Societies* (2 vols). Princeton, NJ: Princeton University Press, 1966.
Lobschied, W., *English and Chinese Dictionary, with the Punti and Mandarin Pronunciation* (4 parts). Hong Kong, 1866–69.
Lopez-Gray, J., *El Catecumenado en la Mision del Japon del XVI*. Rome: Pontifical Gregorian University, 1966.
Marnas, F., *La Religion de Jésus, Iaso Ja-kyo Ressuscitée au Japon dans la Seconde Moitié du XIXeme Siècle*. Paris: Delhomme et Briguet, 1896.
Masefield, John, ed., *The Travels of Marco Polo*. London and New York: Dent, 1954.
Matsubara Shin'ichi, *Bungaku Sōzō no Himitsu*. Shinbisha, 1969.
Matsui Toshihiko, 'Bakumatsu Kango no Imi', *Hiroshima Joshidaigaku Bungakubu Kiyō* 16.
—— 'Kindai Nihon Kango to Kan'yakusho no Kango', *Hiroshima Joshidaigaku Bungakubu Kiyō* 16.
Matsumura Akira, 'Arai Hakuseki to Gaikokugo, Gairaigo no Katakana Hyōki', in Matsumura Akira Kyōju Kanreki Kinenkai, ed., *Matsumura Akira Kyōju Kanreki Kinen Kokugogaku to Kokugoshi*. Meiji Shoin, 1969.
Matsumura Kaiseki, *Shinkō Gojūnen*. Dōkai Jimusho, 1926.
Mauriac, François, 'Dieu et Mammon', in *Mauriac: Oeuvres complètes*, 7. Paris: Bibliothèque Grasset, 1983.
Mioni Seiichirō, 'Kirishitan Kinrei o megutte', *Nihon Rekishi* 308 (1974).
—— 'Kirishitan Kinrei no Saikentō', *Kirishitan Kenkyū* 23 (1983).
Miyachi Masato, 'Haihan Chiken no Seiji Katei', in Banno and Miyachi, eds, *Nihon Kindaishi ni okeru Tenkanki no Kenkyū*.
Miyake Jun, 'Folk Religion', in Hori Ichirō ed., *Japanese Religion*, Abe Yoshiya and David Reid, trans. Charles E. Tuttle, 1972.
Miyazaki Kentarō, 'Tenchi Hajimari no Koto Kō', *Nagasaki Chihō Bunkashi Kenkyū* (March 20, 1988).
—— 'Kakure Kirishitan no Kōsho ni tsuite', *Nagasaki Chihō Bunkashi Kenkyū* (14 July 1992).
Moore James R., *The Post-Darwinian Controversies*. Cambridge, Cambridge University Press, 1979.

Morejon Pedro, *Kirishitan Bunka Kenkyū Shirizu, 10: Nihon Junkyōroku*. Kirishitan Bunka Kenkyūkai, 1974.
Morioka Kenji, *Kindaigo no Seiritsu: Meijiki Goihen*. Meiji Shoin, 1969.
Morioka Kiyomi, 'Gairai Shūkyō no Dochakuka o meguru Gainenteki Seiri', *Shichō* 107 (1972).
—— *Nihon no Kindai Shakai to Kirisutokyō*. Hyōronsha, 1976.
—— 'Ancestor Worship in Contemporary Japan: Continuity and Change', in George A. DeVos and Takao Sofue, eds, *Religion and Family in East Asia*. Los Angeles: University of California Press, 1984.
Morse, Edward S., 'What American Zoologists have done to Evolution, concluded', *Popular Science Monthly* 32 (February 1888).
—— *Dōbutsu Shinkaron*, Ishikawa Chiyomatsu, trans., in Yoshino Sakuzō, ed., *Meiji Bunka Zenshū, 24*. Nihon Hyōronsha, 1930.
Mullins, Mark R., 'The Situation of Christianity in Contemporary Japanese Society', *Japan Christian Quarterly* 55:2 (1989).
—— 'The Transplantation of Religion in Comparative Sociological Perspective', *Japanese Religions* 16:2 (1990).
—— 'Japanese Pentecostalism and the World of the Dead: A Study of Cultural Adaptation in Iesu no Mitama Kyōkai', *Japanese Journal of Religious Studies* 17:4 (1990).
—— 'Christianity as a New Religion: Charisma, Minor Founders, and Indigenous Movements', in Mark R. Mullins, Susumu Shimazono, and Paul Swanson, eds, *Religion and Society in Modern Japan: Selected Readings*. Berkeley, Calif.: Asian Humanities Press, 1993.
Murai Jun, *Kirisutokyō Annai*, 1 Iesu no Mitama Kyōkai, no date.
—— *Seisho Shingaku Konpon Kyōgi*. Iesu no Mitama Kyōkai, 1957.
Murai Sanae, 'Kirishitan Kinsei o meguru Tennō to Tōitsu Kenryoku – Tōitsu Seiken Seiritsu Katei ni okeru', *Shien* 40:2 (1980).
—— *Bakuhansei Seiritsu to Kirishitan Kinsei*. Bunken Shuppan, 1987.
Murakami Yoichirō, 'Seibutsu Shinkaron ni taisuru Nihon no Hannō; Meijiki no Autorain'. *Hikaku Bunka Kenkyū* 5 (1964).
Murata Yasuho, 'Kirishitan Kyōgi to Hōkensei – Jōge no Dōtoku o Chūshin toshite', *Waseda Daigaku Kyōikugakubu Gakujutsu Kenkyū* 18 (1969).
Nakae Chōmin, *Sansuijin Keirin Mondō*, in *Nakae Chōmin Zenshū*, 8. Iwanami Shoten, 1984.
Nakamura Tadashi, 'Shimabara no Ran to Sakoku', in *Iwanami Kōza Nihon Rekishi, 9: Kinsei 1*. Iwanami Shoten, 1975.
Nihon Shiseki Kyōkai, ed., *Iwakura Tomomi Kankei Monjo*. (8 vols). Nihon Shiseki Kyōkai, 1927–1935.
—— ed., *Kido Koin Monjo*. (8 vols). Nihon Shiseki Kyōkai, 1929–31.
—— *Saga Sanenaru Nikki*. Nihon Shiseki Kyōkai, 1933.
Nish, Ian, ed., *Contemporary European Writing on Japan*. London: Paul Norbury, 1987.
Nishiyama Shigeru, 'Indigenization and Transformation of Christianity in a Japanese Community', *Japanese Journal of Religious Studies* 12:1 (1985).
Nitobe Inazō, *The Intercourse Between the United States and Japan: A Historical Sketch,* in *Inazō Nitobe Zenshū, 13*. Kyōbunkan, 1970.
Nosco, Peter, 'Secrecy and the Transmission of Tradition: Issues in the Study of the "Underground" Christians', *Japanese Journal of Religious Studies* 20:1 (1993).

## Select Bibliography

Notehelfer, F.G., 'Ebina Danjō: A Christian Samurai of the Meiji Period'. *Papers on Japan,* 2. Cambridge, Mass.: East Asia Research Centre, Harvard University, 1963.
Notehelfer, F.G., *American Samurai: Captain L. L. Janes and Japan.* Princeton, NJ: Princeton University Press, 1985.
Okamoto Yoshitomo, *The Nanban Art of Japan.* Weatherhill/Heibonsha, 1972.
Ōkuma Shigenobu, *Ōkuma Haku Sekijitsudan.* Rikken Kaishintō Tōhōkyoku, 1985.
Ōta Yūzō, *Kurāku no Ichinen – Sapporo Nōgakkō Shodai Kyōto no Nihon Taiken.* Kyōto: Shōwadō, 1979.
—— *E.S. Mōsu: 'Furuki Nihon'o tsutaeta Shinnichi Kagakusha.* Libro Port, 1988.
Ōuchi Saburō, 'Nihon Kirisutokyōshi ni okeru Shinkaron no Mondai: Uchimura Kanzō o Chūshin ni shite', *Nihon Bunka Kenkyūjo Kenkyū Hōkoku* 14 (March 1978).
Oxford, Wayne H., *The Speeches of Fukuzawa: A Translation and Critical Study.* Hokuseidō, 1973.
Ozaki Mugen, '*Rikugo Zasshi* ni okeru Ukita Kazutami no Riron Katsudō ni tsuite', in Dōshisha Daigaku Jinbunkagaku Kenkyūjo Kirisutokyō Shakai Mondai Kenkyūkai, ed., *Rikugō Zasshi no Kenkyū.* Kyōbunkan, 1984.
Ozawa Saburō, *Nihon Purotesutantoshi Kenkyū.* Tōkai Daigaku Shuppankai, 1965.
—— *Bakumatsu Meiji Yasokyōshi Kenkyū.* Nihon Kirisutokyōdan Shuppankyoku, 1973.
Pacheco, J.F. ed., *Coleccion de Documentos Ineditos Relativos al Descubrimento,* 8. Madrid, 1867.
Peel, J.D.Y., *Herbert Spencer: The Evolution of a Sociologist.* London: Heinemann, 1971.
Pettee, James H., *A Chapter of Mission History of Modern Japan.* Okayama, n.d. c. 1895.
Reader, Ian, *Religion in Contemporary Japan.* Honolulu: University of Hawaii Press, 1991.
Reid, David, 'Japanese Christians and the Ancestors', *Japanese Journal of Religious Studies* 16:4 (1989).
—— *New Wine: The Cultural Shaping of Japanese Christianity.* Berkeley, Calif: Asian Humanities Press, 1991.
'*Rikugō Zasshi* Hakkō no Shui', *Rikugō Zasshi* 1 (October 1880).
Ruiz-de-Medina, Juan, ed., *Documentas del Japon, 1547–1557.* Rome: Instituto Historico de la Compania de Jesus, 1990.
Saba Wataru, *Uemura Masahisa to sono Jidai* (5 vols). Kyōbunkan 1937–38.
Sakaguchi Mitsuhiro,'Bakumatsu-ishinki no Hajaron', *Kirisutokyō Shakai Mondai Kenkyū* 37 (March 1989).
Sakamoto Koremaru, *Meiji Ishin to Kokugakusha,* Daimyōdō, 1993.
—— *Kokka Shintō Keisei Katei no Kenkyū,* Iwanami Shoten, 1994.
Sakamoto Mitsuru et al., *Genshoku Nihon no Bijutsu, 25: Nanban Bijutsu to Yōfūga.* Shōgakkan, 1970.
—— *Nihon no Bijutsu, 80: Shoki Yōfūga.* Shibundō, 1973.
Sakatani Shiroshi, 'On Nurturing the Human Spirit', in Braisted, William R. trans. and ed., *Meiroku Zasshi: Journal of the Japanese Enlightenment.* University of Tokyo Press, 1976.
Sako Jun'ichirō, ed., *Dazai Osamu to Seisho,* Kyōbunkan, 1983.

Sasaki Takayuki, *Hogo Hiroi* (12 vols). Tōkyō Daigaku Shuppankai, 1970.
Satō Kyōji, *Kokugo Goi no Rekishiteki Kenkyū*. Meiji Shoin, 1971.
Satow, Ernest, *A Diplomat in Japan – the Inner History of the Critical Years in the Evolution of Japan when the Ports were Opened and the Monarchy Restored*. London 1921.
Sawa Senka, *Kyūshū Jiken Nagasaki Saibansho Gotō Karidome Nikki*. Tōkyō Daigaku Shiryō Hensanjo.
Scheiner, Irwin, *Christian Converts and Social Protest in Meiji Japan*. Berkeley: University of California Press, 1970.
Schurhammer, George, *Das Kirchliche Sprachproblem in der Japanischen Jesuitenmission des 16 und 17 Jahrhunderts: ein Stuck Ritenfrage*. Mitteilungen der Gesellschaft für Natur und Volkerkunde Ostasiens, 1928.
—— 'Die Jesuitenmissionare des 16 and 17 Jahrhunderts und ihr Einfluss auf die Japanische Malerei', in Schurhammer, *Orientalia*. Rome: Institutum Historicum Societatis Iesu, 1963.
Schütte, J.F., *Introductio ad Historiam Societatis Iesu in Japonia (1549–1650)*. Rome: Institutum Historicum Societatis Iesu, 1968.
—— ed., *Textus Catalogorum Japoniae, 1549–1664*. Rome: Monumenta Historica Societatis Iesu, 1975.
Schwantes, Roberts S., 'Christianity versus Science: A Conflict of Ideas in Meiji Japan', *Far East Quarterly* 12 (February 1953).
Schwartz, Benjamin, *In Search of Wealth and Power: Yen Fu and the West*. Cambridge, Mass.: Harvard University Press, 1964.
*Seiyōjin no Kaita Nihon Chizu: Japan mit den Augen des Westens Gesehen*. OAG, 1993.
Senmoto Masuo, 'Kirishitan Kinsei Kenkyū Nōto', *Nihon Rekishi* 338 (1976).
—— *Shimabara no Ran*. Kyōikusha, 1980.
—— 'Shimabara no Ran to Kirishitan Ikki', in Katō Eiichi, Yamada Tadao, eds, *Kōza Nihon Kinseishi, 2: Sakoku*. Yuhikaku, 1981.
Shiina Rinzō, 'Shūkyō to Bungaku', *Shiina Rinzō Zenshū, 20*. Tōjusha, 1970–79.
Shimizu Koichi, 'Shūmon Aratameyaku Nōto', *Kirisutokyō Shigaku* 30 (1976).
—— comp. 'Kirishitan Kankei Hōsei Shiryōshū'. *Kirishitan Kenkyū* 17 (1977).
—— 'Kirishitan Sonin Hoshōsei ni tsuite', *Kirishitan Kenkyū* 19 (1979).
—— *Kirishitan Kinseishi*. Kyōikusha, 1981.
*Shintei Zōho Shiseki Shūran*. Rinsen Shoten, 1967.
*Shiseki Zassan*. Kokusho Kankōkai, 1911.
*Shūkyō Kankei Hōrei Ichiran*, in Yasumaru, Miyachi, eds, *Nihon Kindai Shisō Taikei*.
Smalley, William A., 'Cultural Implications of an Indigenous Church', in Smalley, ed., *Readings in Missionary Anthropology*. South Pasadena, Calif: William Carey Library, 1974.
Smith, Robert, J., *Ancestor Worship in Contemporary Japan*. Stanford: Stanford University Press, 1974.
Soejima Tanenobu, *Honkō Kokushi Nikki*. Zoku Gunsho Ruiju Kanseikai, 1970.
Staggs, Kathleen M., '"Defend the Nation and Love the Truth": Inoue Enryō and the Revival of Meiji Buddhism', *Monumenta Nipponica* 39 (Autumn 1983).
Sugii Mutsurō, 'Kozaki Hiromichi no Tōkyō Dendō to Rikugō Zasshi no Hakkan', in Dōshisha Daigaku Jinbunkagaku Kenkyūjo Kirisutokyō Shakai Mondai Kenkyūkai, ed., *Nihon no Kindaika to Kirisutokyō*. Shinkyō Shuppansha, 1973.

—— 'Tōkyō Seinenkai no Seiritsu to *Rikugō Zasshi*', in Dōshisha Daigaku Jinbunkagaku Kenkyūjo Kirisutokyō Shakai Mondai Kenkyūkai, ed., *Rikugō Zasshi no Kenkyū*. Kyōbunkan, 1984.
Sugimoto Tsutomu, *Kaitai Shinsho no Jidai*. Waseda Daigaku Shuppankai, 1987.
Sugimoto Y. and Mouer R., *Constructs for Understanding Japan*. London: Kegan Paul International, 1989.
Suzuki Hiroko, 'Meiji Seifu no Kirisutokyō Seisaku – Kōsatsu Tekkyo made no Seiji Katei', *Shigaku Zasshi* 86:2.
Tagita Kōya, *Shōwa Jidai no Senpuku Kirishitan*. Nippon Gakujutsu, 1954.
—— *Study of Acculturation among the Secret Christians of Japan*. Privately published.
Takadō Kaname, 'Kirisutosha no Bungaku no Kanōsei', *Fukuin to Sekai* (December 1966).
—— 'The Challenge of Christian Literature', *Japan Christian Quarterly* 33:2 (Spring 1967).
Takahashi Takako, 'Dopperugengeru-kō', *Bungakkai* 28:4 (April 1974).
Takase Kōichirō, *Kirishitan Jidai no Kenkyū*. Iwanami Shoten, 1977.
Takeda Hideaki, 'Kindai Tennō Saishi Keisei Katei no Ichikōsatsu', in Inoue and Sakamoto, eds, *Nihongata Seikyō Kankei no Tanjō*.
—— 'Meiji Jingikan no Kaikaku Mondai', *Kogukakuin Zasshi* 88: 3 (1988).
Takeda Kiyoko, 'Nihon no Shisō Zasshi: *Rikugō Zasshi*', *Shisō* 462 (December 1962).
—— see also Chō Takeda Kiyoko.
Takeda Tomoju, *'Chinmoku' igo*. Joshi Paolo-kai, 1976.
Tamura Naoomi, *Shinkō Gojūnenshi*. Keiseisha Shoten, 1924.
Taylor, James L., *A Portuguese–English Dictionary* (revised), Stanford: Stanford University Press, 1958.
Teshima Ikurō, *Nihon Minzoku to Genshi Fukuin*. Kirisuto Seisho Juku, 1984.
Thelle, Notto R., *Buddhism and Christianity in Japan: From Conflict to Dialogue, 1854–1899*. Honolulu: University of Hawaii Press, 1987.
Tokoyo Nagatane, *Shinkyō Soshiki Monogatari*, in Yasumaru and Miyachi, eds, *Nihon Kindai Shisō Taikei*.
Tōkyō Teikoku Daigaku, ed., *Dai Nihon Shiryō 12:9*. Tōkyō Teikoku Daigaku, 1906.
Tsuji Zennosuke, *Nihon Bukkyōshi: Kinseihen, 9* (4th reprint edn). Iwanami Shoten, 1970.
Tsukishima Hiroshi, '"Monzenyomi" Kō', *Kokugo to Kokubungaku* 28: 11 (1951).
Tsuruda Yasunari, 'Shimabara ni okeru Kasei no Jisshō', *Kumamoto Shigaku* 31 (1966).
Turnbull, S.R., 'The Veneration of the Martyrs of Ikitsuki (1609–1645) by the "Hidden Christians" of Japan', in Diana Wood, ed., *Studies in Church History, 30: Martyrs and Martyrologies*. Oxford: Blackwell, 1993.
—— *Devotion to Mary among the Hidden Christians of Japan*. Wallingford: Ecumenical Society of the Blessed Virgin Mary, 1993.
—— 'From Catechist to Kami: Martyrs and Mythology among the *Kakure Kirishitan*', *Japanese Religions* 19:1 (1994).
Uchimura Kanzō, 'Sōseiki Daiichi-sho', *Seisho no Kenkyū* 1 and 3 (September and November 1900).
—— 'Yo no Shukyōteki Shōgai no Ippan', *Seisho no Kenkyū* 29 (December 1902).

—— 'Kirisutokyō to Shinka', *Seisho no Kenkyū* 98 (April 1908).
—— *How I Became a Christian: Out of my Diary*, in Yamamoto and Mutō, eds, *The Complete Works of Kanzō Uchimura*, 1. Kyōbunkan, 1971.
—— 'Shūkyō to Kagaku', in *Uchimura Kanzō Zenshū*, 6. Iwanami Shoten, 1980.
—— 'War in Nature', in *Uchimura Kanzō Zenshū*, 12. Iwanami Shoten, 1981.
Uemura Masahisa, *Shinri Ippan*, in *Uemura Masahisa Chosakushū, 4*. Shinkyō Shuppansha, 1966.
Ukita Kazutami, 'Shinkaron to Yūshinron no Kankei', *Rikugō Zasshi* 24 (February 1884).
Urakawa Wasaburō, *Urakami Kirishitanshi*. Zenkoku Shobō, 1943.
Valignano, Alessandro, *Nihon Iezusukaishi Reihō Shishin*. Kirishitan Bunka Kenkyūkai, 1970.
Vizcaino, Sebastian, *Relacion del Viaje hecho para el Descubrimento de las Islas Llamadas 'Ricas de Oro y Plata', Situadas en el Japon*, in Pacheco, ed. *Coleccion de Documentos Ineditos Relativos al Descubrimiento, 8*.
Vlam, Grace, 'Western-Style Secular Painting in Momoyama Japan'. (Unpublished PhD dissertation, University of Michigan, 1976).
—— 'Kings & Heroes: Western-Style Painting in Momoyama Japan', *Antibus Asiae* 39: 2–4 (1977).
*Vocabulario da Lingua de Iapam*. Nagasaki, 1603.
Volpe, A., *I Kakure, Religione e Societa in Giappone*. Reggio Emilia: One Way, 1992.
Watanabe Kazuyasu, 'Katō Hiroyuki no iwayuru "Tenkō": Sono Shisōshiteki Ichizuke', *Nihon Shisōshi Kenkyū* 5 (May 1971).
Watanabe Masao and Ōse Yōko, 'Meiji shoki no Gakujutsu Zasshi to Shinkaron', *Kagakushi Kenkyū* 88 (Winter 1968).
—— *O-yatoi Beikokujin Kagaku Kyōshi*. Kōdansha, 1976.
—— *The Japanese and Western Science*, Otto Theodor Benfey, trans. Philadelphia: University of Pennsylvania Press, 1990.
Watase Tsunekichi, *Ebina Danjō-sensei*. Ryūginsha, 1938.
Wayman, Dorothy G., *Edward Sylvester Morse: A Biography*. Cambridge, Mass.: Harvard University Press, 1942.
Williams, Mark, 'Kōteiteki na Hitei: Endō Bungaku ni okeru Zoku no Seika', in Yamagata Kazumi, ed., *Sei naru Mono to Sōzōryoku*. Sairyūsha, 1994.
—— 'Shadows of the Former Self: Images of Christianity in Contemporary Japanese Literature', (Unpublished PhD dissertation University of California: Berkeley, 1991).
Yamagata Kazumi, 'Eien naru Joshō-ron: Kirisutokyō Bungaku no Kanōsei toshite Yomu', *Kirisutokyō Bungaku Kenkyū* 5 (1988).
Yamamori, Tetsunao, *Church Growth in Japan: A Study in the Development of Eight Denominations, 1859–1939*. South Pasadena, Calif: William Carey Library, 1974.
Yamashita Shigekazu, *Supensā to Nihon Kindai*. Ochanomizu Shobō, 1983.
Yasumaru Yoshio and Miyachi Masato, eds, *Nihon Kindai Shisō Taikei, 25: Shyūkyō to Kokka*. Iwanami Shoten, 1988.
Yasuno Shinko, *Bateren Tsuihōrei*. Nihon Edeitāsukūru Shuppanbu, 1989.
Yinger, Milton J., *The Scientific Study of Religion*. Toronto: Collier-Macmillan, 1970.
Yoshimura Toyotake, 'Kinsei Shoki Kumamotohan ni okeru Kirishitan Kinsei no Tenkai', *Shigaku Kenkyū* 149 (1980).

Yoshinare Akiko, *Ebina Danjō no Seiji Shisō*. Tōkyō Daigaku Shuppankai, 1982.
Yoshiyama Hiroshi, ed., *Mitama ni Michibikarete: Sōritsu Sanjūnenshi*. Japan Assemblies of God, 1979.
Young, Richard Fox, 'Abortion, Grief and Consolation: Prolegomena to a Christian Response to *Mizuko Kuyo*', *Japan Christian Quarterly* 55:1 (1989).
Yūki Diego, 'Fukusha Machado Shinpu no Saigo no Tabi', a talk presented at the Kirishitan Bunka Kenkyūkai, Sophia University (15 November 1992).
*Zokuzoku Gunshoruijū*. Kokusho Kankōkai, 1907.

# Index

Acts of Pilate, 69–70
Adam Arakawa, 56, 57
Age of Reason, 108
Akutagawa Ryūnosuke, 163–4
Almeida, Luis de, 124
Amakusa, 54–9, 68
Anesaki Masaharu, 104
Arabic Infancy Gospel, 69–70
Arai Hakuseki, 22–4
Arima Harunobu, 55–7
Arima Harunobu-ki, 57
Arima Kiroku, 55
Arima Korō Monogatari, 57
Arima Naozumi, 55–7, 58
Arishima Takeo, 163
Ariyoshi Sawako, 167
The Assumption, 32, 35

Baba Tatsui, 112
Ballagh, James, 109
Barreto, Manuel, 11–12, 15–16
Bastian Calendar, 126–7
bateren, 47–53, 59–60
The Battle of Lepanto, 40–1
Beatitudes, 15–16
bōja, 96
Bon, 150–1
Brown, Samuel, 26, 109
Buddhist art, 39
Buddhist–Christian Conference, 101–2
Bushido, 143
byōbu, 31, 36, 39–42

Cabral, Francisco, 34
Caldarola, Carlo, 7, 143, 151
Catholicism, 1–2,
Chinese, 24–5
Christianity
  Buddhism and, 67–8
  Buddhism in the 1870s and, 86, 89–90
  Buddhism in the 1890s and, 94–102
  Buddhism in the twentieth century and, 102–6
  fumie and, 134
  indigenous social forms of, 139–55
  Japanese language and, 8–29
  literature in Japan and, 156–72
  Meiji Restoration and, 75–93
  see also Catholicism, Kakure Kirishitan, Kumamoto Band, Protestant mission, Sapporo Band, Yokohama Band
chōkata, 127–8, 130, 131
Civitates Orbis Terrarum, 33, 42
Clark, W.S., 108
Cleric and Two Children, 39
Conference of Religionists, see Buddhist–Christian Conference
Contemptus Mundi, 21

Daikyō Goshui, 88–9
Daiseikai, 146
Darwin, Charles, 99, 107, 114
Date Munenari, 77
Dazai Osamu, 165–7
DeForest, J.H., 98
Doctrina Cristan, 13–14, 15–22, 24, 66, 129
doppelgänger, 171
Dōshisha, 100, 108, 110, 115
Dostoevsky, Fyodor, 158–9, 169–70

Ebina Danjō, 109–10, 116–17
Ebisawa, Arimichi, 2, 16, 26
Ecce Homo, 34
Emperor Meiji, 79, 82, 83–5
Endō Shūsaku, 156–61, 167–72
enzetsukai, 115
Etō Shinpei, 87, 89
Evola Screen, 11, 13
evolution, 107–21, see also The Origin of Species

Faulds, Henry, 114
Freud, Sigmund, 168
Frois, Luis, 32, 35, 36
Fukaya Katsumi, 54
Fukuba Bisei, 79, 81, 82, 83, 84, 87–8, 89
Furuno Kiyoto, 125

Gago, Baltasaar, 10, 12, 17
Gakugei Shirin, 115
Genshi Fukuin (Original Gospel), see Makuya
Gesshō, 96
Gide, André, 169
Gōdō irei sai, 150–1
gohō, 95
gokoku, 95

# Index

*Gospel of Nicodemus*, 69
Gotō, 64, 80, 123–5, 127–8, 134
Gotō Shōjirō, 82, 89
Green, D.C., 98
Greene, Graham, 157
Gulick, John, 114
Gulick, O.H., 97

Hasegawa Sahyoe, 55–6, 58
Hepburn, J.C., 26
Hidden Christians, *see* Kakure Kirishitan
Hirata Atsutane, 25, 83
Holtom, D.C., 142, 151
Honzui Shonin, 57–8
Hori Ichirō, 124
Hosokawa Tadaoki, 51
Huxley, Thomas, 99, 107, 113

*Iesu no Mitama Kyōkai* (Spirit of Jesus Church), 140, 144–52
Inoue Enryō, 112, 114
Inoue Hisashi, 167
Inoue Kaoru, 75
Ise, 79, 88
*Ishū Bōgyo ni tsuki Mikomi*, 89
Iwakura Tomomi, 76, 78, 80, 87, 89, 90
Iwamoto Yoshiharu, 160

Janes, Capt. L.L., 108, 109
Japan Bible Church, 144
Jesuits, 8, 24, 26, 31–4, 35, 37, 38, 68–72, 130
*Jingikan*, 82–3, 84, 87–8
Joan, Mancio, 37
João, Pedro, 37
*Jitsugaku*, 109
Jung, Carl, 168

Kadowaki Shigeaya, 82, 87–8
Kagawa Toyohiko, 167
*Kakure Kirishitan*, 3–4, 63–74, 75–9, 122–36
  differing names used to describe, 63, 122, 132
  geography of, 66
  location of communities, 122–5
  *tengu* and, 67
  unwritten tradition, 128–36
  written texts, 126–36
  *see also orashio, Tenchi Hajimari no Koto*, Urakami
Kamei Katsuichirō, 159, 166
Kanō Eitoku, 33
Kanō Motohide, 31
Kanō Pedro, 38

Katō Hiroyuki, 112
Katō Kiyomasa, 55
Kawaguchi, Z., 134
Keene, Donald, 166
*Kenkokusaku*, 87
Kido Kōin, 75, 77, 78–9, 80–1, 86, 87, 89
Kimura, Leonardo, 37
*Kirishitan no Fukkatsu*, 131
*Kirishitan*, the meaning of, 46–7, 48–9
*Kirisutokyō Annai*, 148
*Kirisutokyō Nenkan*, 140
Kishimoto Nobuta, 104
Kitamura Tōkoku, 161–2
*Kōgisho*, 81
*Kōmō Zatsuwa*, 24–5
Konchiin Sūden, 51
Konishi Yukinaga, 55–6
Kozaki Hiromichi, 110, 115, 117
Kūkai, 129
Kumamoto Band, 109–10, 114, 116
*Kumamoto Yōgakkō*, 108
Kunikida Doppo, 163
*Kyōbushō*, 89
*Kyōdōkyoku*, 81, 90

Lourenço, Brother, 124

*Makuya* (Tabernacle of Christ), 140, 143, 144
*Mappa Mundi*, 42
Martins, Pedro, 36
Masamune Hakuchō, 162–3
Mataichi, Domingo, 65
*Mater Dolorosa*, 32
Matsudaira, Viscount, 101
Matsukura Shigemasa, 55
Matsumura Kaiseki, 114
Mauriac, François, 157, 169
*Meiroku Zasshi*, 108
Mitford, Algernon, 78
Miura Shumon, 167
Miura Ayako, 167
*Monzenyomi*, 17–19
Morejon, Pedro, 52
Morse, Edward, 111–13, 115
*Mukyōkai*, 4, 140, 143, 151
Murai Jun, 144–9
Murai Suwa, 145–6
Mushanokōji Saneatsu, 165

Nagasaki, 32, 36, 56, 58, 75, 78, 80, 82–7, 88, 97, 113, 122–3
Namura Gendō, 25
*nanban bijutsu*, 31–2
Nanzan Institute for Religion and Culture, 105

# Index

Naozumi, 55–7, 58
*Natara*, 134–6
Natsume Sōseki, 163–4
NCC Centre for the Study of Japanese Religions, 105
NHK survey on Japanese Religious consciousness, 139
Niccolo, Giovanni, 34, 35–6, 37
Nikkyō, 39
Nishida Kitarō, 94, 104–5
Nishitani Keiji, 94
Nitobe Inazō, 110, 139–40, 151
Niwa, Jacobo, 37
Nobutaka, 37, 39

Oda Nobunaga, 34
Ogawa Kunio, 167
Okamoto Daihachi, 55
Ōkubo Toshimichi, 80–1, 87
Ōkuma Shigenobu, 77, 78, 87
Ōkuni Takamasa, 79, 85
Ōmura Sumiyasu, 124
Ono Jusshin, 81, 84, 88
*Oranda Gekasho*, 22
*Oranda Jii*, 25
*Orashio no Shiori*, 130–4
*orashio*, 24, 126–8
*The Origin of Species*, 107
Ōuchi Yoshinaga, 10
Ōuchi Yoshitaka, 33
Our Lady of the Rosary, 37–8, 41

painting, Western-style, 80
Parkes, Sir Harry, 76, 78, 80, 86
Pedro João, 37
Petit-Jean, Bernard, 64, 65
Portuguese, 16, 22–4, 47
proscription, 46–62, 76
 removal of, 89–90, 98
Protestant mission, 9, 24–6, 86
Protestant missionaries and the evolution controversy, 107–19

Reader, Ian, 124
*Rei Sanka*, 149–50
Renan, Ernest, 99
Ricci, Matteo, 23, 25, 42
*Rikugō Zasshi*, 109, 115–16
Romanes, George, 114
Rosary, *Tenchi Hajimari* and, 66
*Ruizoku Aratame*, 60
Russo-Japanese War, 102

Saemon, 57–8
*Saido riyaku*, 14

*saisei itchi*, 79, 81, 82, 83, 85, 87
*Sanctos no Gosagyō*, 11, 13, 14
Sapporo Band, 109–10, 114
*Sapporo Nōgakkō*, 108
*The Saviour*, 34, 83
Sawa Nobuyoshi, 75, 76, 85–6
Sebastian, 126–7
*Seimei no Hikari*, 144
*Seisho Shingaku*, 147, 149
*seminario*, 34, 36
*Senkyōshi*, 82, 84, 85–6, 87–9
Shiga Naoya, 165
Shiina Rinzō, 159, 167, 172
Shimabara Rebellion, 47, 50, 52, 53–60
Shimaji Mokurai, 89
Shimao Toshio, 159, 167
Shimazaki Tōson, 163–5
Shimazu Takahisa, 33
*Shin Bukkyō*, 100
*Shindensai*, 84
*Shinkyō Yōshi*, 84, 88
*Shinri Ippan*, 117
Shinto, 79, 81–8, 90
*Shirakaba-ha* (White Birch Society), 166
*shishōsetsu*, 166
Shizuoka, Luis, 37
shrines, 82–3, 85–6, 88
*Shūmon Aratameyaku*, 60
Sino-Japanese war, 100, 102
Sono Ayako, 167

Tagita Kōya, 64, 66, 67–8, 71
Taichiku Mancio, 37
Takadō Kaname, 167
Takahashi Takako, 167, 171
Tamura Naoomi, 115
Tanabe Hajime, 94
Tanaka Kōtarō, 167
*Tenchi Hajimari no Koto*, 3, 63–74, 126
Terazawa Hirotaka, 57
terminology, 10, 12, 13–14, 15–17, 20–2
Teshima Ikurō, 143–4
Tokudaiji Sanenori, 84
Tokugawa Hidetada, 33, 36
Tokugawa Ieyasu, 33, 36, 55
Tokyo Conference, 82
*Tōkyō Seinenkai*, 115
*Tōryū Denki Yōsatsu Nukigaki*, 22
*Tōyō Gakugei Zasshi*, 115–16
Toyotomi Hideyoshi, 35, 42, 51, 52–3, 55
True Jesus Church, 145
Tsuji Zennosuke, 96
Tsuruda Yasunari, 59
Tsuwano, 79

## Index

Uchimura Kanzō, 4, 109–10, 114, 117–18, 157, 161, 167
Uemura Masahisa, 109, 115, 117–18, 161, 167
Ukita Kazutami, 116
Urakami, 64, 75–9, 80, 85, 86, 87, 90
Urakawa Wasaburō, 131

Valignano, Alessandro, 11, 34
Vatican Council, Second, 94
Verbeck, Guido, 97, 108
Veronica, 68–9
Vicarious Baptism, 149–50
*Virgin and Child*, 32
Vizcaino, Sebastian, 33

Wartime Conference of Religionists, 103
Wilberforce, Bishop, 113
*Woman Playing the Lute*, 39

World Council of Churches, 94
World Parliament of Religions, 100

Xavier, St Francis, 8–10, 22, 31, 33, 38

Yajirō, 10
*Yakken*, 25
Yamada Emonsaku, 37
Yashiro Seiichi, 167
*Yasuoka Shōtarō*, 167
Yatabe Ryōkichi, 108, 111
*Yōgo On'yakusen*, 25
Yokohama Band, 109, 114
Yokoi Shōnan, 80
Yokoi Tokio, 100
Yuasa Hangetsu, 160

Zen, 105